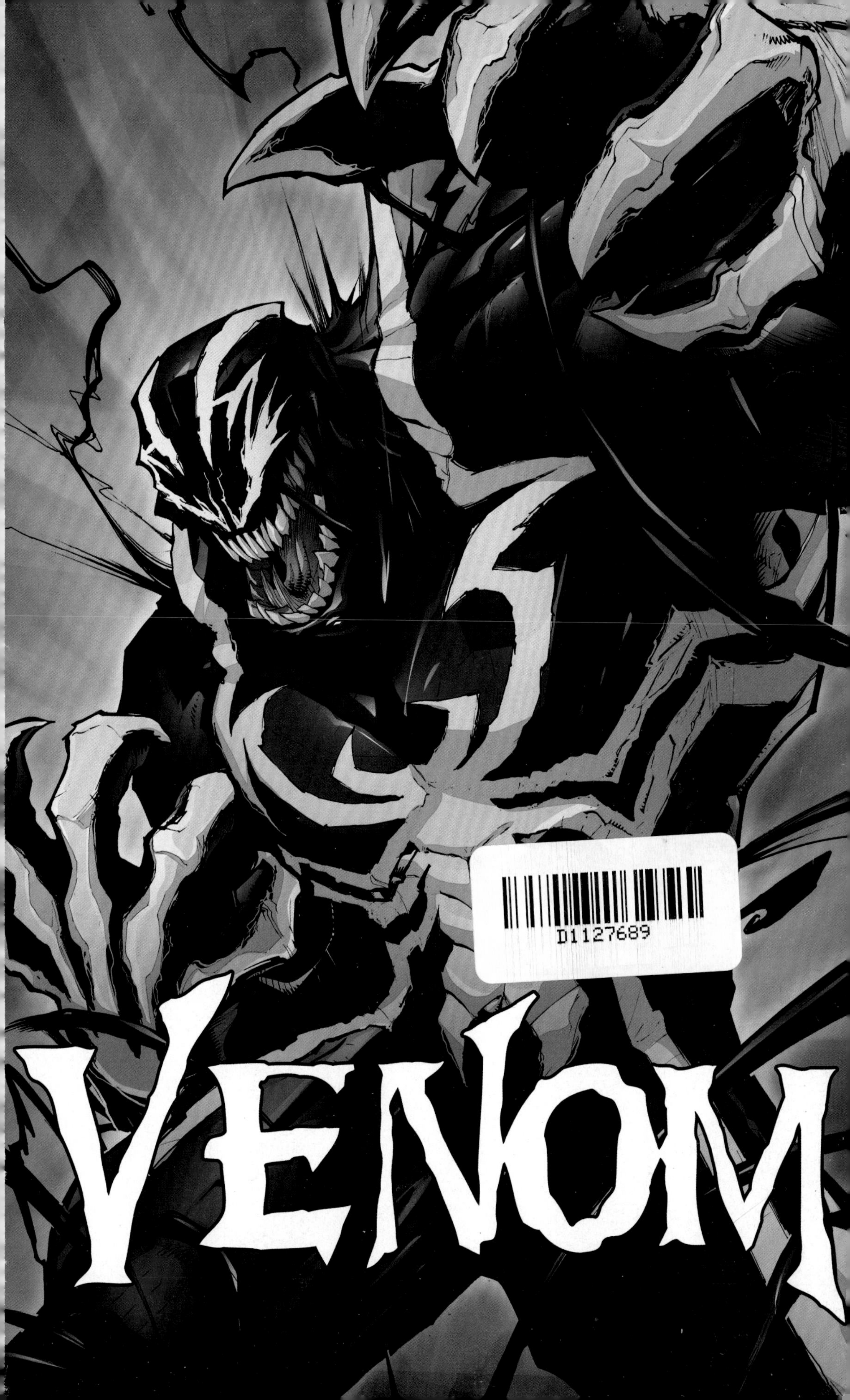
VENOM

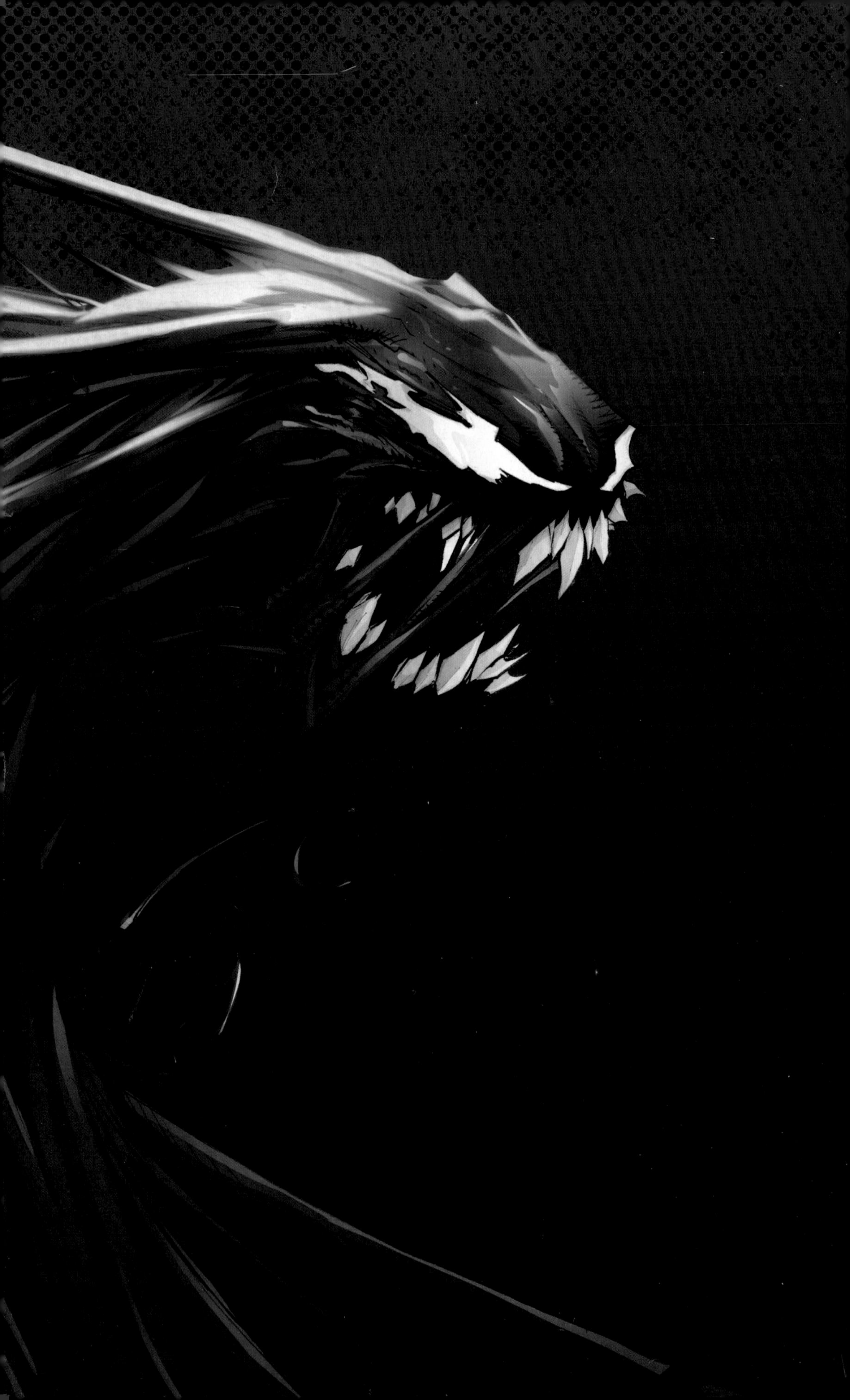

VENOM

MIKE COSTA
WRITER

GERARDO SANDOVAL (#1-6)
WITH **JUANAN RAMÍREZ** (#4) & **IBAN COELLO** (#5)
ARTISTS

VICTOR OLAZABA (#4)
INKER

DONO SÁNCHEZ-ALMARA
WITH **ISRAEL SILVA** & **ANDRES MOSSA** (#5)
COLOR ARTISTS

VC's CLAYTON COWLES
LETTERER

GERARDO SANDOVAL
COVER ART

ALLISON STOCK
ASSISTANT EDITOR

DEVIN LEWIS
EDITOR

NICK LOWE
EXECUTIVE EDITOR

SPECIAL THANKS TO **VICTOR NAVA**

COLLECTION EDITOR **MARK D. BEAZLEY** :: ASSISTANT EDITOR **CAITLIN O'CONNELL**
ASSOCIATE MANAGING EDITOR **KATERI WOODY** :: SENIOR EDITOR, SPECIAL PROJECTS **JENNIFER GRÜNWALD**
VP PRODUCTION & SPECIAL PROJECTS **JEFF YOUNGQUIST** :: SVP PRINT, SALES & MARKETING **DAVID GABRIEL**
BOOK DESIGNER **JAY BOWEN**

EDITOR IN CHIEF **AXEL ALONSO** :: CHIEF CREATIVE OFFICER **JOE QUESADA**
PRESIDENT **DAN BUCKLEY** :: EXECUTIVE PRODUCER **ALAN FINE**

VENOM VOL. 1: HOMECOMING. Contains material originally published in magazine form as VENOM #1-6. First printing 2017. ISBN# 978-1-302-90602-3. Published by MARVEL WORLDWIDE, INC., a subsidiary of MARVEL ENTERTAINMENT, LLC. OFFICE OF PUBLICATION: 135 West 50th Street, New York, NY 10020. **Printed in Canada.** DAN BUCKLEY, President, Marvel Entertainment; JOE QUESADA, Chief Creative Officer; TOM BREVOORT, SVP of Publishing; DAVID BOGART, SVP of Business Affairs & Operations, Publishing & Partnership; C.B. CEBULSKI, VP of Brand Management & Development, Asia; DAVID GABRIEL, SVP of Sales & Marketing, Publishing; JEFF YOUNGQUIST, VP of Production & Special Projects; DAN CARR, Executive Director of Publishing Technology; ALEX MORALES, Director of Publishing Operations; SUSAN CRESPI, Production Manager; STAN LEE, Chairman Emeritus. For information regarding advertising in Marvel Comics or on Marvel.com, please contact Vit DeBellis, Integrated Sales Manager, at vdebellis@marvel.com. For Marvel subscription inquiries, please call 888-511-5480. **Manufactured between 4/21/2017 and 5/23/2017 by SOLISCO PRINTERS, SCOTT, QC, CANADA.**

10 9 8 7 6 5 4 3 2 1

YEARS AGO, THINKING HE WAS DONNING A NEW COSTUME, PETER PARKER (A.K.A. THE AMAZING SPIDER-MAN) ACCIDENTALLY BONDED WITH A UNIQUE ALIEN BEING CALLED A SYMBIOTE.

WHEN PETER REALIZED THE COSTUME WAS MAKING HIM ANGRIER AND MORE AGGRESSIVE AND ACTUALLY A LIVING ORGANISM, A MEMBER OF AN ALIEN SPECIES CALLED THE KLYNTAR, HE REJECTED IT, LEAVING THE CREATURE FEELING BETRAYED AND ALONE ON A FOREIGN WORLD.

BUT DURING THEIR TIME TOGETHER, THE SYMBIOTE HAD ACCESS TO SPIDER-MAN'S GENETIC CODE, AND AS A RESULT CAN NOW GRANT WHOMEVER IT BONDS WITH SKILLS SIMILAR TO THOSE OF ITS FIRST HOST: WALL CRAWLING, THE POWER TO GENERATE BIORGANIC WEBBING, AND UNIQUE ABILITIES TO SHAPE-SHIFT AND TURN INVISIBLE.

THE SYMBIOTE HAS HAD MANY HOSTS OVER THE YEARS, SOME NOBLE, SOME NEFARIOUS. AND THOUGH IT HAS BEEN A LETHAL PROTECTOR, A GOVERNMENT AGENT, AND A GUARDIAN OF THE GALAXY, IT WILL ALWAYS REMAIN...

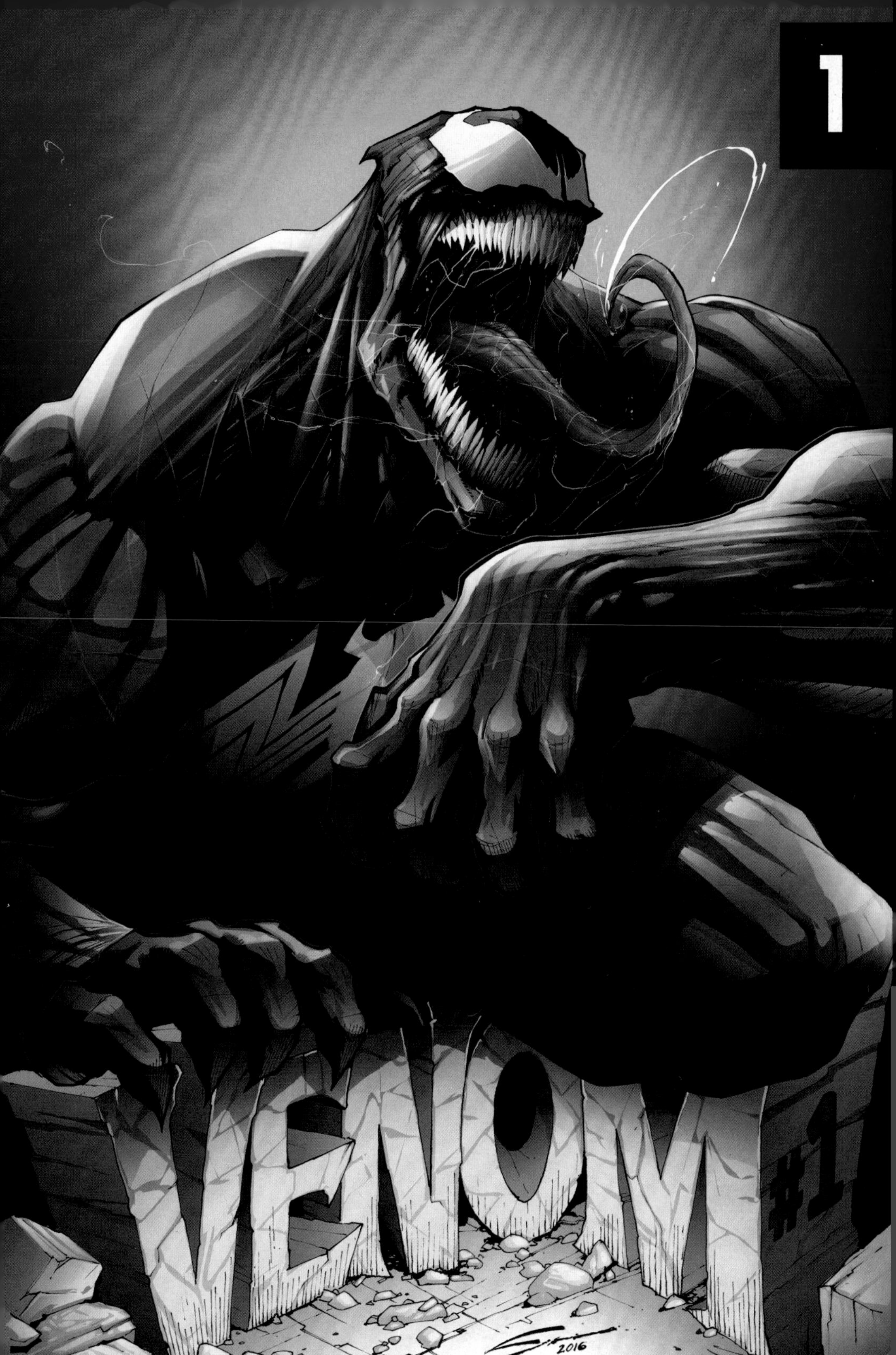
1
VENOM
#1
2016

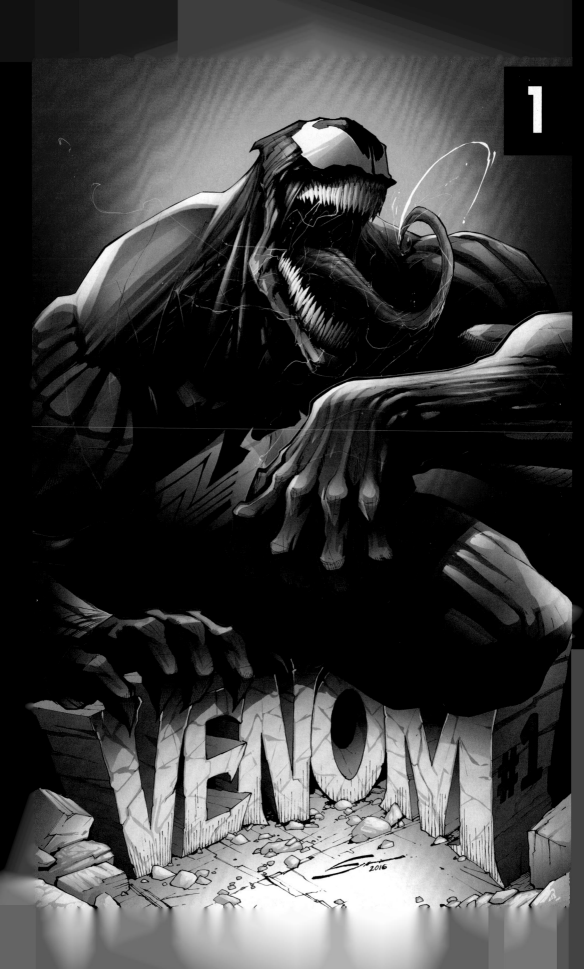

ONE THING THIS WORLD HAS TAUGHT ME...

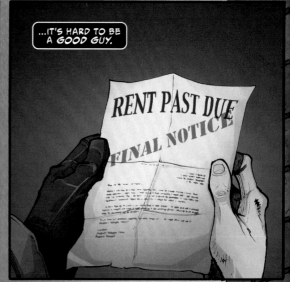

...IT'S HARD TO BE A *GOOD GUY*.

RENT PAST DUE
FINAL NOTICE

BAD GUYS HAVE IT MUCH EASIER. GIVEN A MEASURE OF POWER, IT'S EASIER TO USE IT SELFISHLY. IT'S EASIER TO TAKE THAN TO GIVE.

I'VE LEARNED IT TAKES *STRENGTH* TO DO WHAT'S RIGHT. AND POWER IS *NOT* STRENGTH.

Tony

You still looking for work?

Meet @ diner in an hour.

WHAT'S WORSE IS THAT STRENGTH, I'VE LEARNED, TAKES *HELP*.

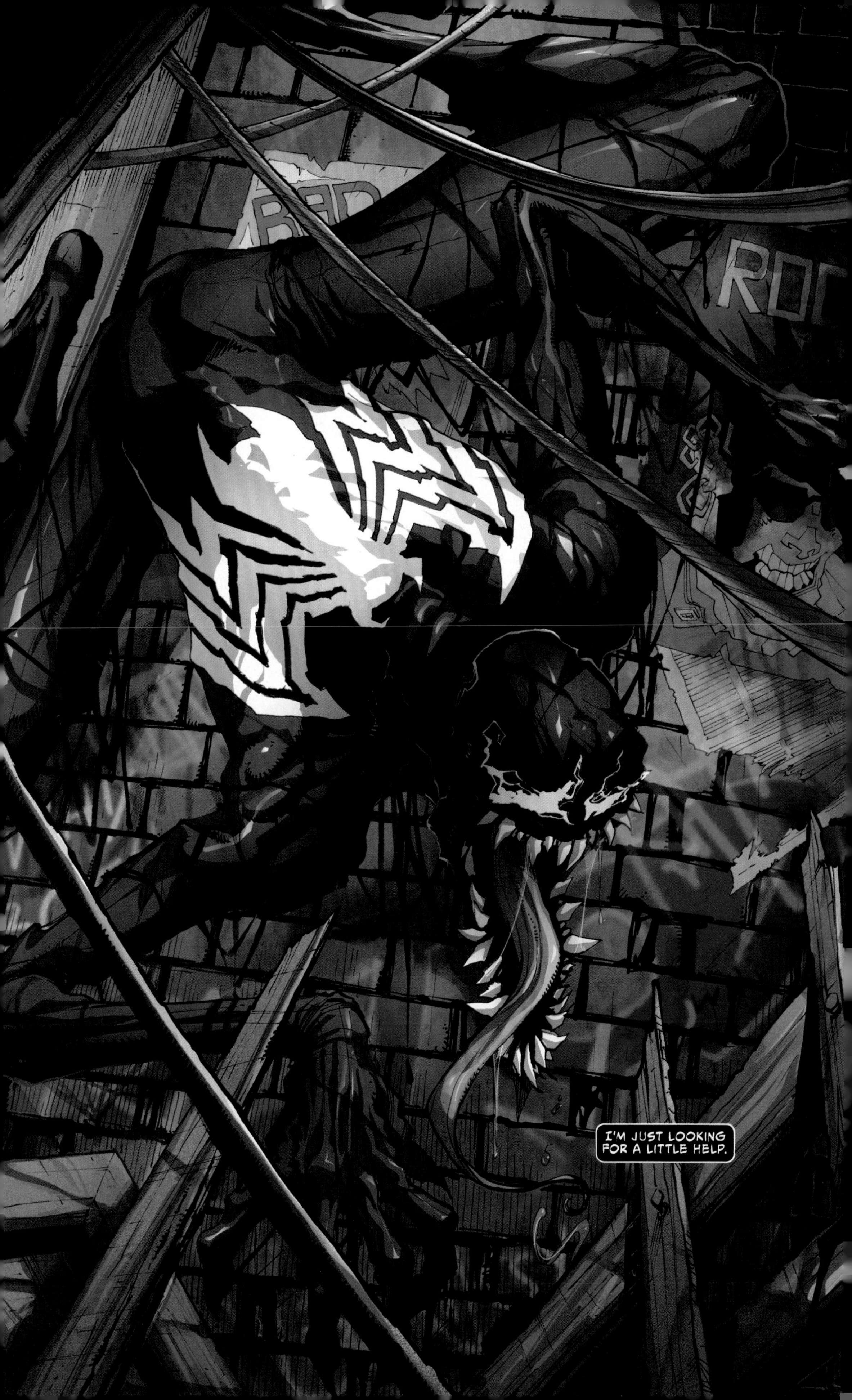
I'M JUST LOOKING FOR A LITTLE HELP.

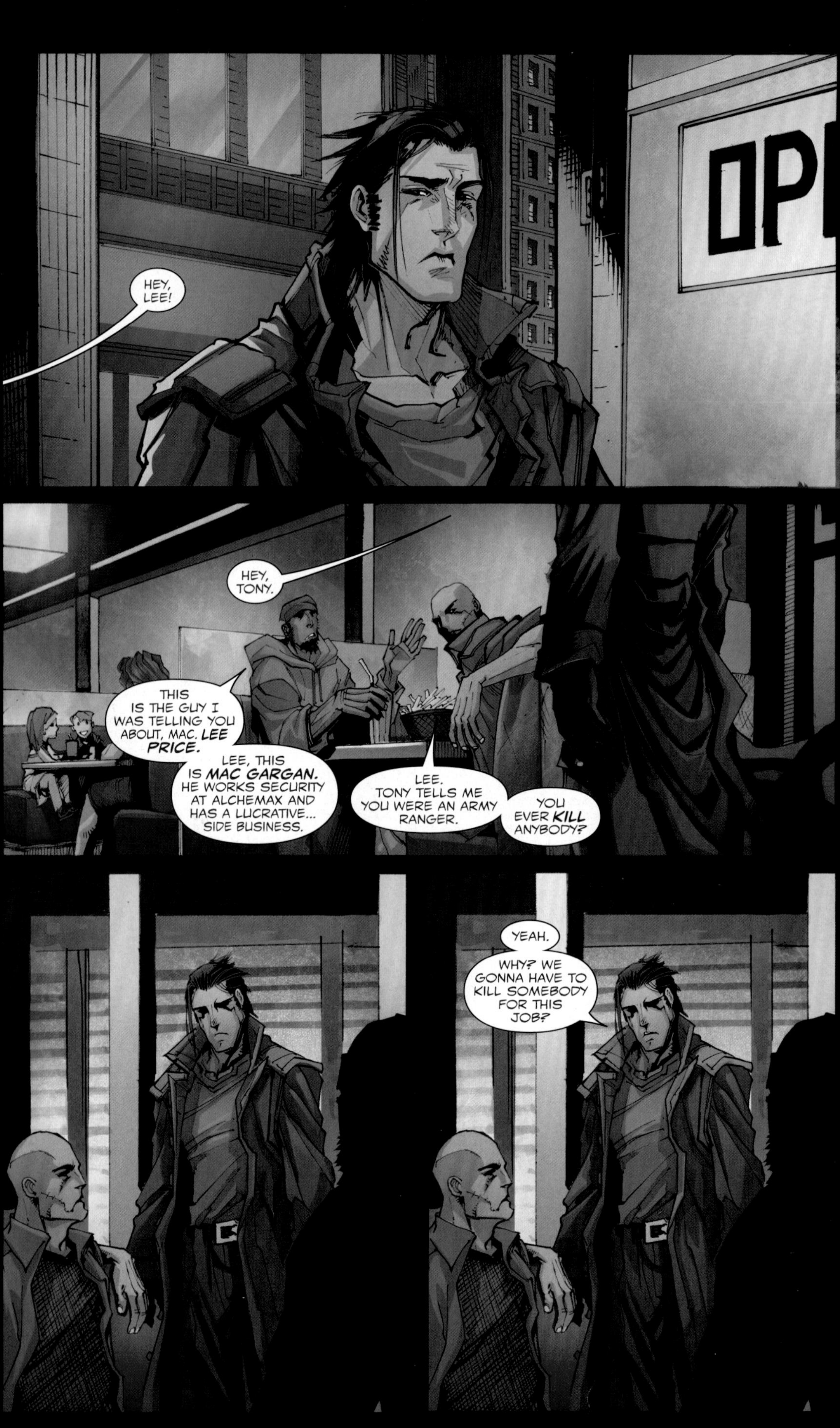
HEY, LEE!
OP
HEY, TONY.
THIS IS THE GUY I WAS TELLING YOU ABOUT, MAC. LEE PRICE.
LEE, THIS IS MAC GARGAN. HE WORKS SECURITY AT ALCHEMAX AND HAS A LUCRATIVE... SIDE BUSINESS.
LEE. TONY TELLS ME YOU WERE AN ARMY RANGER.
YOU EVER KILL ANYBODY?
YEAH.
WHY? WE GONNA HAVE TO KILL SOMEBODY FOR THIS JOB?

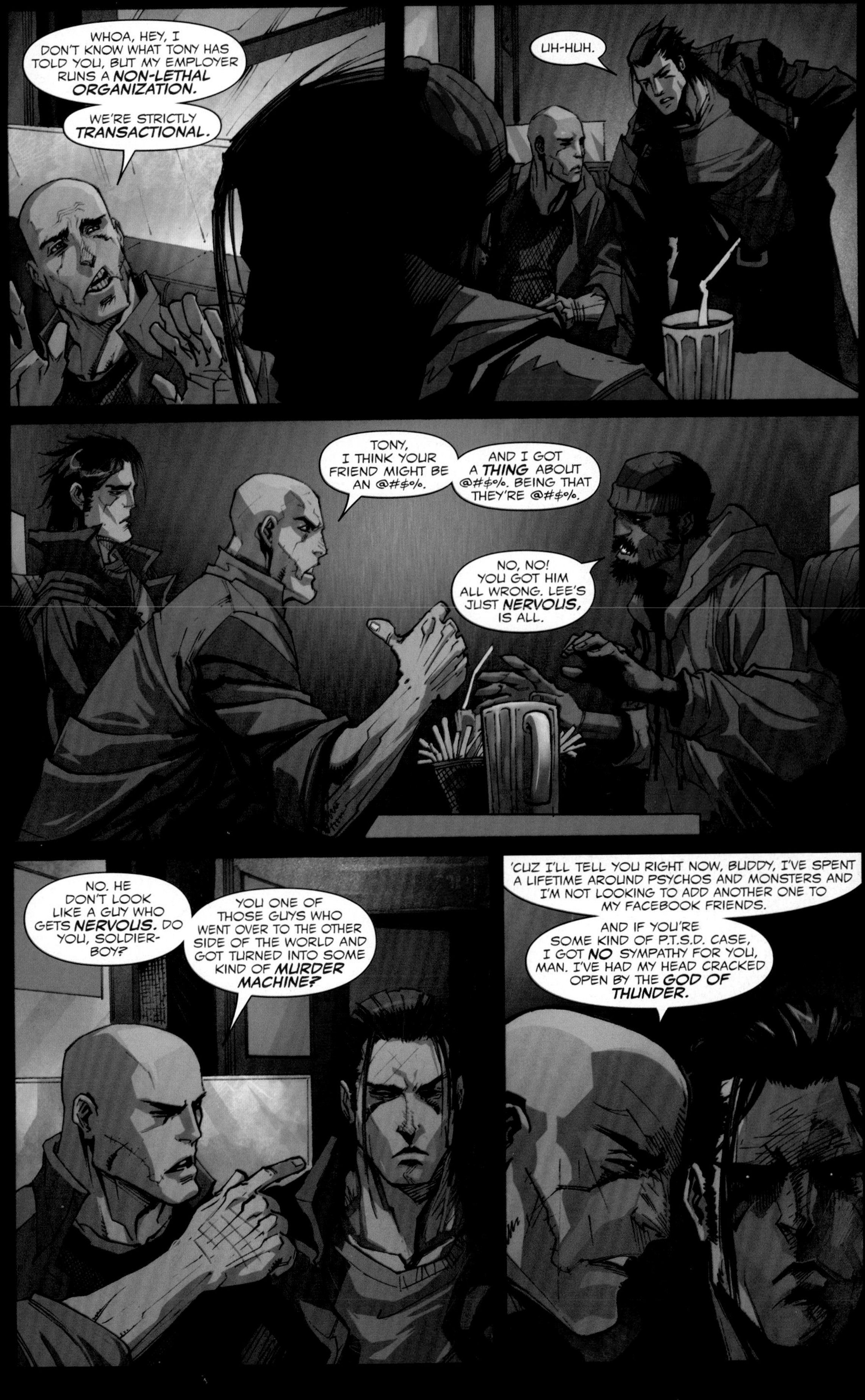
WHOA, HEY, I DON'T KNOW WHAT TONY HAS TOLD YOU, BUT MY EMPLOYER RUNS A NON-LETHAL ORGANIZATION.
WE'RE STRICTLY TRANSACTIONAL.
UH-HUH.
TONY, I THINK YOUR FRIEND MIGHT BE AN @#$%.
AND I GOT A THING ABOUT @#$%. BEING THAT THEY'RE @#$%.
NO, NO! YOU GOT HIM ALL WRONG. LEE'S JUST NERVOUS, IS ALL.
NO. HE DON'T LOOK LIKE A GUY WHO GETS NERVOUS. DO YOU, SOLDIER-BOY?
YOU ONE OF THOSE GUYS WHO WENT OVER TO THE OTHER SIDE OF THE WORLD AND GOT TURNED INTO SOME KIND OF MURDER MACHINE?
'CUZ I'LL TELL YOU RIGHT NOW, BUDDY, I'VE SPENT A LIFETIME AROUND PSYCHOS AND MONSTERS AND I'M NOT LOOKING TO ADD ANOTHER ONE TO MY FACEBOOK FRIENDS.
AND IF YOU'RE SOME KIND OF P.T.S.D. CASE, I GOT NO SYMPATHY FOR YOU, MAN. I'VE HAD MY HEAD CRACKED OPEN BY THE GOD OF THUNDER.

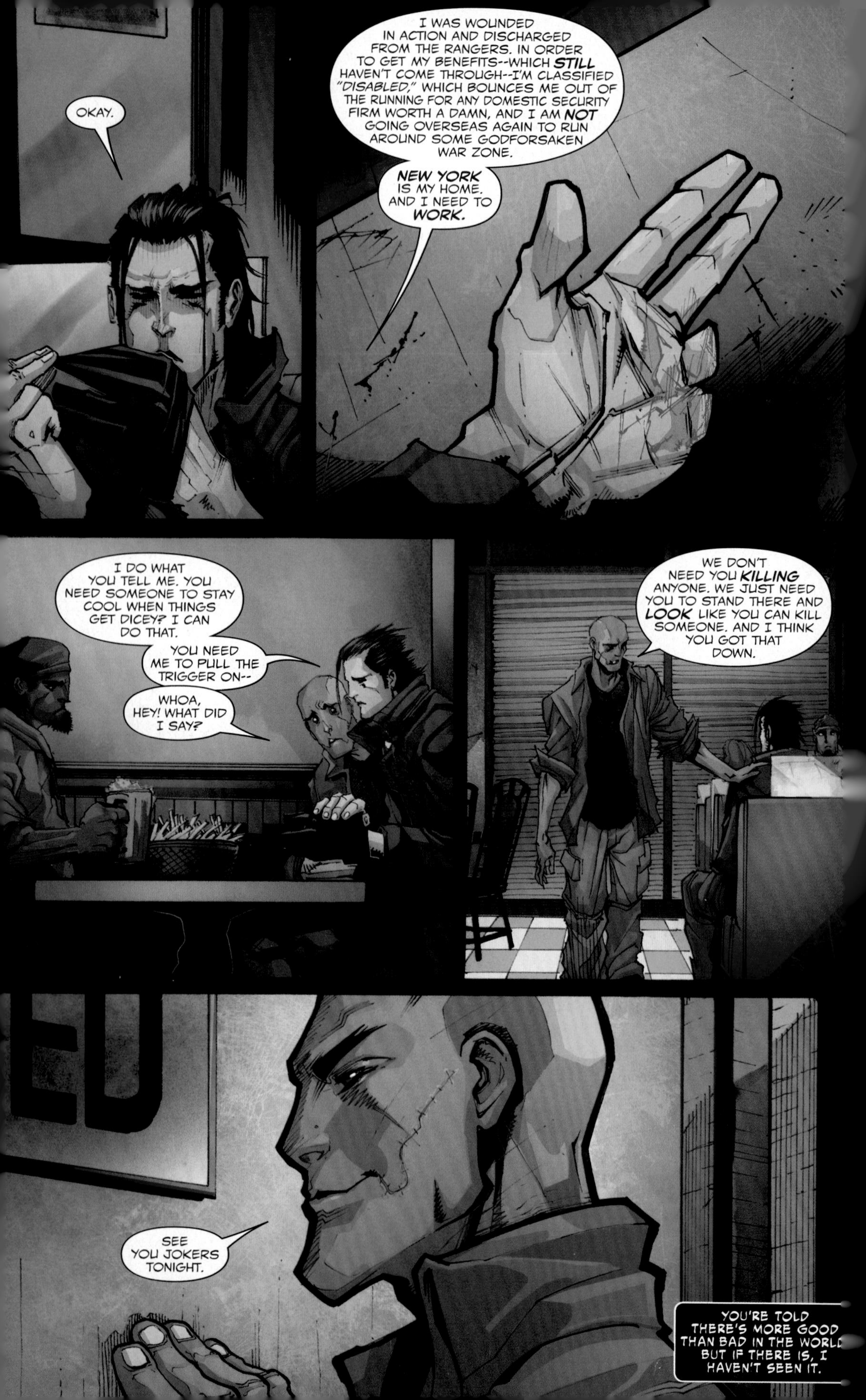

OKAY.
I WAS WOUNDED IN ACTION AND DISCHARGED FROM THE RANGERS. IN ORDER TO GET MY BENEFITS--WHICH STILL HAVEN'T COME THROUGH--I'M CLASSIFIED "DISABLED," WHICH BOUNCES ME OUT OF THE RUNNING FOR ANY DOMESTIC SECURITY FIRM WORTH A DAMN, AND I AM NOT GOING OVERSEAS AGAIN TO RUN AROUND SOME GODFORSAKEN WAR ZONE.
NEW YORK IS MY HOME. AND I NEED TO WORK.
I DO WHAT YOU TELL ME. YOU NEED SOMEONE TO STAY COOL WHEN THINGS GET DICEY? I CAN DO THAT.
YOU NEED ME TO PULL THE TRIGGER ON--
WHOA, HEY! WHAT DID I SAY?
WE DON'T NEED YOU KILLING ANYONE. WE JUST NEED YOU TO STAND THERE AND LOOK LIKE YOU CAN KILL SOMEONE. AND I THINK YOU GOT THAT DOWN.
ED
SEE YOU JOKERS TONIGHT.
YOU'RE TOLD THERE'S MORE GOOD THAN BAD IN THE WORLD BUT IF THERE IS, I HAVEN'T SEEN IT.

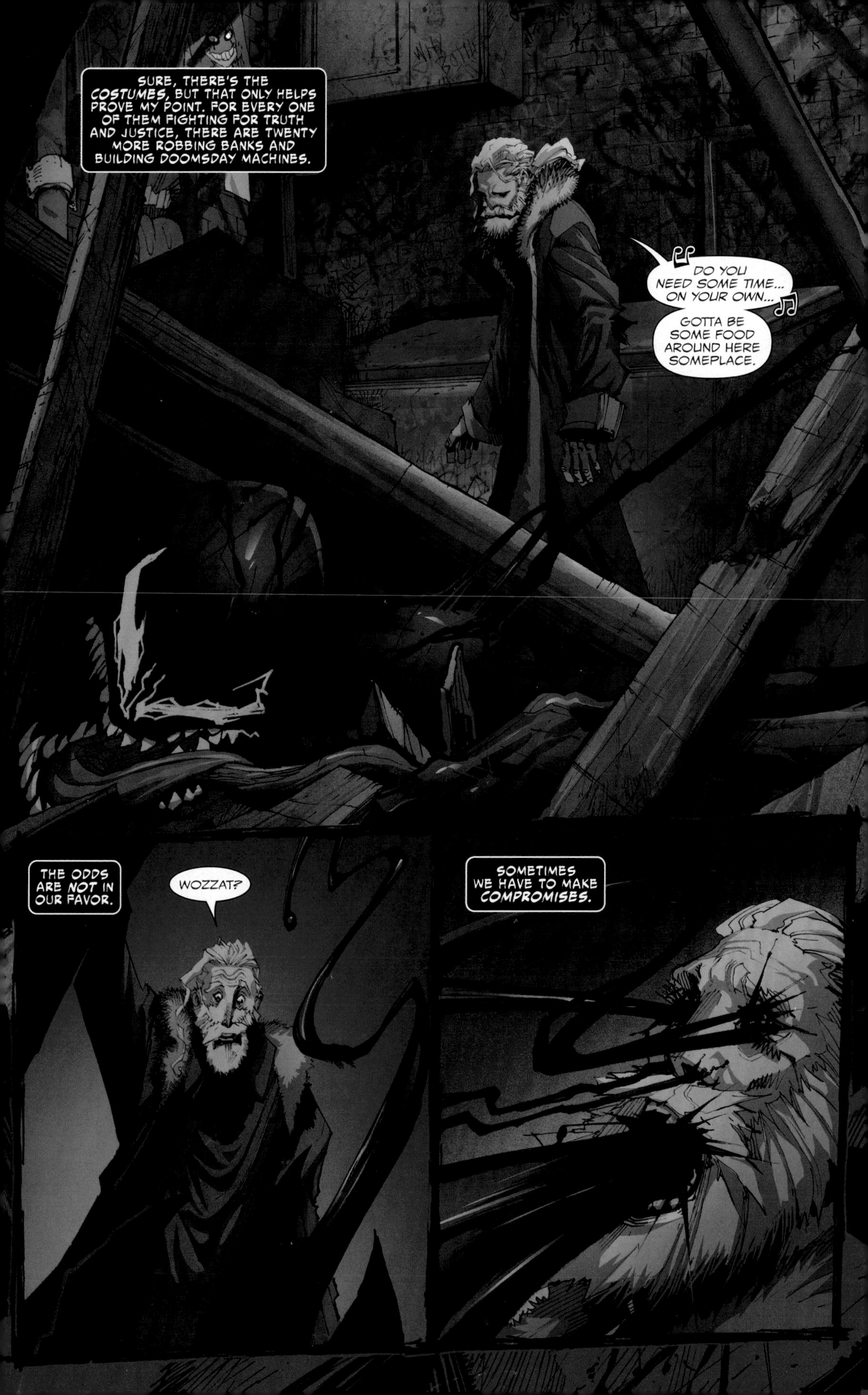
SURE, THERE'S THE COSTUMES, BUT THAT ONLY HELPS PROVE MY POINT. FOR EVERY ONE OF THEM FIGHTING FOR TRUTH AND JUSTICE, THERE ARE TWENTY MORE ROBBING BANKS AND BUILDING DOOMSDAY MACHINES.
DO YOU NEED SOME TIME... ON YOUR OWN...
GOTTA BE SOME FOOD AROUND HERE SOMEPLACE.
THE ODDS ARE NOT IN OUR FAVOR.
WOZZAT?
SOMETIMES WE HAVE TO MAKE COMPROMISES.

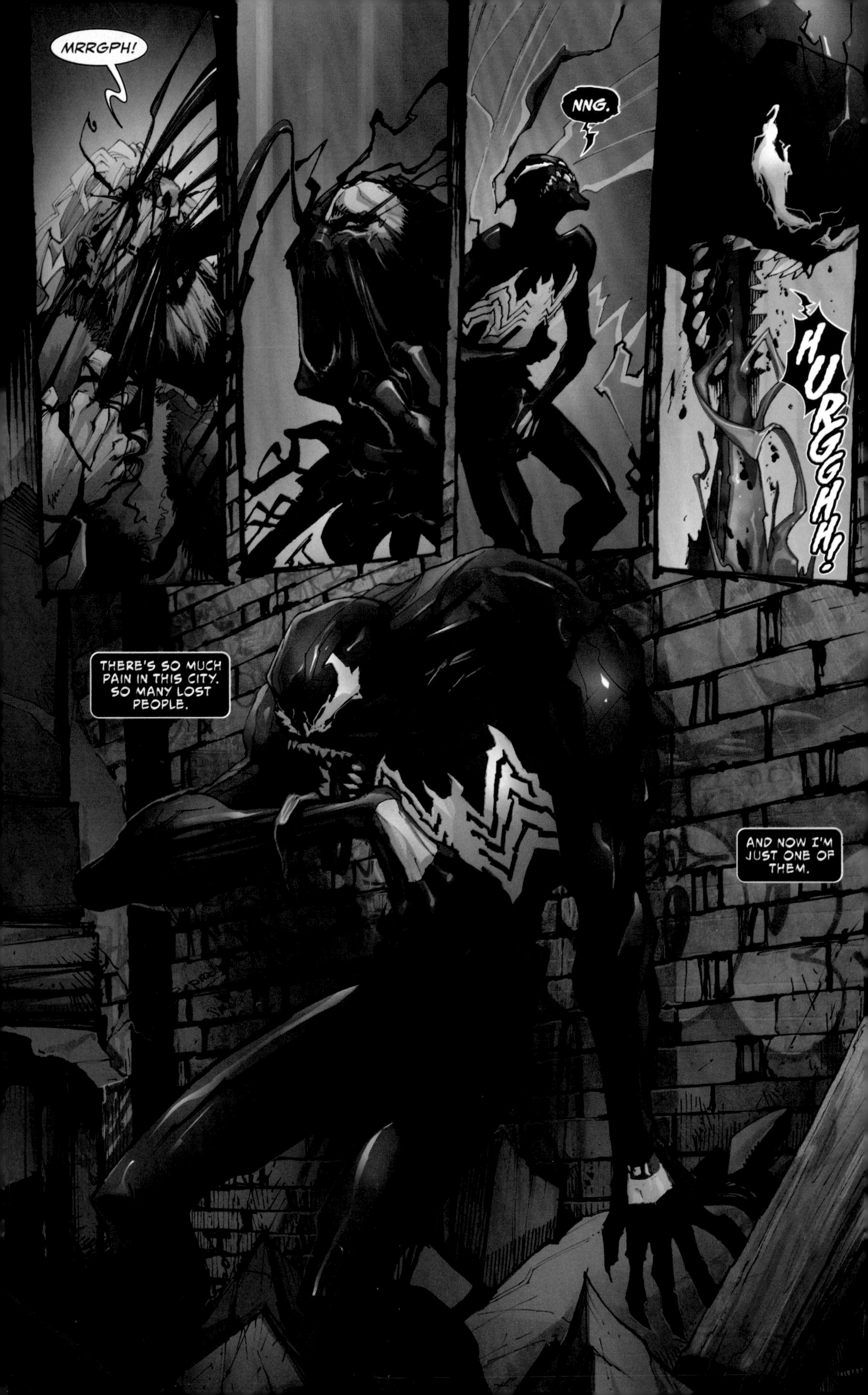
MRRGPH!
NNG.
HURGGHH!
THERE'S SO MUCH PAIN IN THIS CITY. SO MANY LOST PEOPLE.
AND NOW I'M JUST ONE OF THEM.

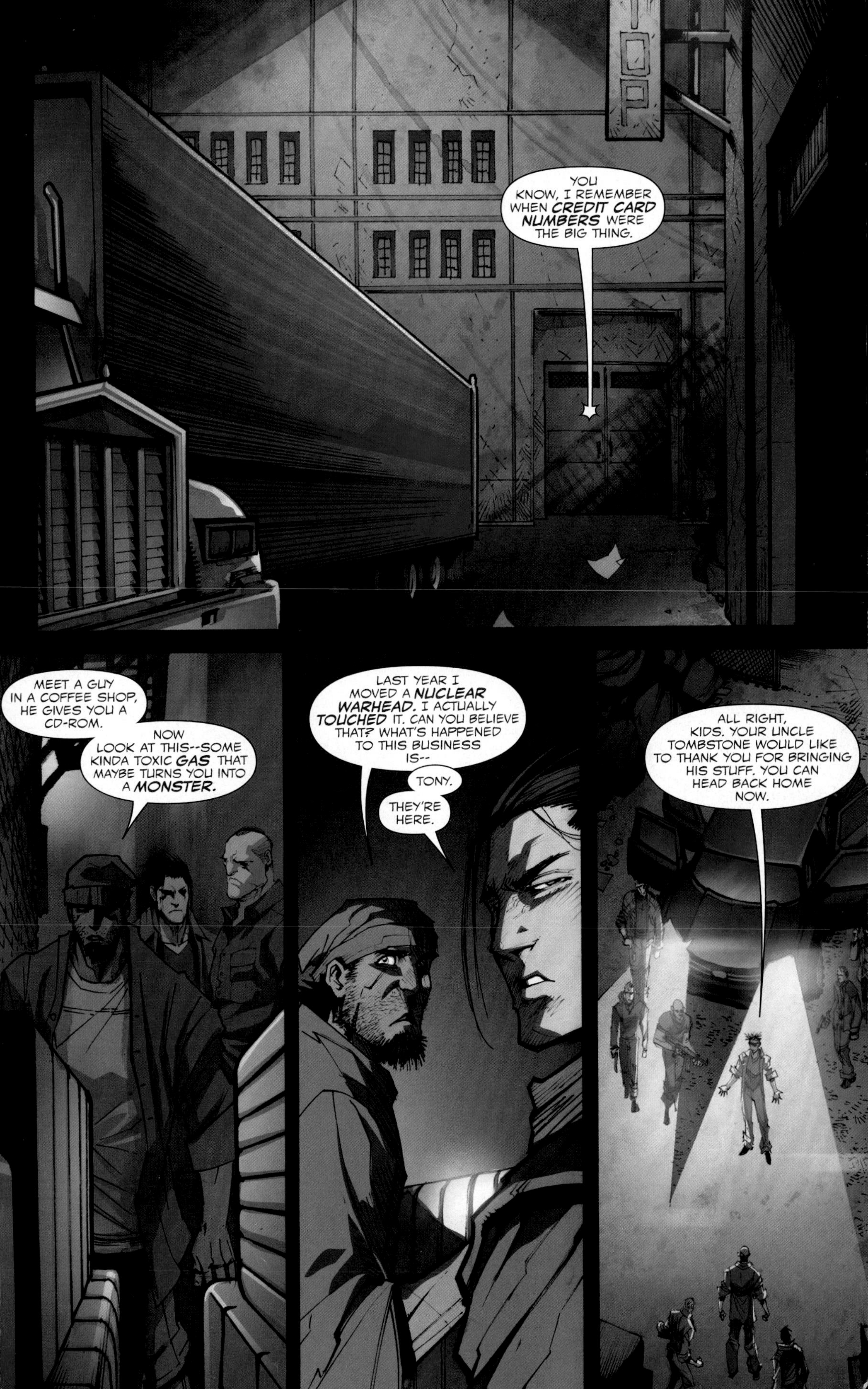
YOU KNOW, I REMEMBER WHEN CREDIT CARD NUMBERS WERE THE BIG THING.
MEET A GUY IN A COFFEE SHOP, HE GIVES YOU A CD-ROM.
NOW LOOK AT THIS--SOME KINDA TOXIC GAS THAT MAYBE TURNS YOU INTO A MONSTER.
LAST YEAR I MOVED A NUCLEAR WARHEAD. I ACTUALLY TOUCHED IT. CAN YOU BELIEVE THAT? WHAT'S HAPPENED TO THIS BUSINESS IS--
TONY.
THEY'RE HERE.
ALL RIGHT, KIDS. YOUR UNCLE TOMBSTONE WOULD LIKE TO THANK YOU FOR BRINGING HIS STUFF. YOU CAN HEAD BACK HOME NOW.

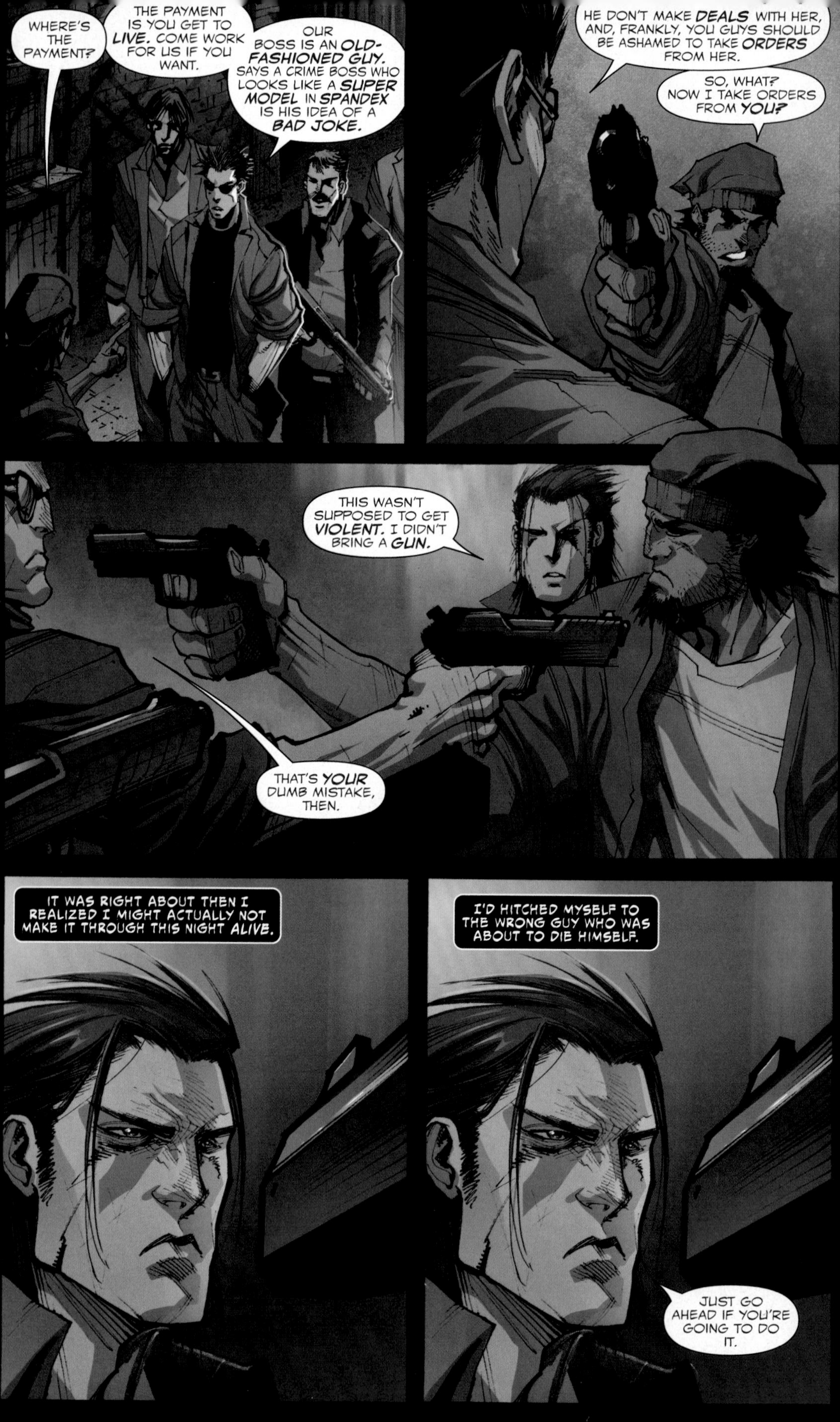
WHERE'S THE PAYMENT?
THE PAYMENT IS YOU GET TO LIVE. COME WORK FOR US IF YOU WANT.
OUR BOSS IS AN OLD-FASHIONED GUY. SAYS A CRIME BOSS WHO LOOKS LIKE A SUPER MODEL IN SPANDEX IS HIS IDEA OF A BAD JOKE.
HE DON'T MAKE DEALS WITH HER, AND, FRANKLY, YOU GUYS SHOULD BE ASHAMED TO TAKE ORDERS FROM HER.
SO, WHAT? NOW I TAKE ORDERS FROM YOU?
THIS WASN'T SUPPOSED TO GET VIOLENT. I DIDN'T BRING A GUN.
THAT'S YOUR DUMB MISTAKE, THEN.
IT WAS RIGHT ABOUT THEN I REALIZED I MIGHT ACTUALLY NOT MAKE IT THROUGH THIS NIGHT ALIVE.
I'D HITCHED MYSELF TO THE WRONG GUY WHO WAS ABOUT TO DIE HIMSELF.
JUST GO AHEAD IF YOU'RE GOING TO DO IT.

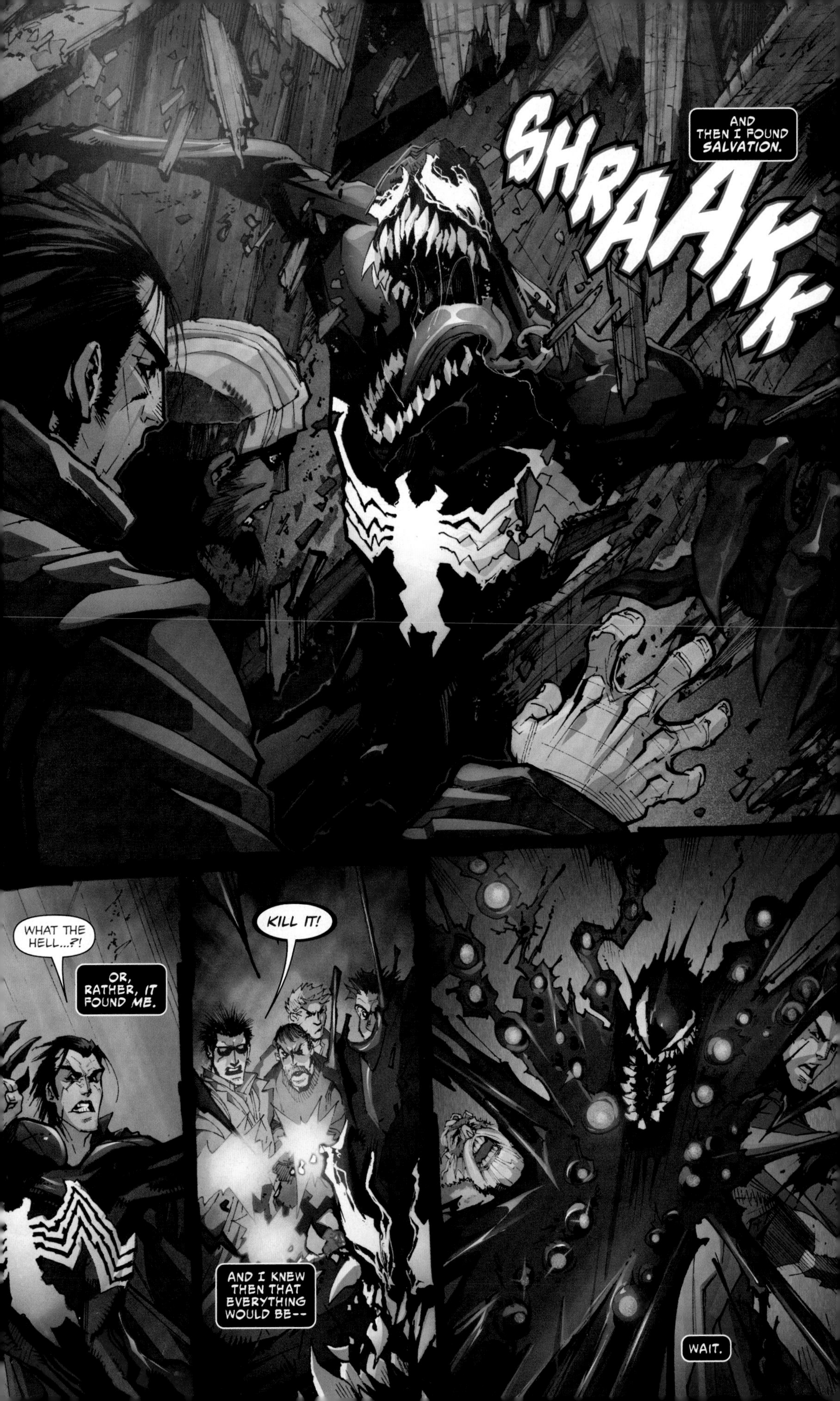
SHRAAKK
AND THEN I FOUND SALVATION.
WHAT THE HELL...?!
OR, RATHER, IT FOUND ME.
KILL IT!
AND I KNEW THEN THAT EVERYTHING WOULD BE--
WAIT.

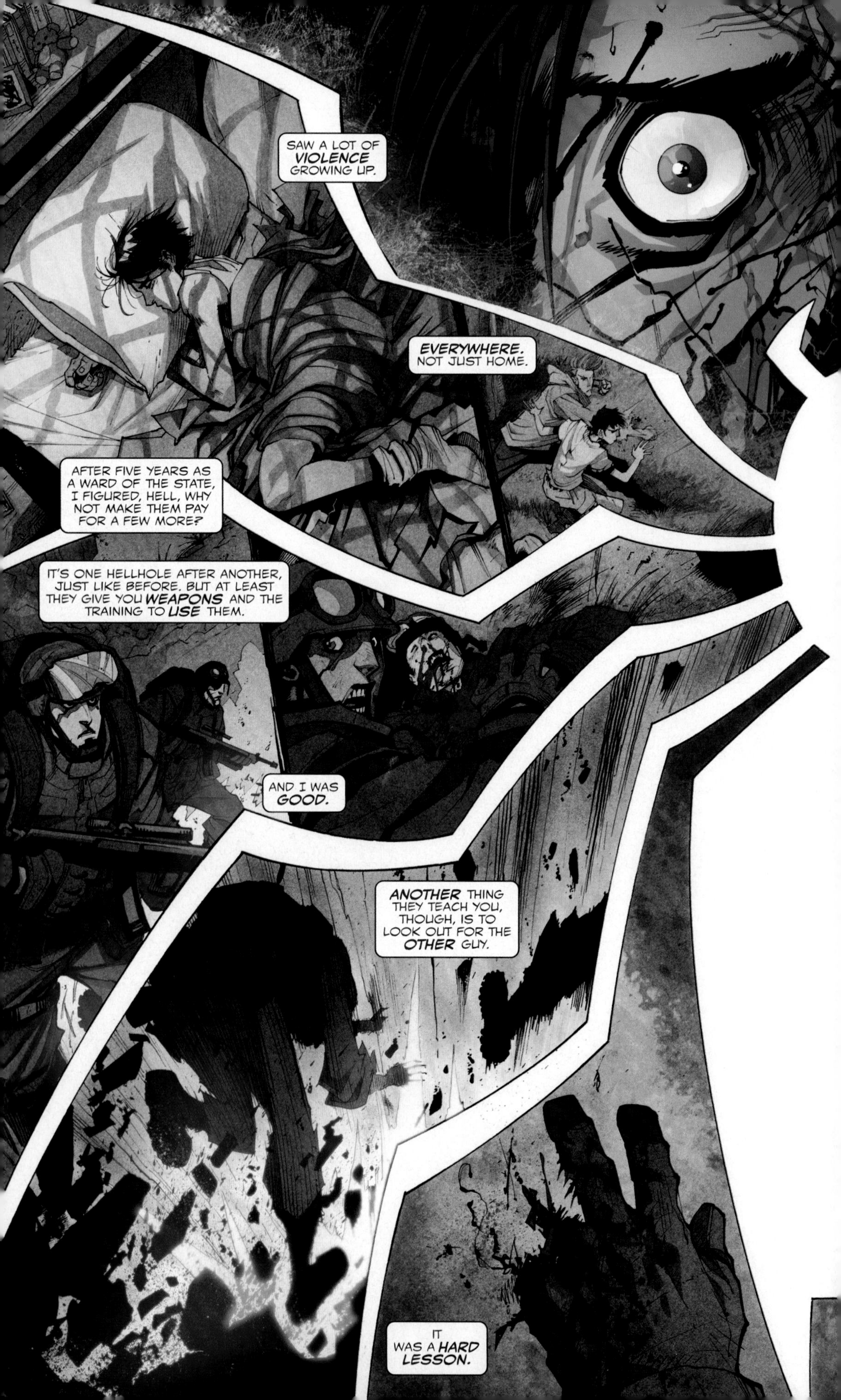

SAW A LOT OF VIOLENCE GROWING UP.
EVERYWHERE. NOT JUST HOME.
AFTER FIVE YEARS AS A WARD OF THE STATE, I FIGURED, HELL, WHY NOT MAKE THEM PAY FOR A FEW MORE?
IT'S ONE HELLHOLE AFTER ANOTHER, JUST LIKE BEFORE. BUT AT LEAST THEY GIVE YOU WEAPONS AND THE TRAINING TO USE THEM.
AND I WAS GOOD.
ANOTHER THING THEY TEACH YOU, THOUGH, IS TO LOOK OUT FOR THE OTHER GUY.
IT WAS A HARD LESSON.

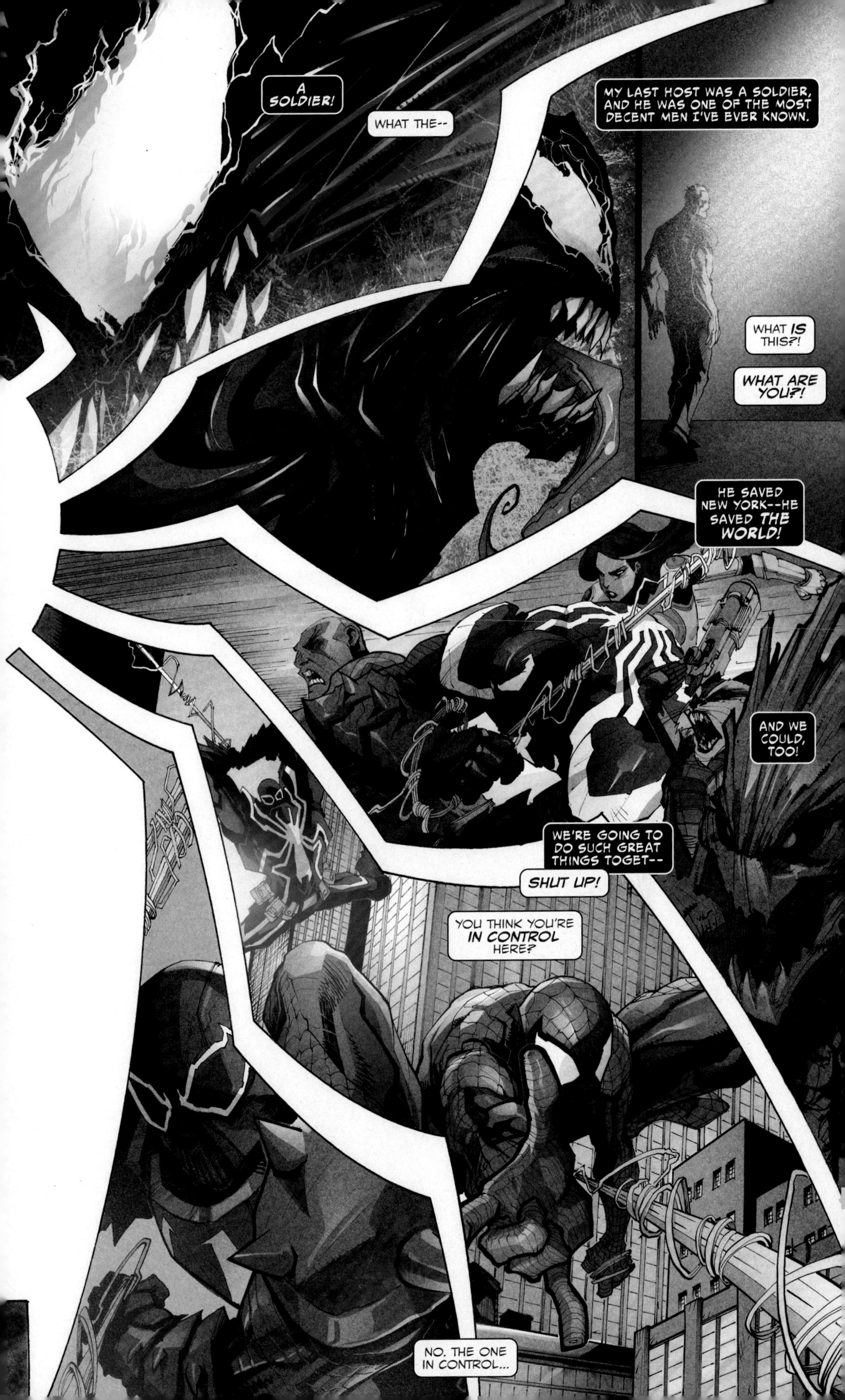
A SOLDIER!
WHAT THE--
MY LAST HOST WAS A SOLDIER, AND HE WAS ONE OF THE MOST DECENT MEN I'VE EVER KNOWN.
WHAT IS THIS?!
WHAT ARE YOU?!
HE SAVED NEW YORK--HE SAVED THE WORLD!
AND WE COULD, TOO!
WE'RE GOING TO DO SUCH GREAT THINGS TOGET--
SHUT UP!
YOU THINK YOU'RE IN CONTROL HERE?
NO. THE ONE IN CONTROL...

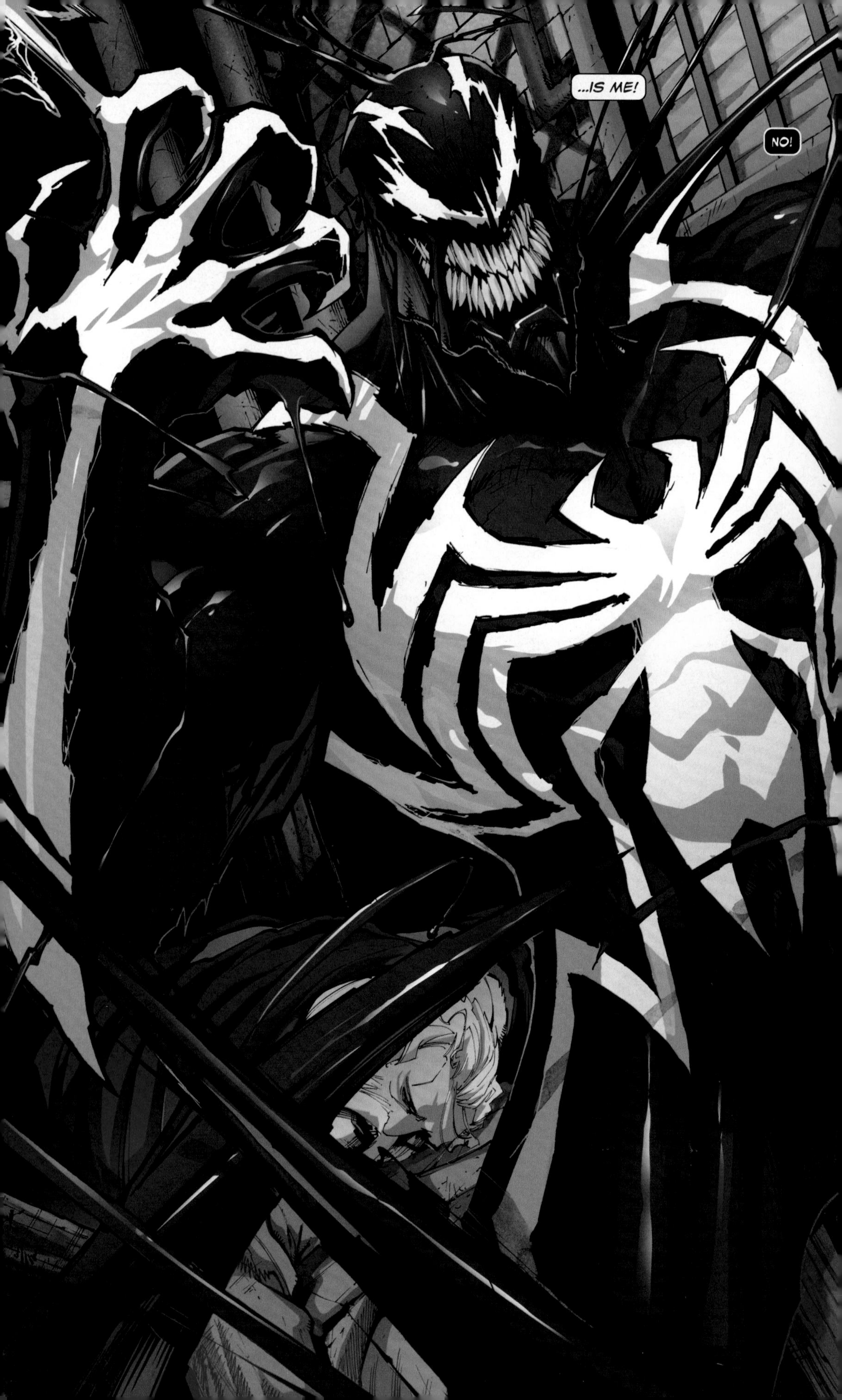
...IS ME!
NO!

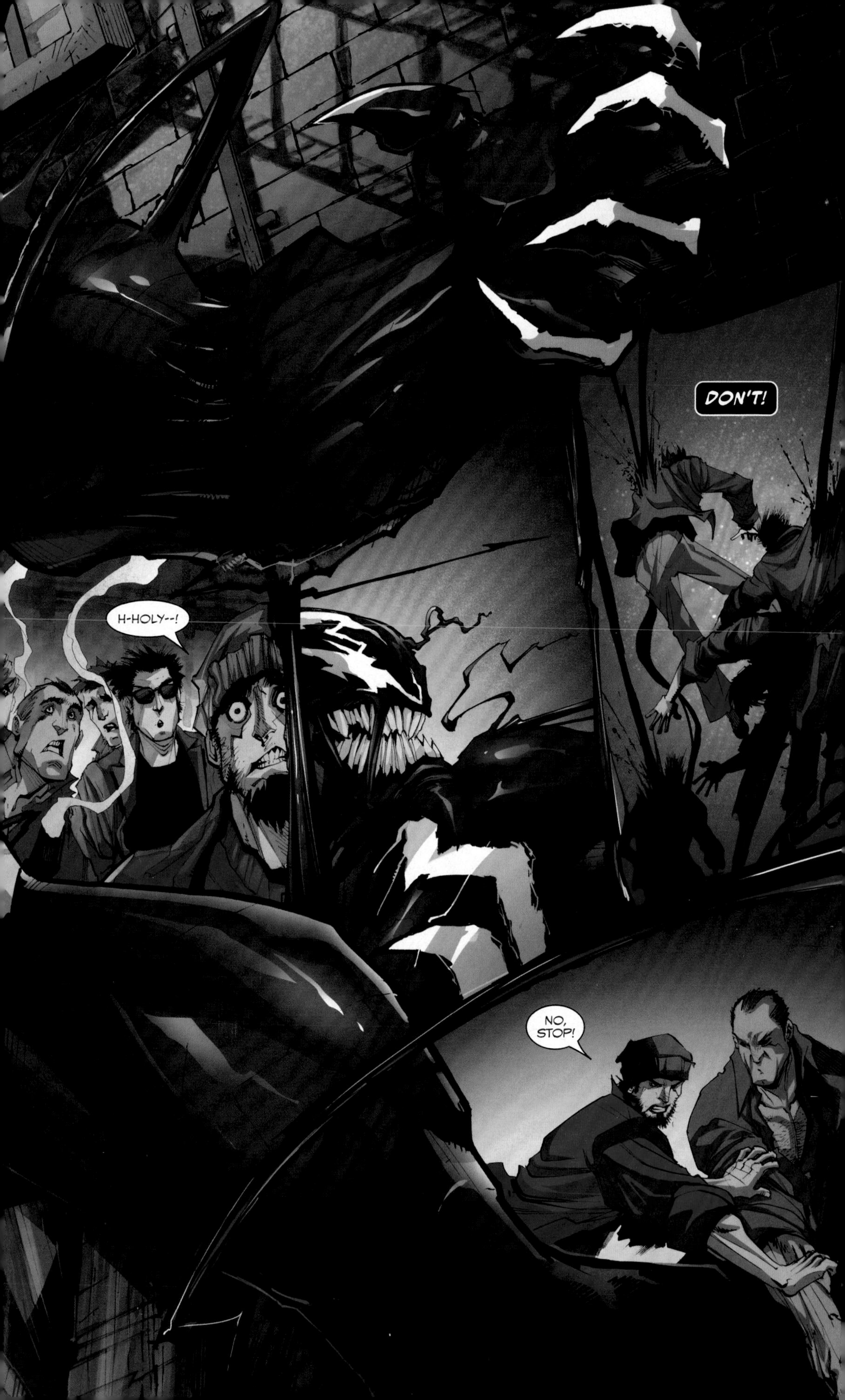
DON'T!
H-HOLY--!
NO, STOP!

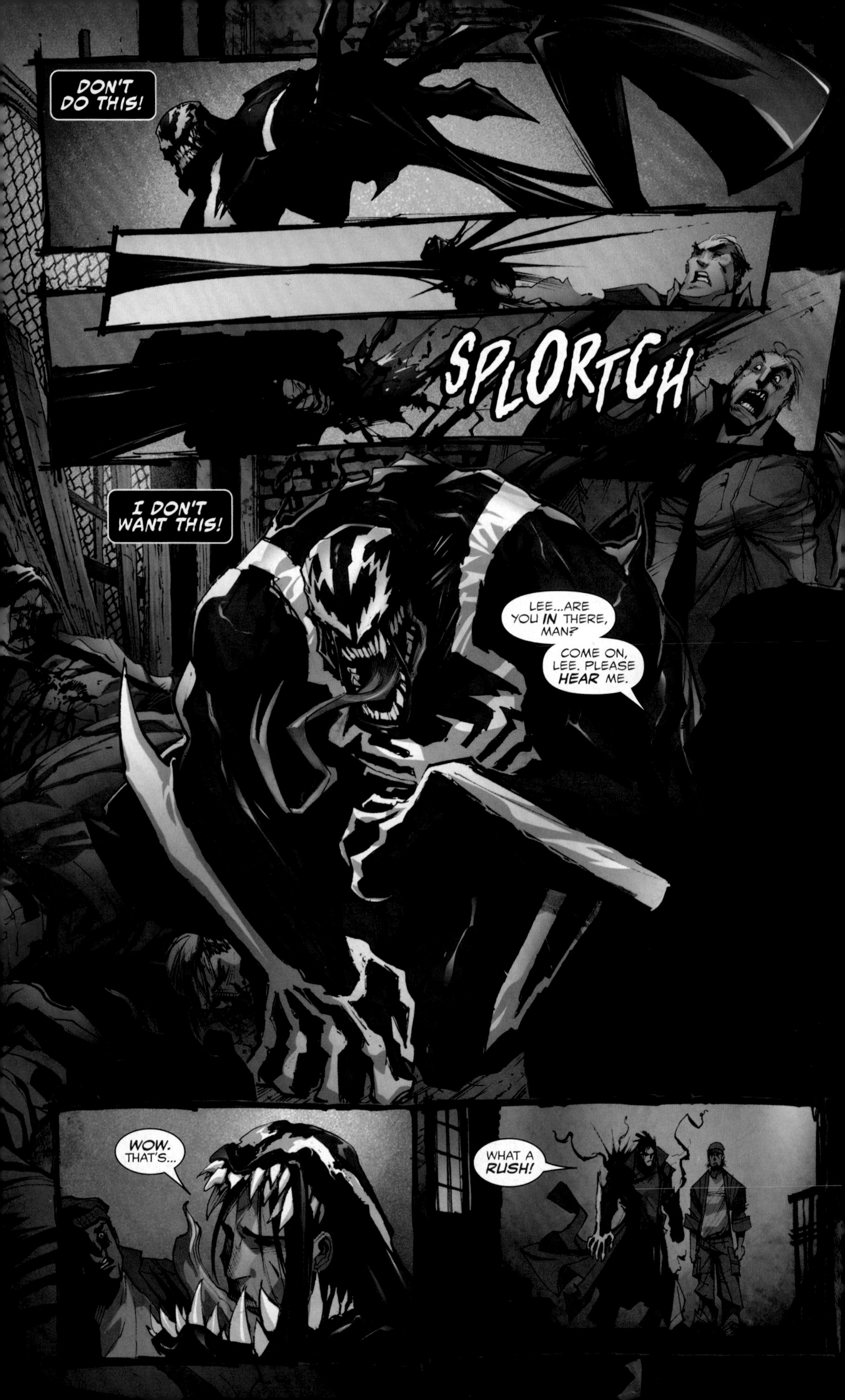
DON'T DO THIS!
SPLORTCH
I DON'T WANT THIS!
LEE...ARE YOU IN THERE, MAN?
COME ON, LEE. PLEASE HEAR ME.
WOW. THAT'S...
WHAT A RUSH!

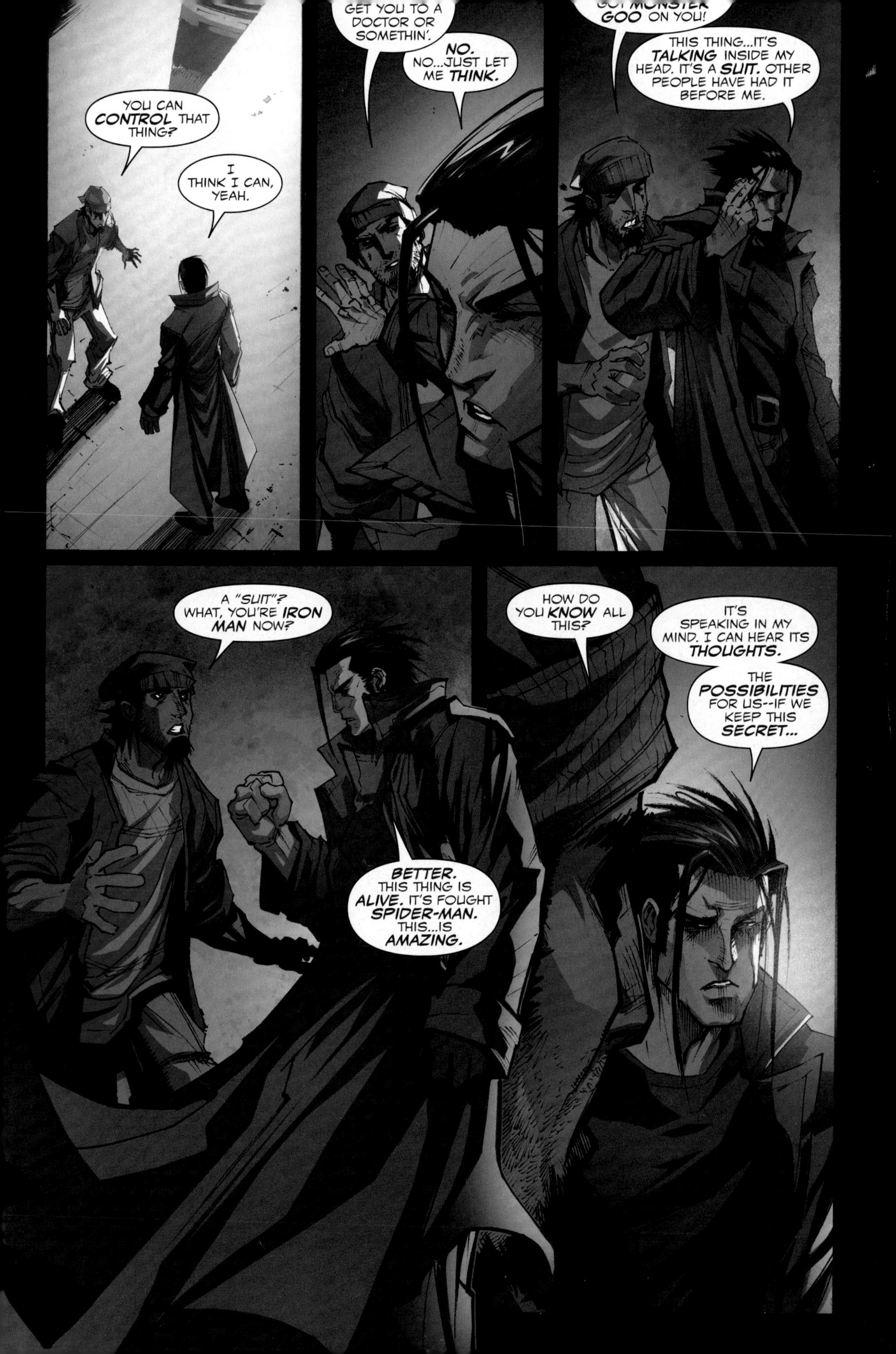
YOU CAN CONTROL THAT THING?
I THINK I CAN, YEAH.
GET YOU TO A DOCTOR OR SOMETHIN'.
NO. NO...JUST LET ME THINK.
MONSTER GOO ON YOU!
THIS THING...IT'S TALKING INSIDE MY HEAD. IT'S A SUIT. OTHER PEOPLE HAVE HAD IT BEFORE ME.
A "SUIT"? WHAT, YOU'RE IRON MAN NOW?
BETTER. THIS THING IS ALIVE. IT'S FOUGHT SPIDER-MAN. THIS...IS AMAZING.
HOW DO YOU KNOW ALL THIS?
IT'S SPEAKING IN MY MIND. I CAN HEAR ITS THOUGHTS.
THE POSSIBILITIES FOR US--IF WE KEEP THIS SECRET...

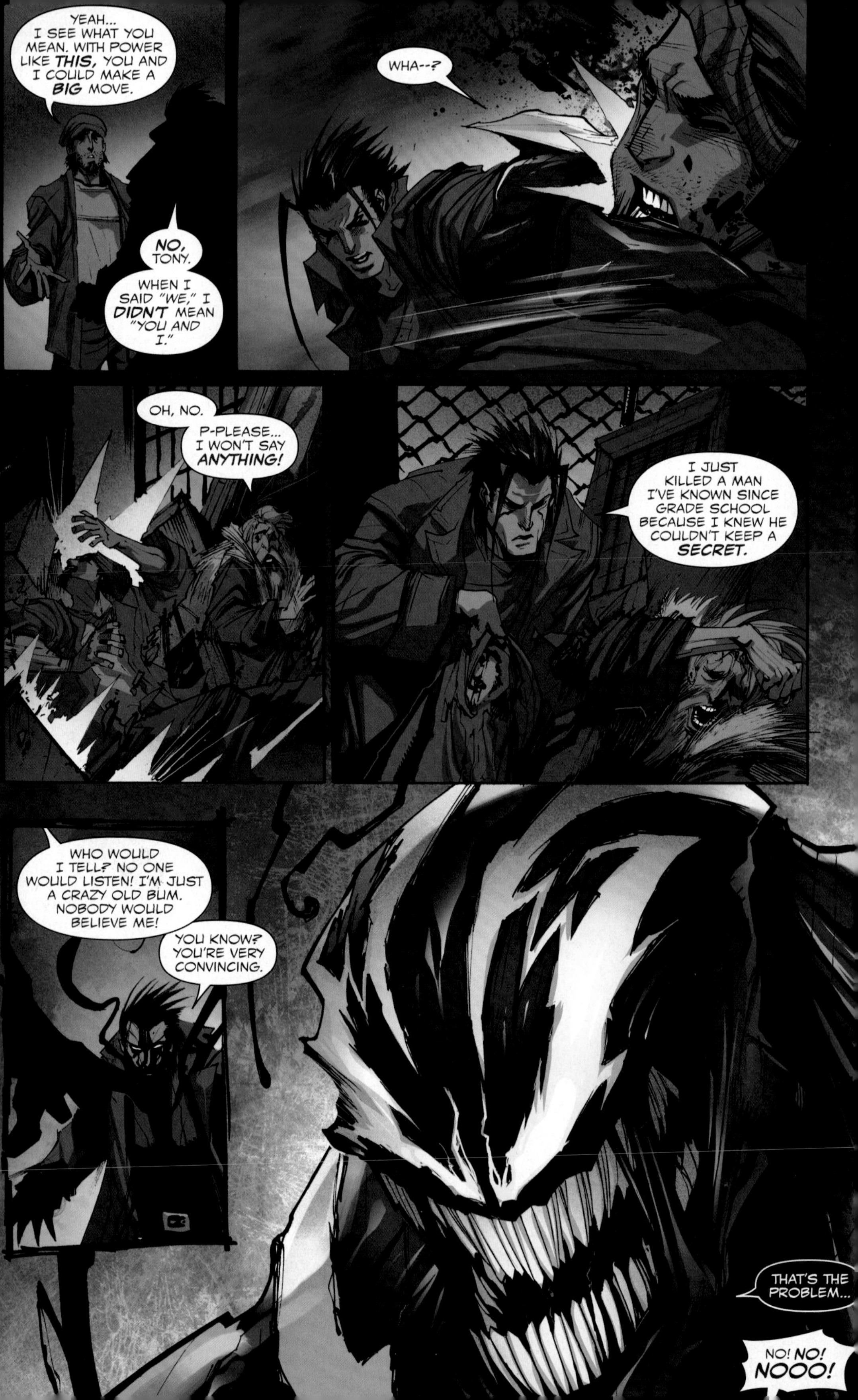
YEAH... I SEE WHAT YOU MEAN. WITH POWER LIKE THIS, YOU AND I COULD MAKE A BIG MOVE.
NO, TONY.
WHEN I SAID "WE," I DIDN'T MEAN "YOU AND I."
WHA--?
OH, NO.
P-PLEASE... I WON'T SAY ANYTHING!
I JUST KILLED A MAN I'VE KNOWN SINCE GRADE SCHOOL BECAUSE I KNEW HE COULDN'T KEEP A SECRET.
WHO WOULD I TELL? NO ONE WOULD LISTEN! I'M JUST A CRAZY OLD BUM. NOBODY WOULD BELIEVE ME!
YOU KNOW? YOU'RE VERY CONVINCING.
THAT'S THE PROBLEM...
NO! NO! NOOO!

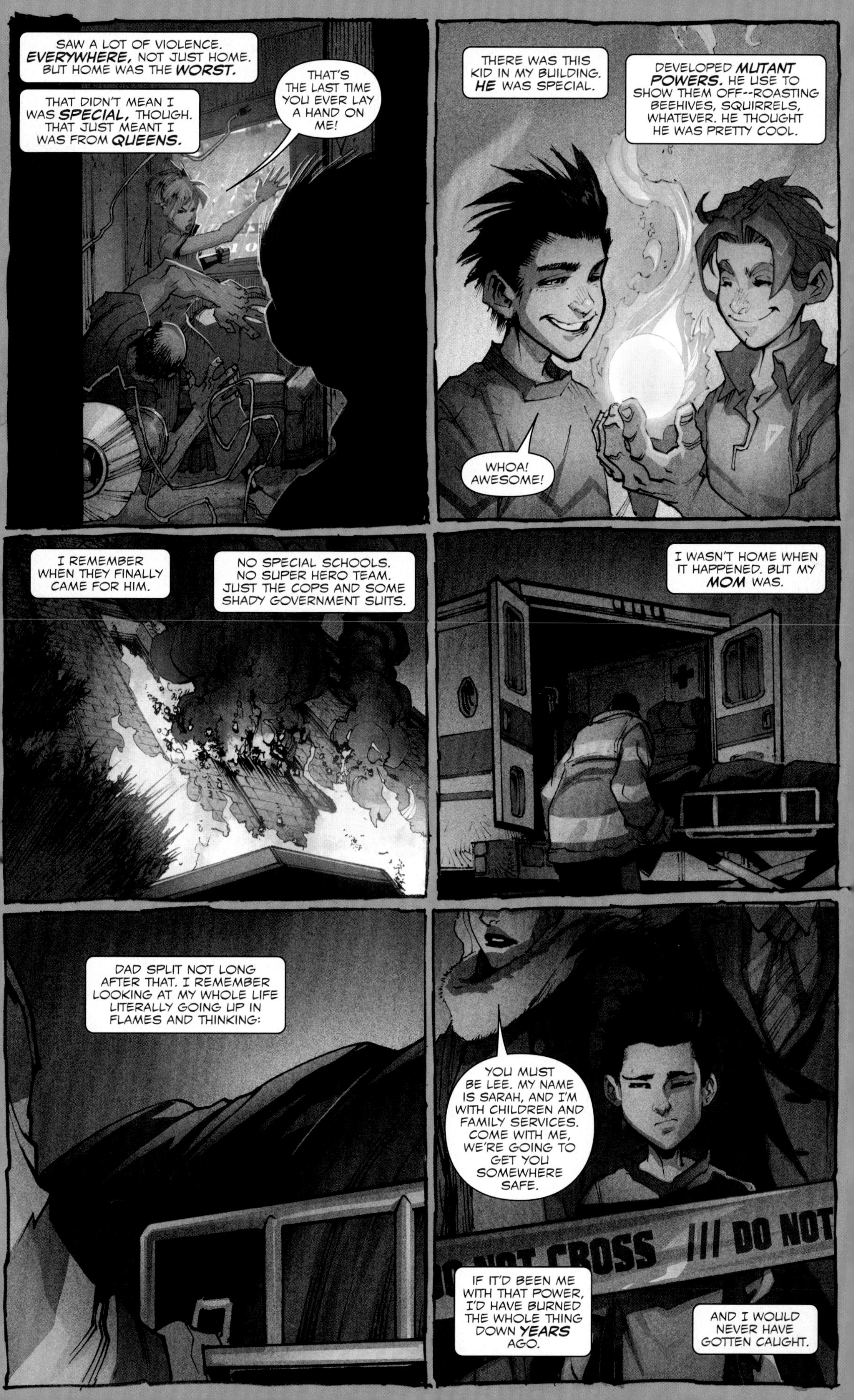
SAW A LOT OF VIOLENCE. EVERYWHERE, NOT JUST HOME. BUT HOME WAS THE WORST.
THAT DIDN'T MEAN I WAS SPECIAL, THOUGH. THAT JUST MEANT I WAS FROM QUEENS.
THAT'S THE LAST TIME YOU EVER LAY A HAND ON ME!
THERE WAS THIS KID IN MY BUILDING. HE WAS SPECIAL.
DEVELOPED MUTANT POWERS. HE USE TO SHOW THEM OFF--ROASTING BEEHIVES, SQUIRRELS, WHATEVER. HE THOUGHT HE WAS PRETTY COOL.
WHOA! AWESOME!
I REMEMBER WHEN THEY FINALLY CAME FOR HIM.
NO SPECIAL SCHOOLS. NO SUPER HERO TEAM. JUST THE COPS AND SOME SHADY GOVERNMENT SUITS.
I WASN'T HOME WHEN IT HAPPENED. BUT MY MOM WAS.
DAD SPLIT NOT LONG AFTER THAT. I REMEMBER LOOKING AT MY WHOLE LIFE LITERALLY GOING UP IN FLAMES AND THINKING:
YOU MUST BE LEE. MY NAME IS SARAH, AND I'M WITH CHILDREN AND FAMILY SERVICES. COME WITH ME, WE'RE GOING TO GET YOU SOMEWHERE SAFE.
CROSS /// DO NOT
IF IT'D BEEN ME WITH THAT POWER, I'D HAVE BURNED THE WHOLE THING DOWN YEARS AGO.
AND I WOULD NEVER HAVE GOTTEN CAUGHT.

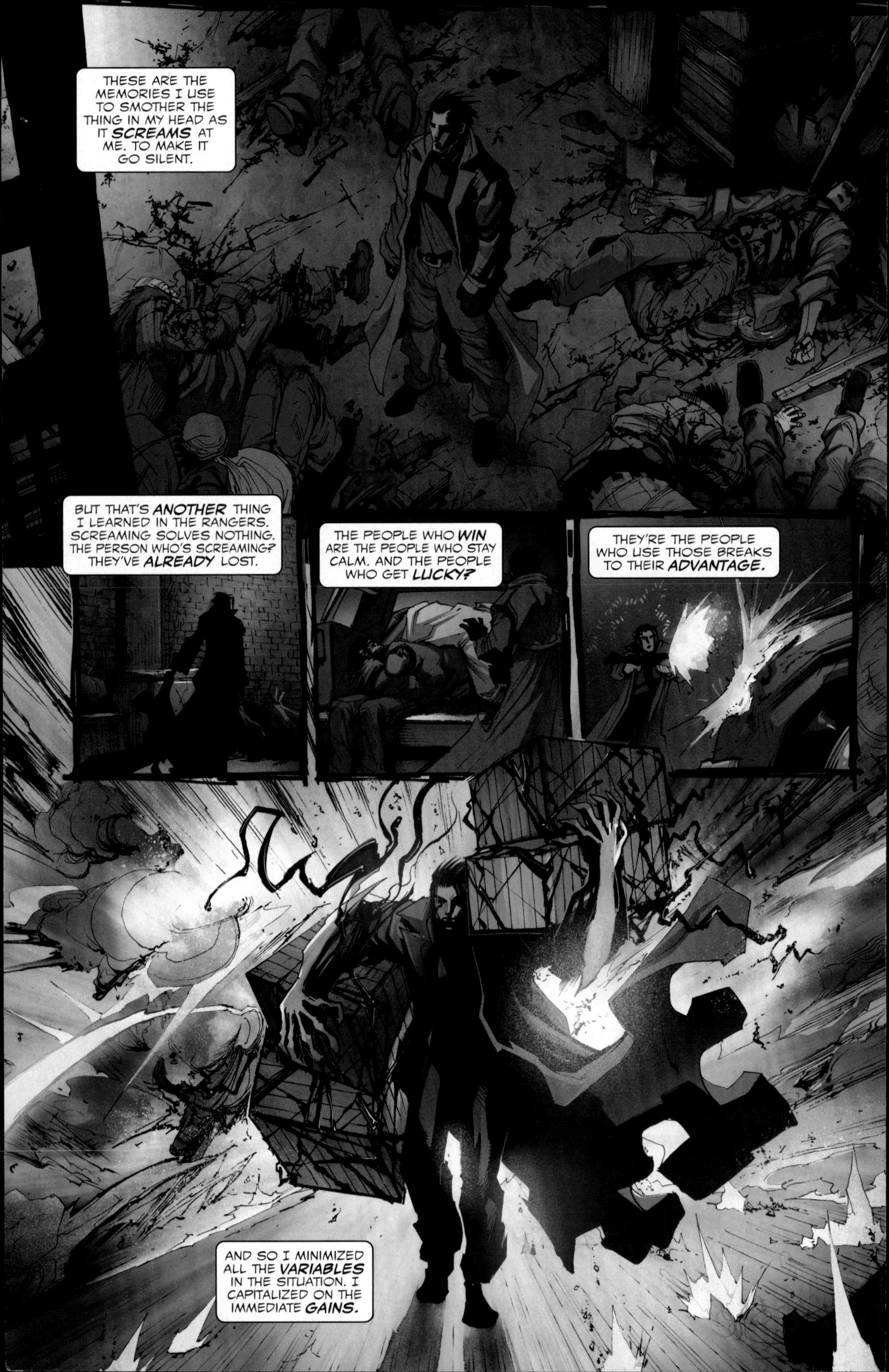
THESE ARE THE MEMORIES I USE TO SMOTHER THE THING IN MY HEAD AS IT SCREAMS AT ME. TO MAKE IT GO SILENT.
BUT THAT'S ANOTHER THING I LEARNED IN THE RANGERS. SCREAMING SOLVES NOTHING. THE PERSON WHO'S SCREAMING? THEY'VE ALREADY LOST.
THE PEOPLE WHO WIN ARE THE PEOPLE WHO STAY CALM. AND THE PEOPLE WHO GET LUCKY?
THEY'RE THE PEOPLE WHO USE THOSE BREAKS TO THEIR ADVANTAGE.
AND SO I MINIMIZED ALL THE VARIABLES IN THE SITUATION. I CAPITALIZED ON THE IMMEDIATE GAINS.

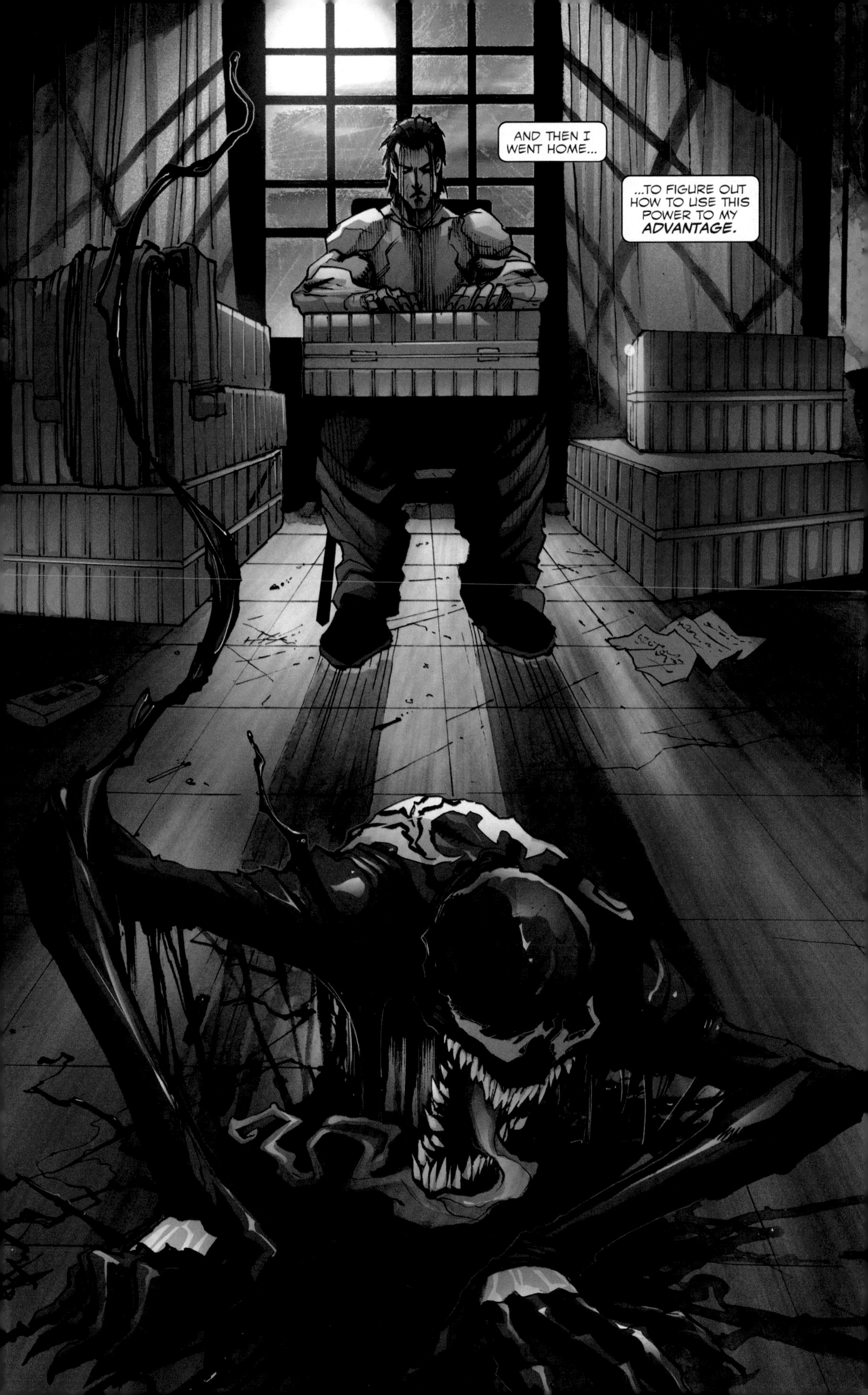
AND THEN I WENT HOME...
...TO FIGURE OUT HOW TO USE THIS POWER TO MY ADVANTAGE.

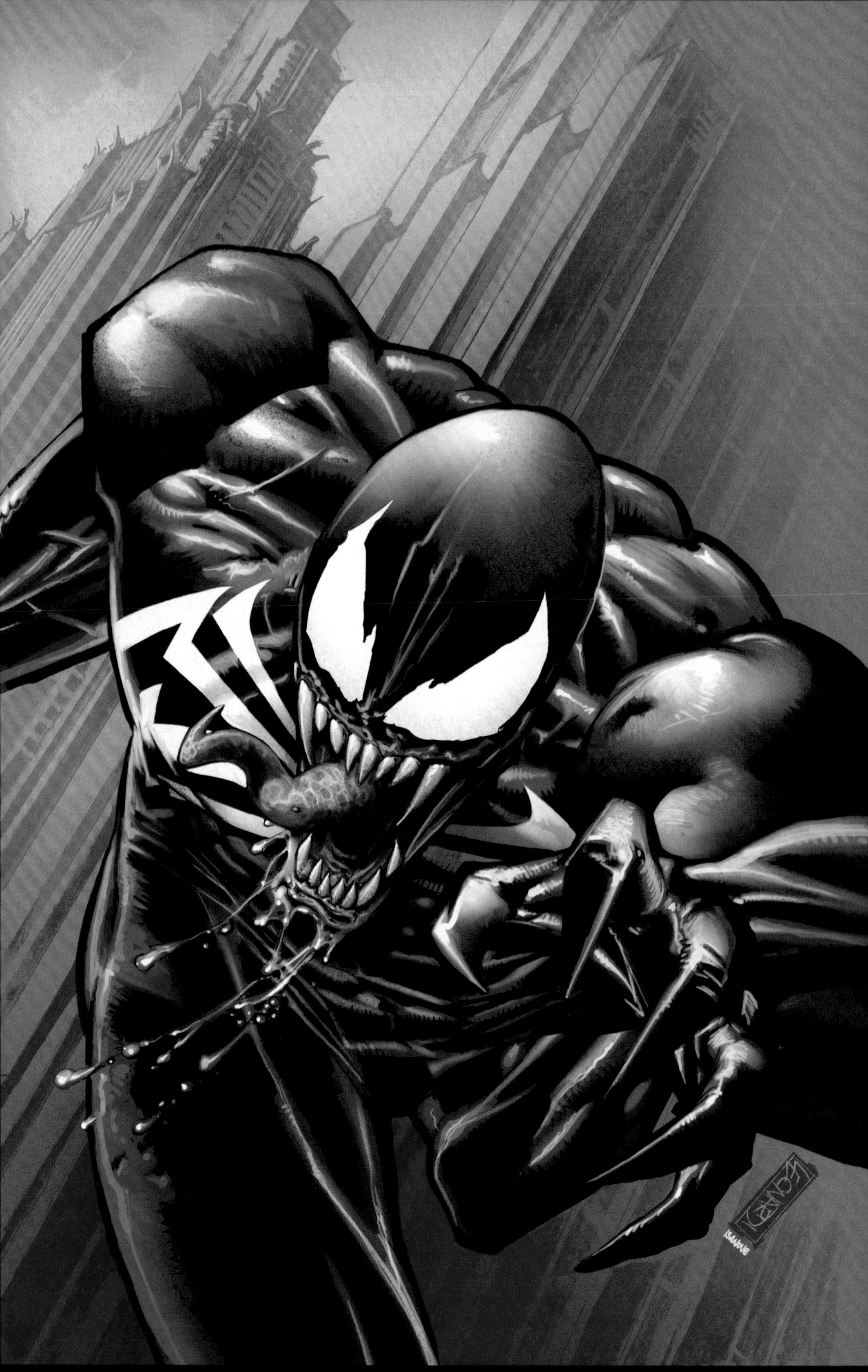

#1 VARIANT BY **RICK LEONARDI & RICHARD ISANOVE**

2

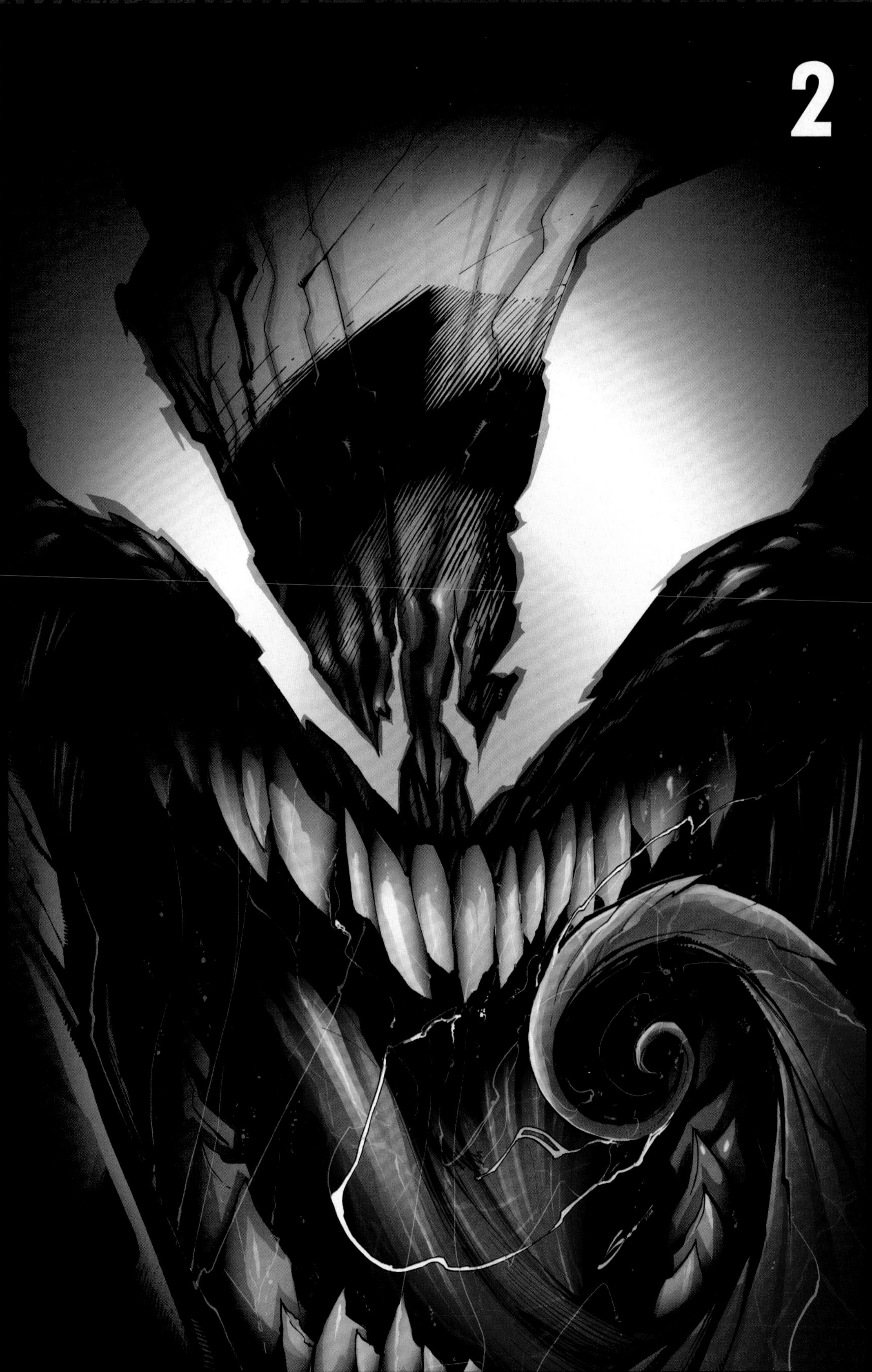

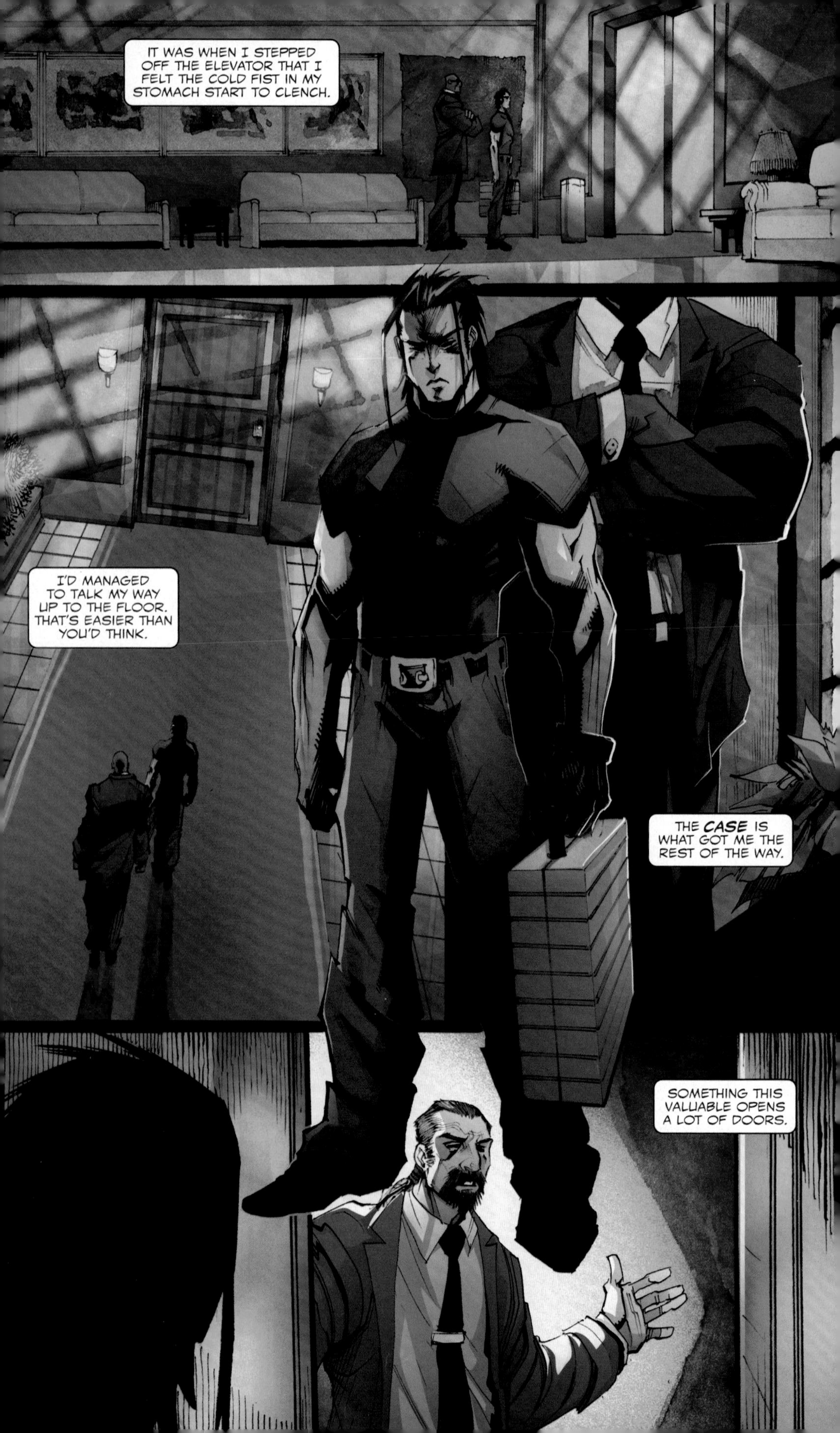
IT WAS WHEN I STEPPED OFF THE ELEVATOR THAT I FELT THE COLD FIST IN MY STOMACH START TO CLENCH.
I'D MANAGED TO TALK MY WAY UP TO THE FLOOR. THAT'S EASIER THAN YOU'D THINK.
THE CASE IS WHAT GOT ME THE REST OF THE WAY.
SOMETHING THIS VALUABLE OPENS A LOT OF DOORS.

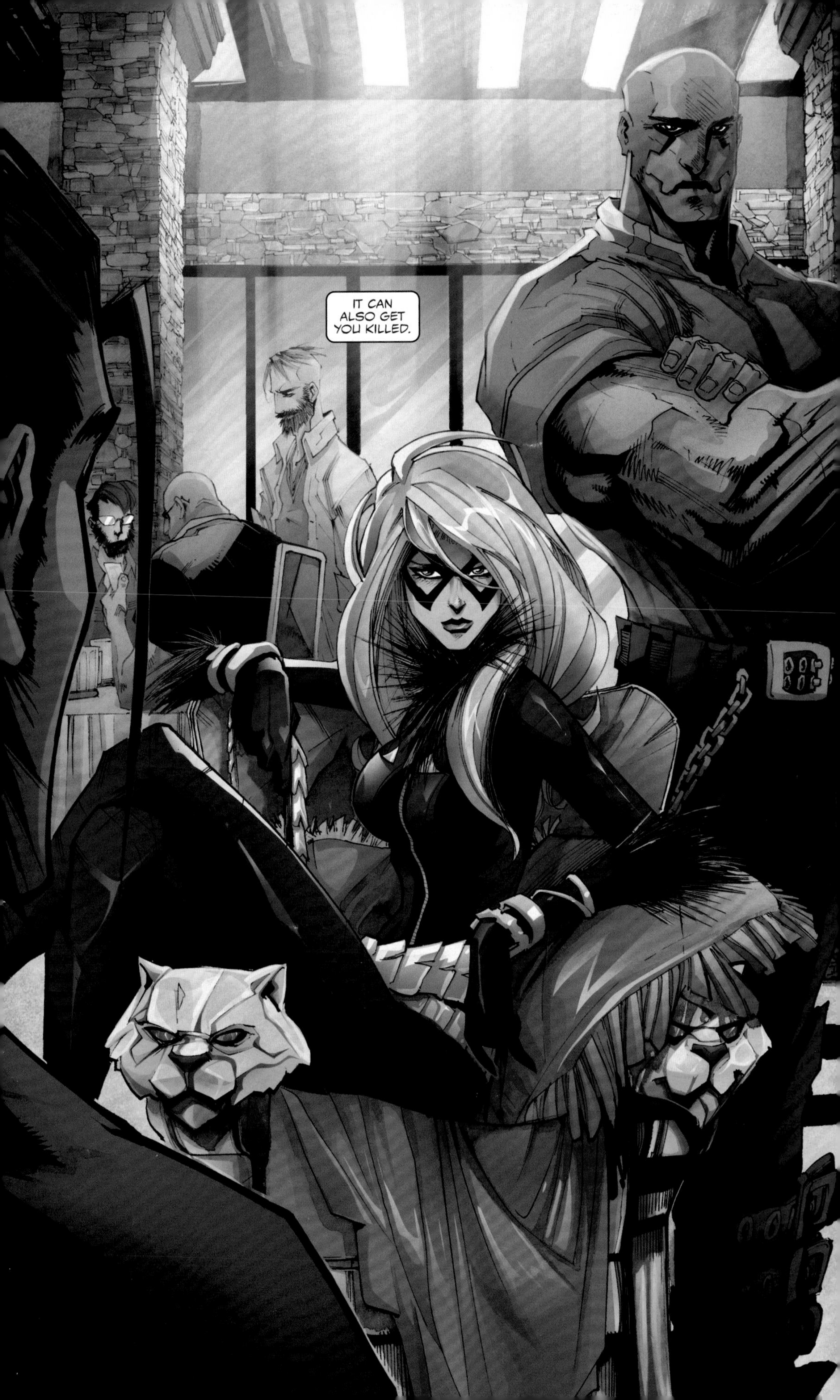
IT CAN ALSO GET YOU KILLED.

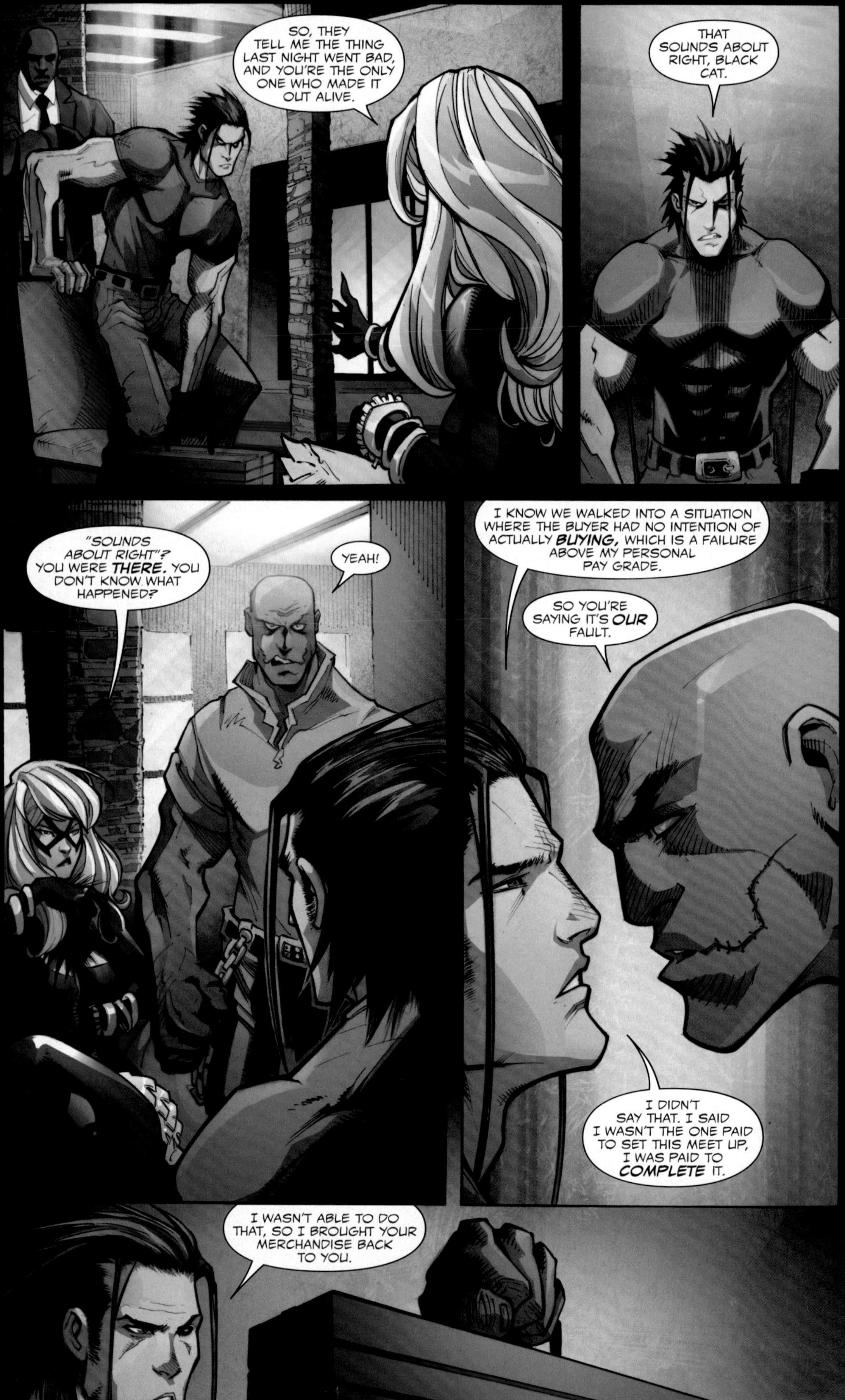

SO, THEY TELL ME THE THING LAST NIGHT WENT BAD, AND YOU'RE THE ONLY ONE WHO MADE IT OUT ALIVE.
THAT SOUNDS ABOUT RIGHT, BLACK CAT.
"SOUNDS ABOUT RIGHT"? YOU WERE THERE. YOU DON'T KNOW WHAT HAPPENED?
YEAH!
I KNOW WE WALKED INTO A SITUATION WHERE THE BUYER HAD NO INTENTION OF ACTUALLY BUYING, WHICH IS A FAILURE ABOVE MY PERSONAL PAY GRADE.
SO YOU'RE SAYING IT'S OUR FAULT.
I DIDN'T SAY THAT. I SAID I WASN'T THE ONE PAID TO SET THIS MEET UP, I WAS PAID TO COMPLETE IT.
I WASN'T ABLE TO DO THAT, SO I BROUGHT YOUR MERCHANDISE BACK TO YOU.

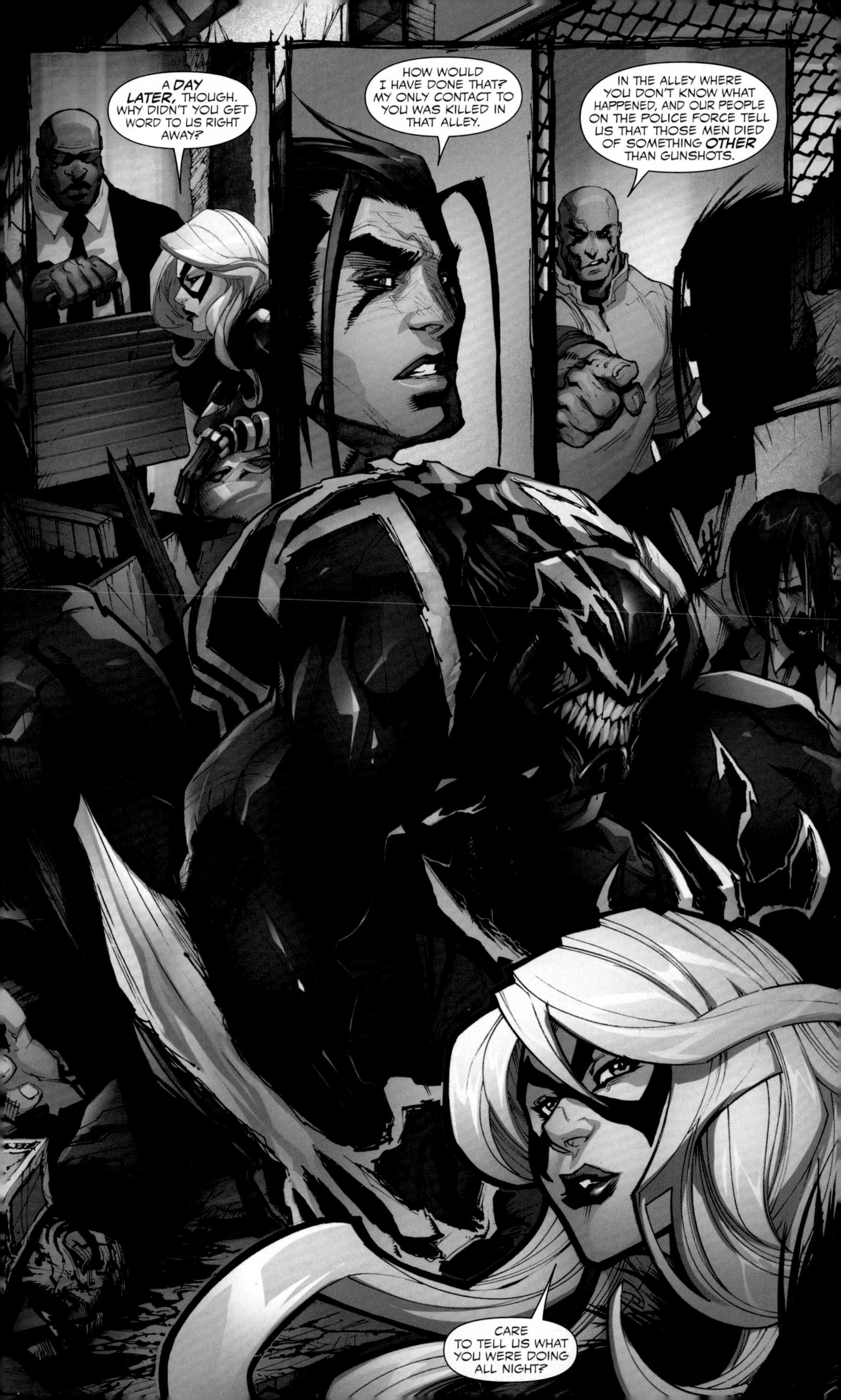
A DAY LATER, THOUGH. WHY DIDN'T YOU GET WORD TO US RIGHT AWAY?
HOW WOULD I HAVE DONE THAT? MY ONLY CONTACT TO YOU WAS KILLED IN THAT ALLEY.
IN THE ALLEY WHERE YOU DON'T KNOW WHAT HAPPENED, AND OUR PEOPLE ON THE POLICE FORCE TELL US THAT THOSE MEN DIED OF SOMETHING OTHER THAN GUNSHOTS.
CARE TO TELL US WHAT YOU WERE DOING ALL NIGHT?

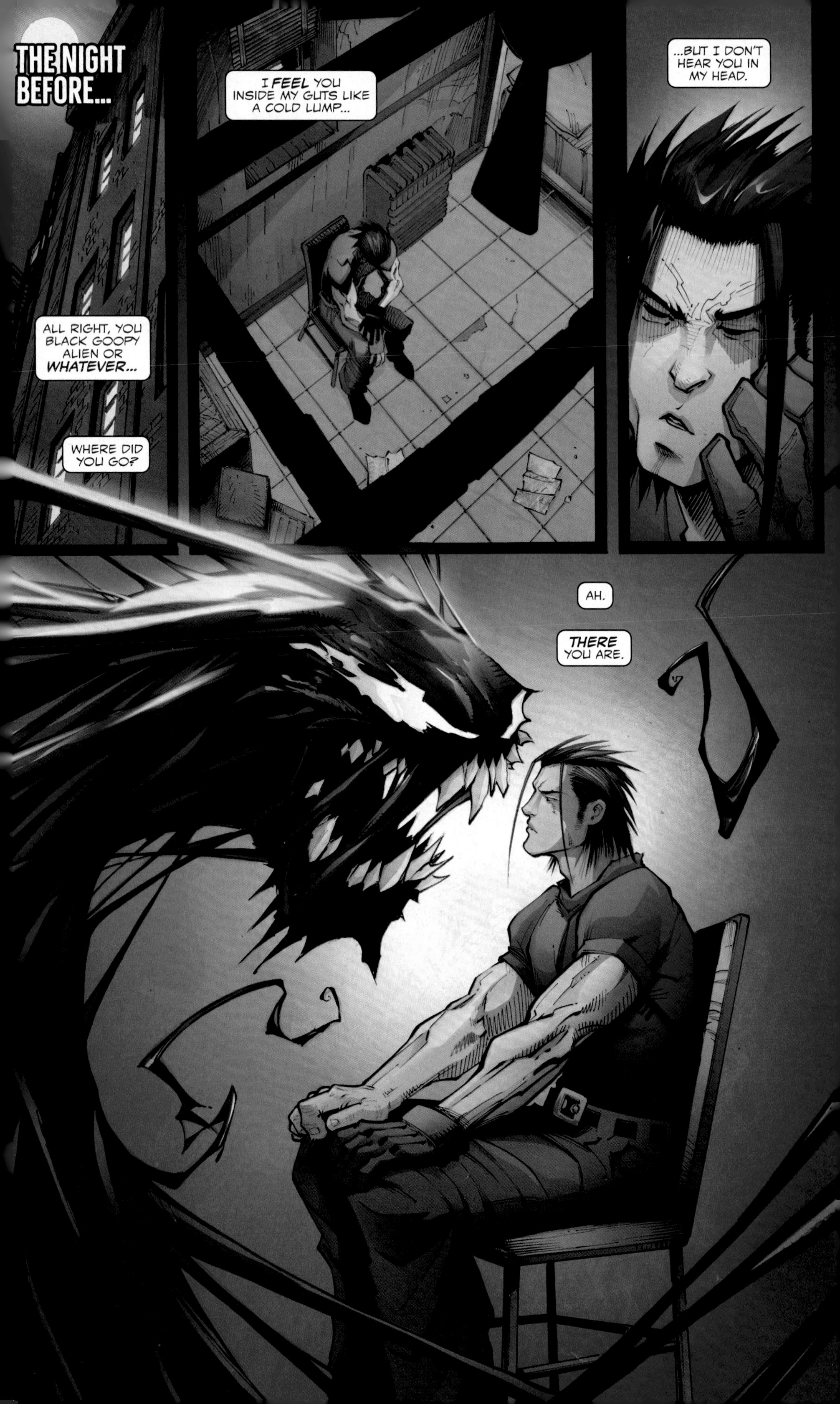
THE NIGHT BEFORE...
I FEEL YOU INSIDE MY GUTS LIKE A COLD LUMP...
...BUT I DON'T HEAR YOU IN MY HEAD.
ALL RIGHT, YOU BLACK GOOPY ALIEN OR WHATEVER...
WHERE DID YOU GO?
AH.
THERE YOU ARE.

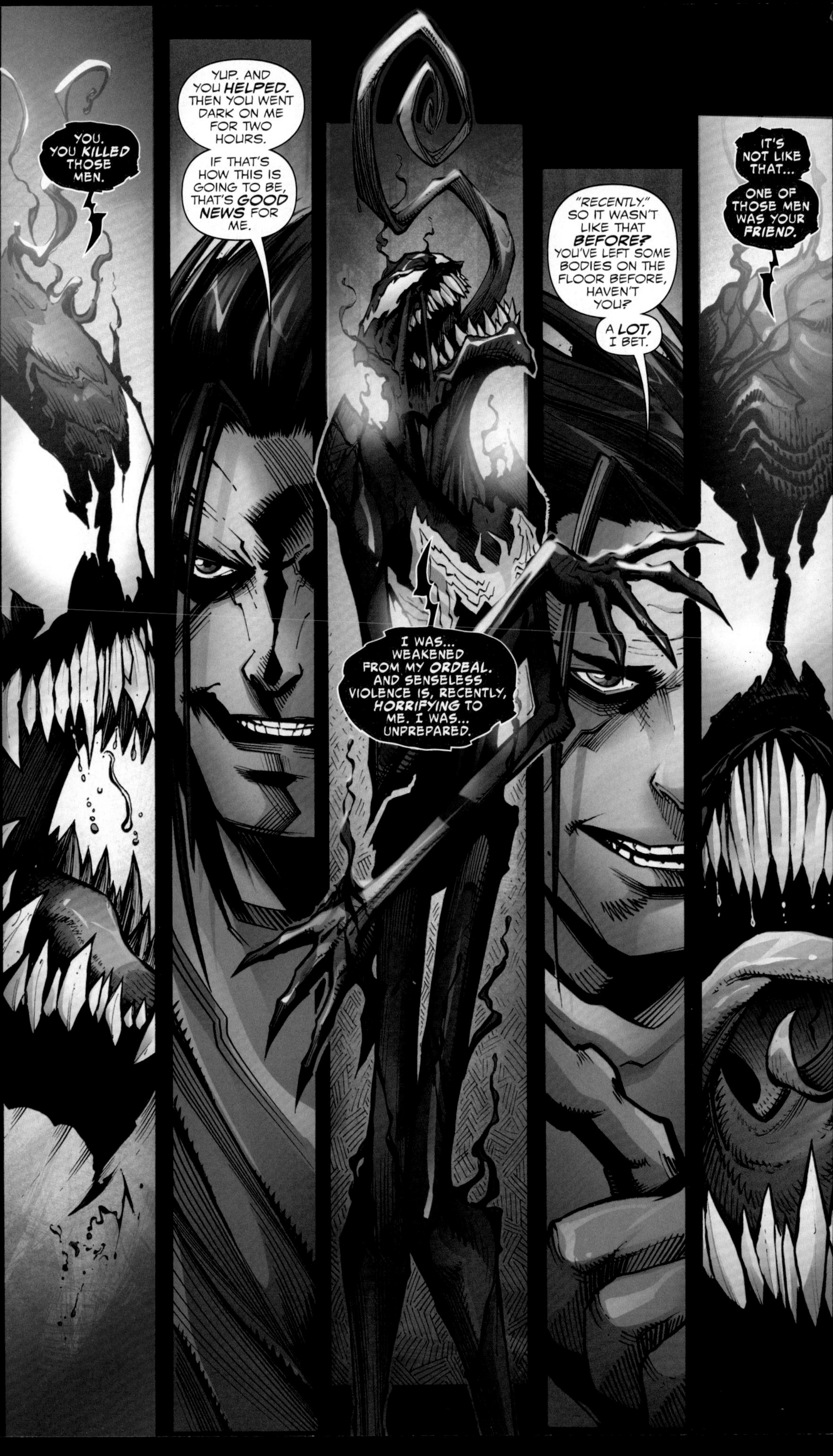
YOU. YOU KILLED THOSE MEN.
YUP. AND YOU HELPED. THEN YOU WENT DARK ON ME FOR TWO HOURS.
IF THAT'S HOW THIS IS GOING TO BE, THAT'S GOOD NEWS FOR ME.
I WAS... WEAKENED FROM MY ORDEAL. AND SENSELESS VIOLENCE IS, RECENTLY, HORRIFYING TO ME. I WAS... UNPREPARED.
"RECENTLY." SO IT WASN'T LIKE THAT BEFORE? YOU'VE LEFT SOME BODIES ON THE FLOOR BEFORE, HAVEN'T YOU?
A LOT, I BET.
IT'S NOT LIKE THAT...
ONE OF THOSE MEN WAS YOUR FRIEND.

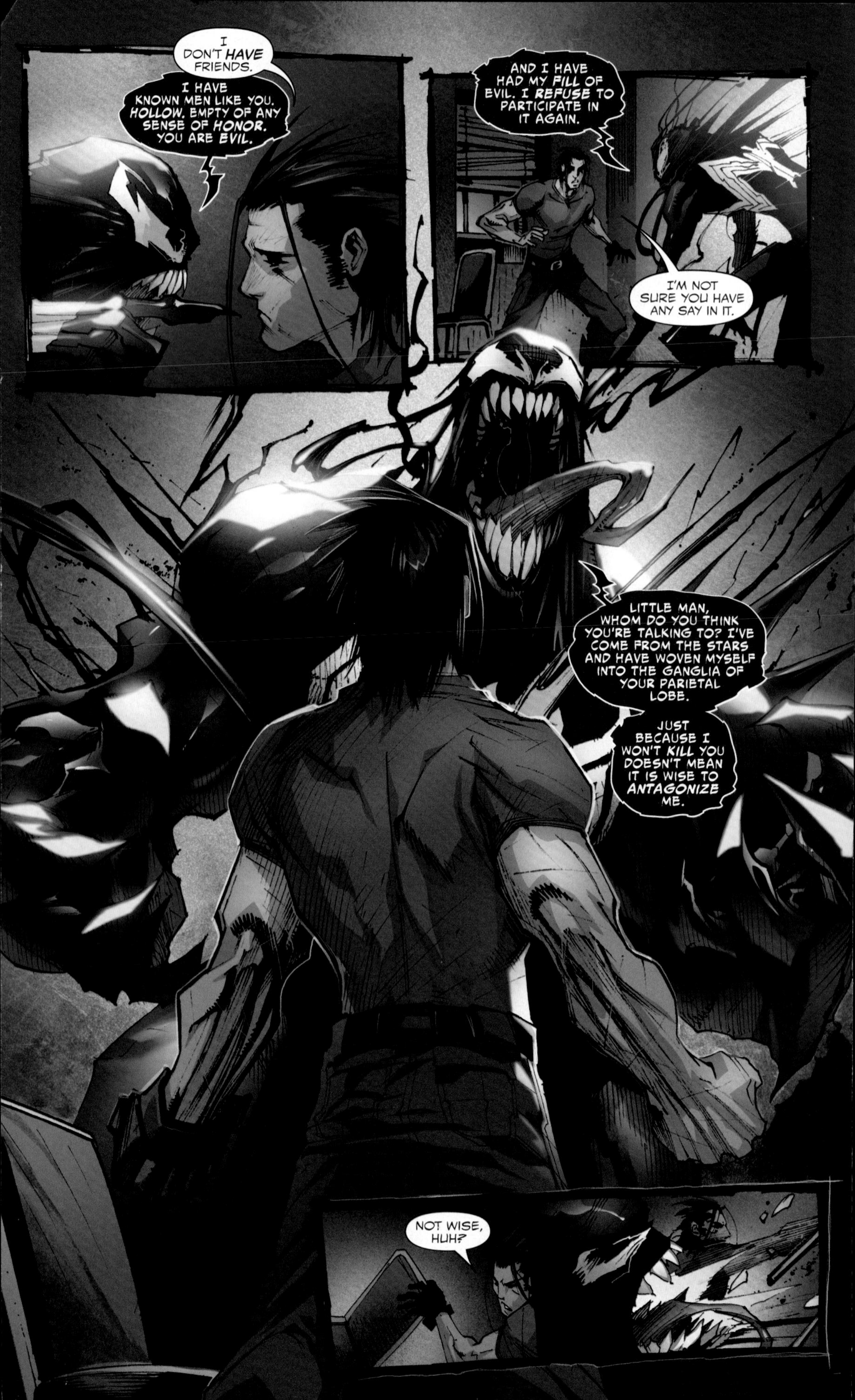
I DON'T HAVE FRIENDS.
I HAVE KNOWN MEN LIKE YOU. HOLLOW. EMPTY OF ANY SENSE OF HONOR. YOU ARE EVIL.
AND I HAVE HAD MY FILL OF EVIL. I REFUSE TO PARTICIPATE IN IT AGAIN.
I'M NOT SURE YOU HAVE ANY SAY IN IT.
LITTLE MAN, WHOM DO YOU THINK YOU'RE TALKING TO? I'VE COME FROM THE STARS AND HAVE WOVEN MYSELF INTO THE GANGLIA OF YOUR PARIETAL LOBE.
JUST BECAUSE I WON'T KILL YOU DOESN'T MEAN IT IS WISE TO ANTAGONIZE ME.
NOT WISE, HUH?

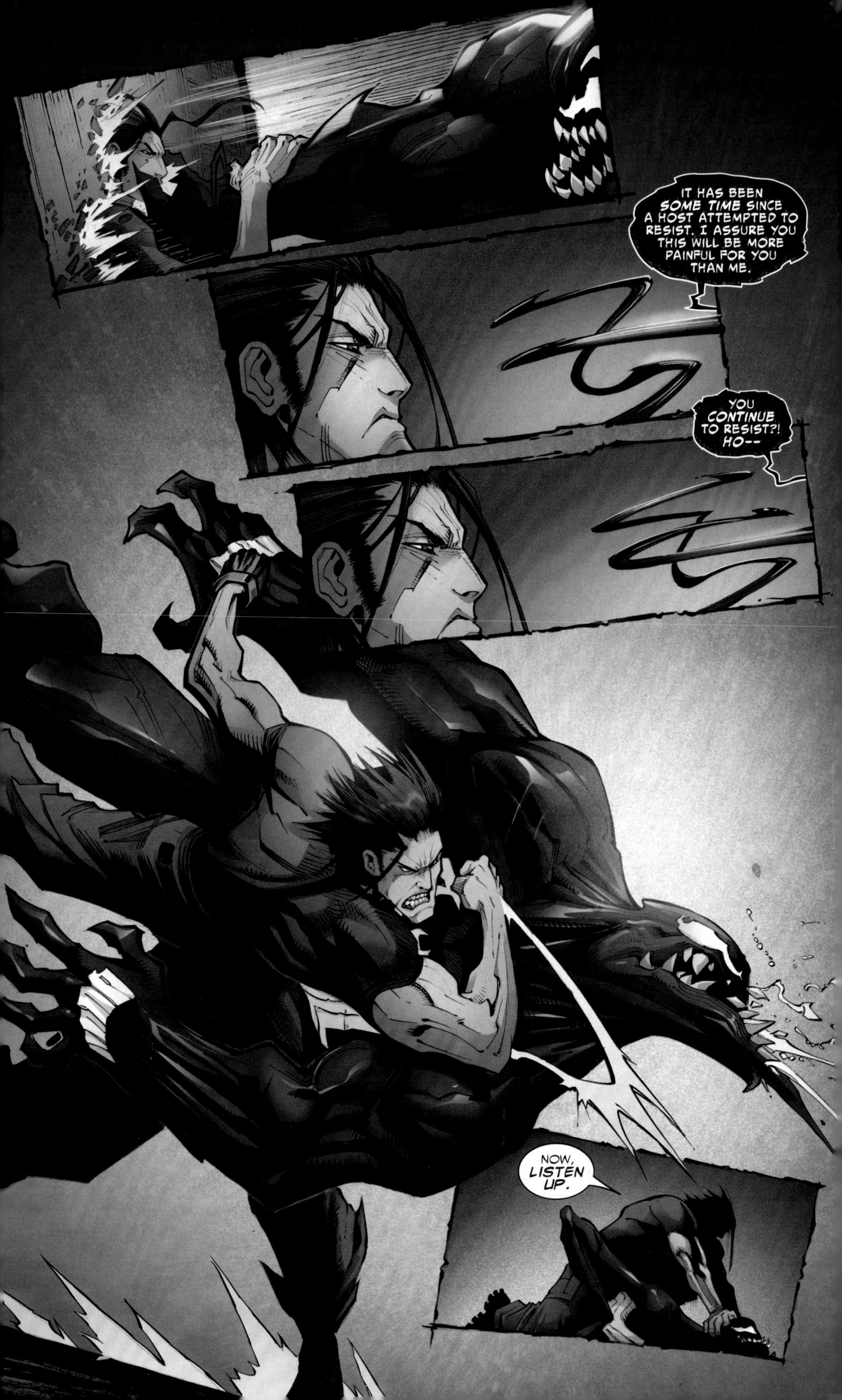
IT HAS BEEN SOME TIME SINCE A HOST ATTEMPTED TO RESIST. I ASSURE YOU THIS WILL BE MORE PAINFUL FOR YOU THAN ME.
YOU CONTINUE TO RESIST?! HO--
NOW, LISTEN UP.

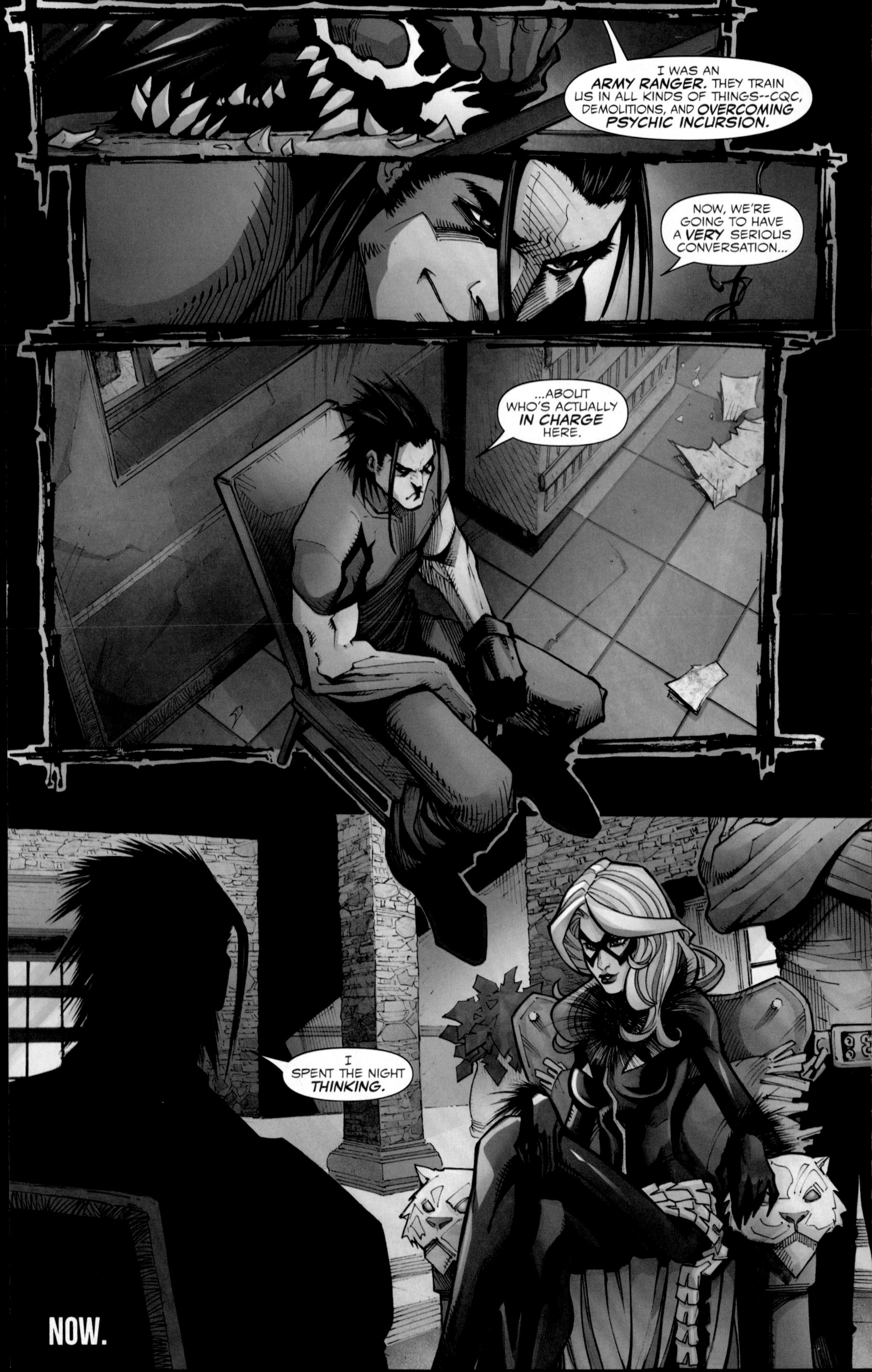
I WAS AN ARMY RANGER. THEY TRAIN US IN ALL KINDS OF THINGS--CQC, DEMOLITIONS, AND OVERCOMING PSYCHIC INCURSION.
NOW, WE'RE GOING TO HAVE A VERY SERIOUS CONVERSATION...
...ABOUT WHO'S ACTUALLY IN CHARGE HERE.
NOW.
I SPENT THE NIGHT THINKING.

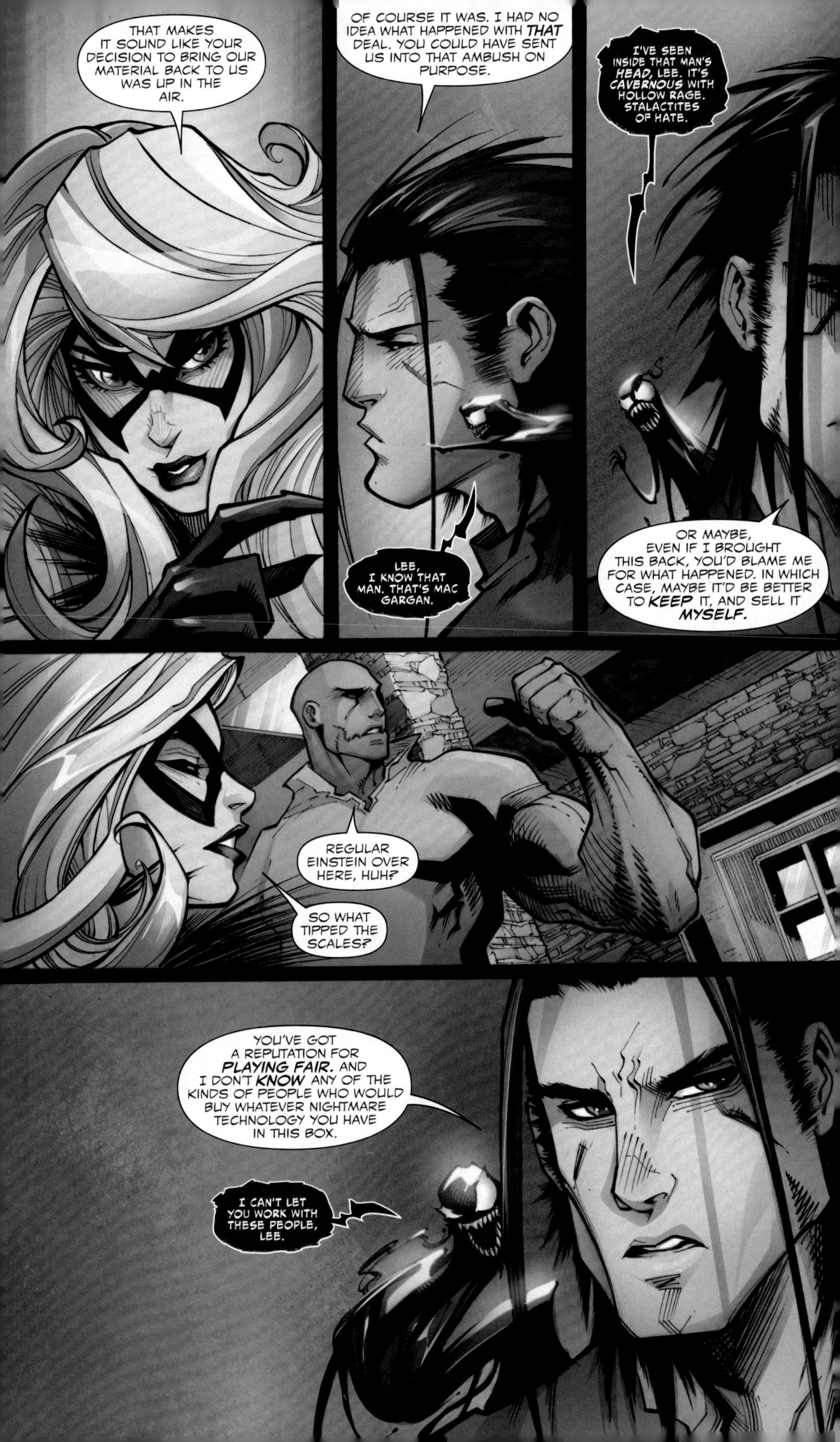
THAT MAKES IT SOUND LIKE YOUR DECISION TO BRING OUR MATERIAL BACK TO US WAS UP IN THE AIR.
OF COURSE IT WAS. I HAD NO IDEA WHAT HAPPENED WITH THAT DEAL. YOU COULD HAVE SENT US INTO THAT AMBUSH ON PURPOSE.
LEE, I KNOW THAT MAN. THAT'S MAC GARGAN.
I'VE SEEN INSIDE THAT MAN'S HEAD, LEE. IT'S CAVERNOUS WITH HOLLOW RAGE. STALACTITES OF HATE.
OR MAYBE, EVEN IF I BROUGHT THIS BACK, YOU'D BLAME ME FOR WHAT HAPPENED. IN WHICH CASE, MAYBE IT'D BE BETTER TO KEEP IT, AND SELL IT MYSELF.
REGULAR EINSTEIN OVER HERE, HUH?
SO WHAT TIPPED THE SCALES?
YOU'VE GOT A REPUTATION FOR PLAYING FAIR. AND I DON'T KNOW ANY OF THE KINDS OF PEOPLE WHO WOULD BUY WHATEVER NIGHTMARE TECHNOLOGY YOU HAVE IN THIS BOX.
I CAN'T LET YOU WORK WITH THESE PEOPLE, LEE.

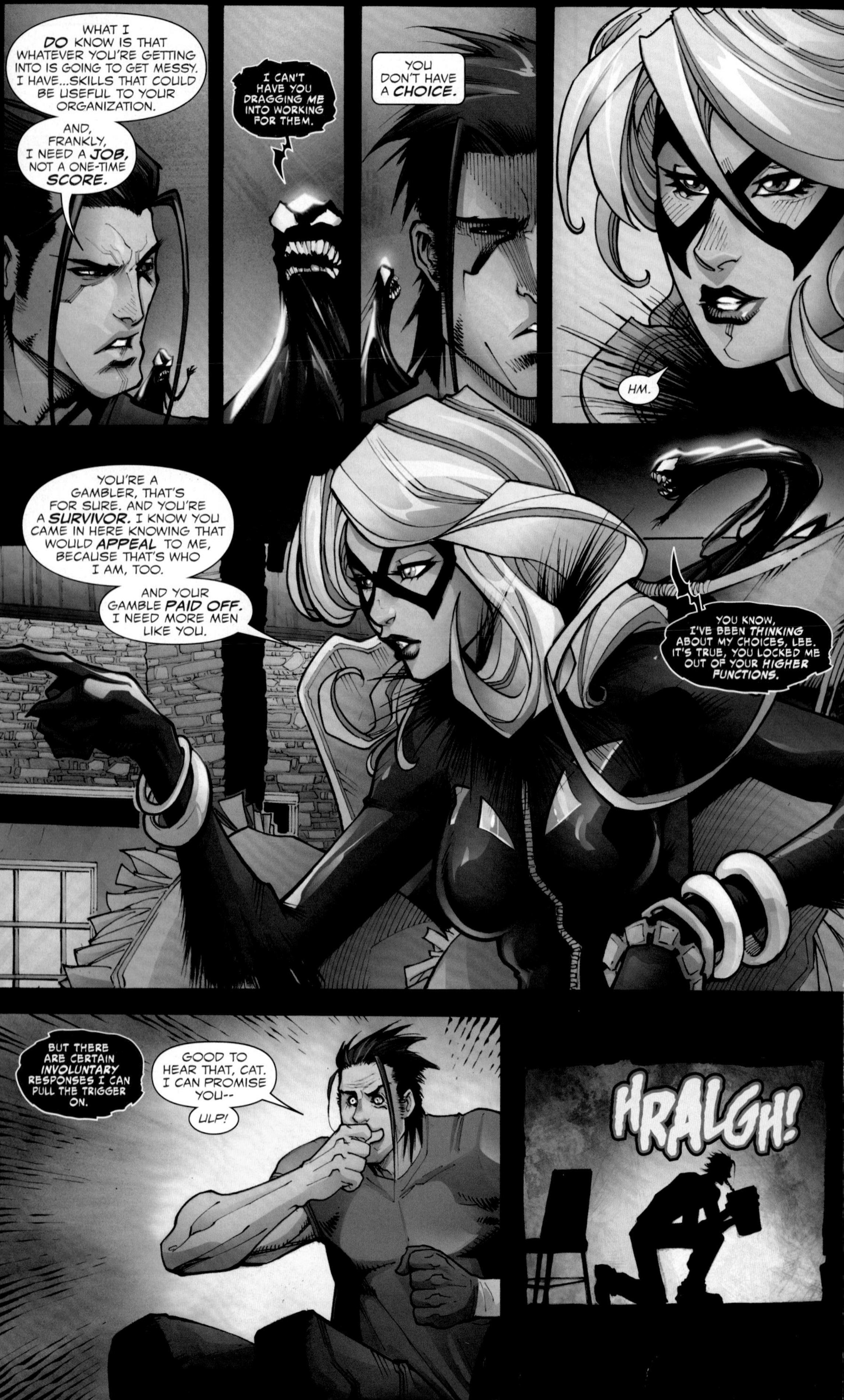

WHAT I DO KNOW IS THAT WHATEVER YOU'RE GETTING INTO IS GOING TO GET MESSY. I HAVE...SKILLS THAT COULD BE USEFUL TO YOUR ORGANIZATION.
AND, FRANKLY, I NEED A JOB, NOT A ONE-TIME SCORE.
I CAN'T HAVE YOU DRAGGING ME INTO WORKING FOR THEM.
YOU DON'T HAVE A CHOICE.
HM.
YOU'RE A GAMBLER, THAT'S FOR SURE. AND YOU'RE A SURVIVOR. I KNOW YOU CAME IN HERE KNOWING THAT WOULD APPEAL TO ME, BECAUSE THAT'S WHO I AM, TOO.
AND YOUR GAMBLE PAID OFF. I NEED MORE MEN LIKE YOU.
YOU KNOW, I'VE BEEN THINKING ABOUT MY CHOICES, LEE. IT'S TRUE, YOU LOCKED ME OUT OF YOUR HIGHER FUNCTIONS.
BUT THERE ARE CERTAIN INVOLUNTARY RESPONSES I CAN PULL THE TRIGGER ON.
GOOD TO HEAR THAT, CAT. I CAN PROMISE YOU--
ULP!
HRALGH!

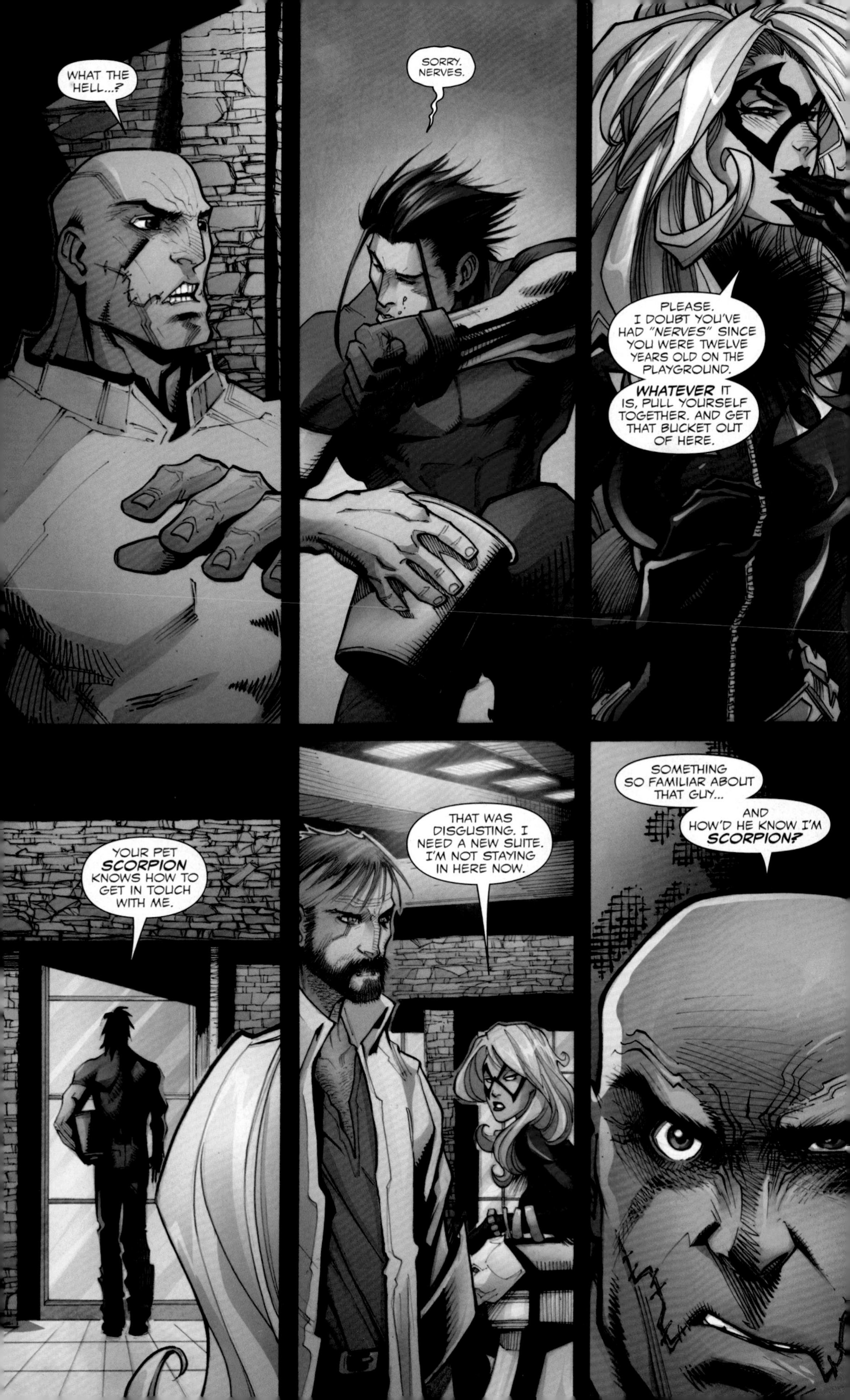
WHAT THE HELL...?
SORRY. NERVES.
PLEASE. I DOUBT YOU'VE HAD "NERVES" SINCE YOU WERE TWELVE YEARS OLD ON THE PLAYGROUND.
WHATEVER IT IS, PULL YOURSELF TOGETHER. AND GET THAT BUCKET OUT OF HERE.
YOUR PET SCORPION KNOWS HOW TO GET IN TOUCH WITH ME.
THAT WAS DISGUSTING. I NEED A NEW SUITE. I'M NOT STAYING IN HERE NOW.
SOMETHING SO FAMILIAR ABOUT THAT GUY...
AND HOW'D HE KNOW I'M SCORPION?

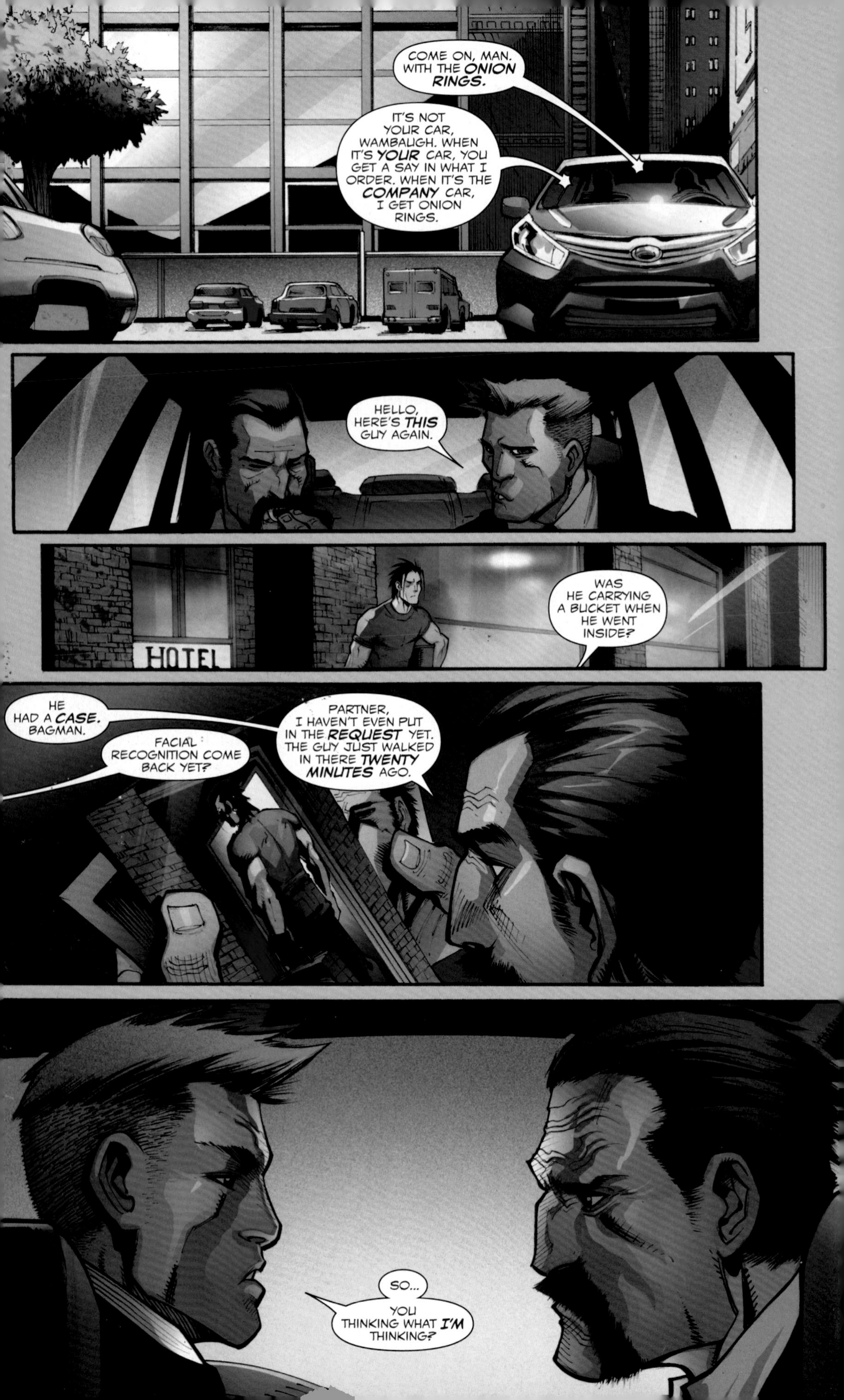
COME ON, MAN. WITH THE ONION RINGS.
IT'S NOT YOUR CAR, WAMBAUGH. WHEN IT'S YOUR CAR, YOU GET A SAY IN WHAT I ORDER. WHEN IT'S THE COMPANY CAR, I GET ONION RINGS.
HELLO, HERE'S THIS GUY AGAIN.
HOTEL
WAS HE CARRYING A BUCKET WHEN HE WENT INSIDE?
HE HAD A CASE. BAGMAN.
FACIAL RECOGNITION COME BACK YET?
PARTNER, I HAVEN'T EVEN PUT IN THE REQUEST YET. THE GUY JUST WALKED IN THERE TWENTY MINUTES AGO.
SO...
YOU THINKING WHAT I'M THINKING?

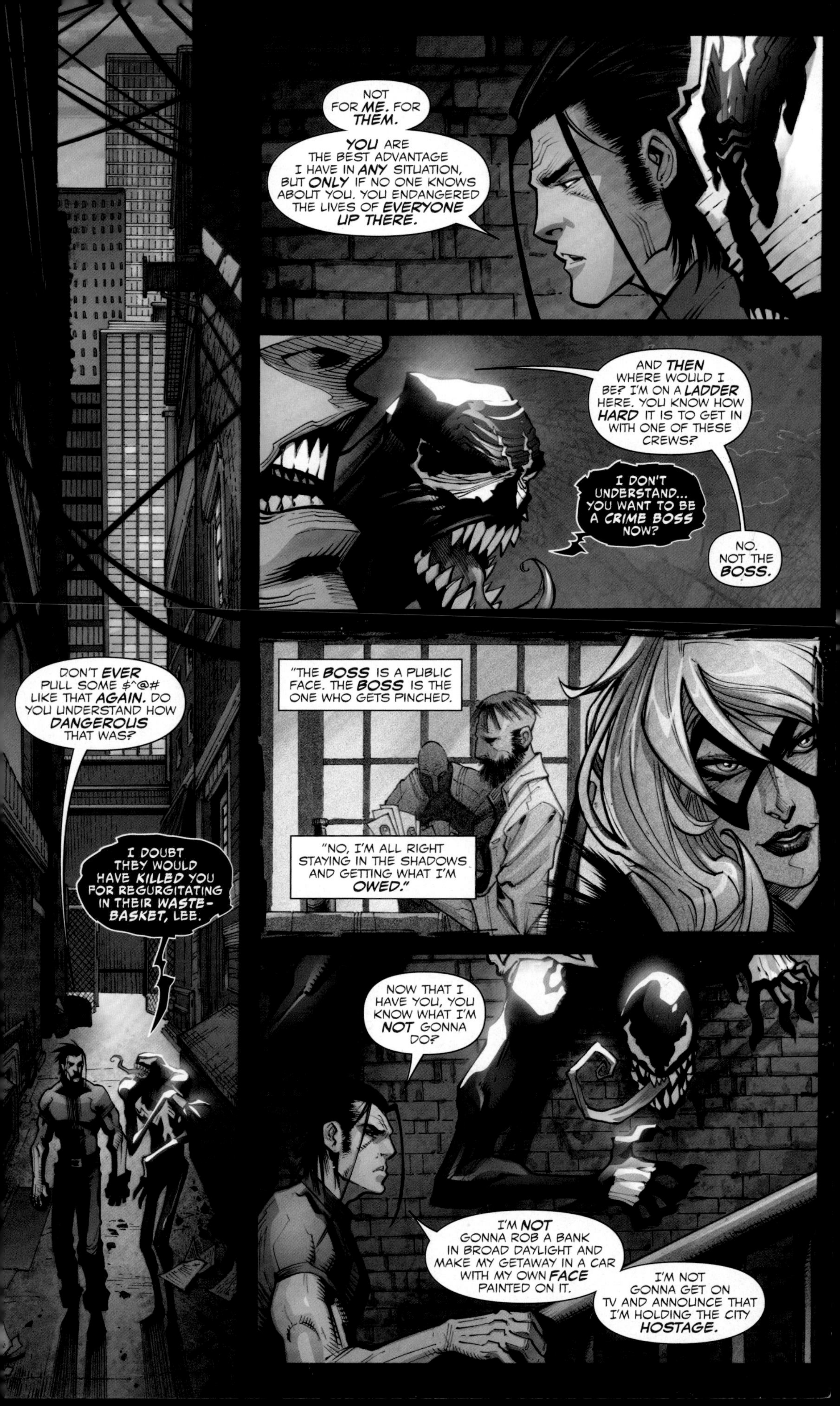
NOT FOR ME. FOR THEM.
YOU ARE THE BEST ADVANTAGE I HAVE IN ANY SITUATION, BUT ONLY IF NO ONE KNOWS ABOUT YOU. YOU ENDANGERED THE LIVES OF EVERYONE UP THERE.
AND THEN WHERE WOULD I BE? I'M ON A LADDER HERE. YOU KNOW HOW HARD IT IS TO GET IN WITH ONE OF THESE CREWS?
I DON'T UNDERSTAND... YOU WANT TO BE A CRIME BOSS NOW?
NO. NOT THE BOSS.
"THE BOSS IS A PUBLIC FACE. THE BOSS IS THE ONE WHO GETS PINCHED.
"NO, I'M ALL RIGHT STAYING IN THE SHADOWS AND GETTING WHAT I'M OWED."
DON'T EVER PULL SOME $^@# LIKE THAT AGAIN. DO YOU UNDERSTAND HOW DANGEROUS THAT WAS?
I DOUBT THEY WOULD HAVE KILLED YOU FOR REGURGITATING IN THEIR WASTE-BASKET, LEE.
NOW THAT I HAVE YOU, YOU KNOW WHAT I'M NOT GONNA DO?
I'M NOT GONNA ROB A BANK IN BROAD DAYLIGHT AND MAKE MY GETAWAY IN A CAR WITH MY OWN FACE PAINTED ON IT.
I'M NOT GONNA GET ON TV AND ANNOUNCE THAT I'M HOLDING THE CITY HOSTAGE.

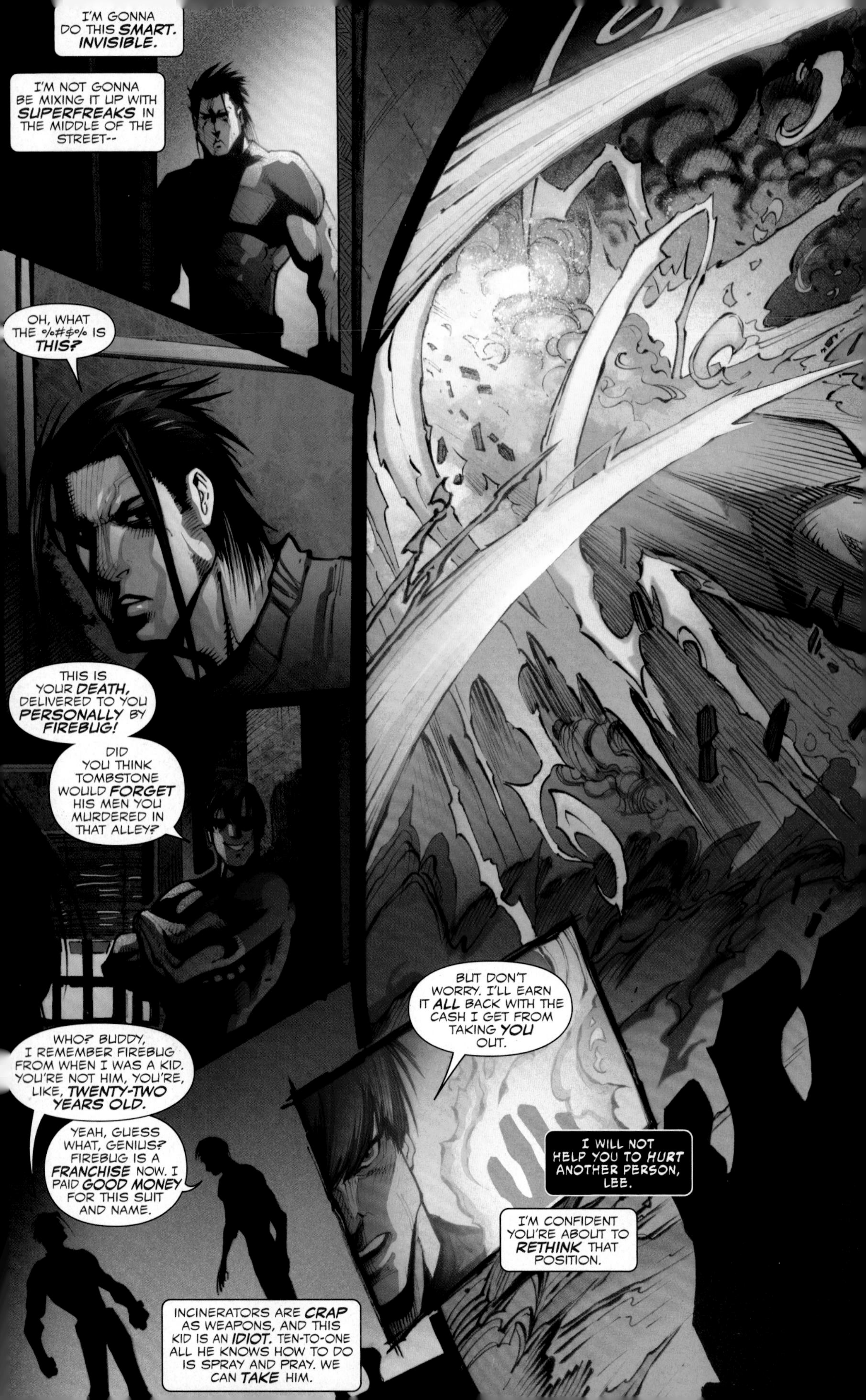
I'M GONNA DO THIS SMART. INVISIBLE.
I'M NOT GONNA BE MIXING IT UP WITH SUPERFREAKS IN THE MIDDLE OF THE STREET--
OH, WHAT THE %#$% IS THIS?
THIS IS YOUR DEATH, DELIVERED TO YOU PERSONALLY BY FIREBUG!
DID YOU THINK TOMBSTONE WOULD FORGET HIS MEN YOU MURDERED IN THAT ALLEY?
WHO? BUDDY, I REMEMBER FIREBUG FROM WHEN I WAS A KID. YOU'RE NOT HIM, YOU'RE, LIKE, TWENTY-TWO YEARS OLD.
YEAH, GUESS WHAT, GENIUS? FIREBUG IS A FRANCHISE NOW. I PAID GOOD MONEY FOR THIS SUIT AND NAME.
INCINERATORS ARE CRAP AS WEAPONS, AND THIS KID IS AN IDIOT. TEN-TO-ONE ALL HE KNOWS HOW TO DO IS SPRAY AND PRAY. WE CAN TAKE HIM.
BUT DON'T WORRY. I'LL EARN IT ALL BACK WITH THE CASH I GET FROM TAKING YOU OUT.
I WILL NOT HELP YOU TO HURT ANOTHER PERSON, LEE.
I'M CONFIDENT YOU'RE ABOUT TO RETHINK THAT POSITION.

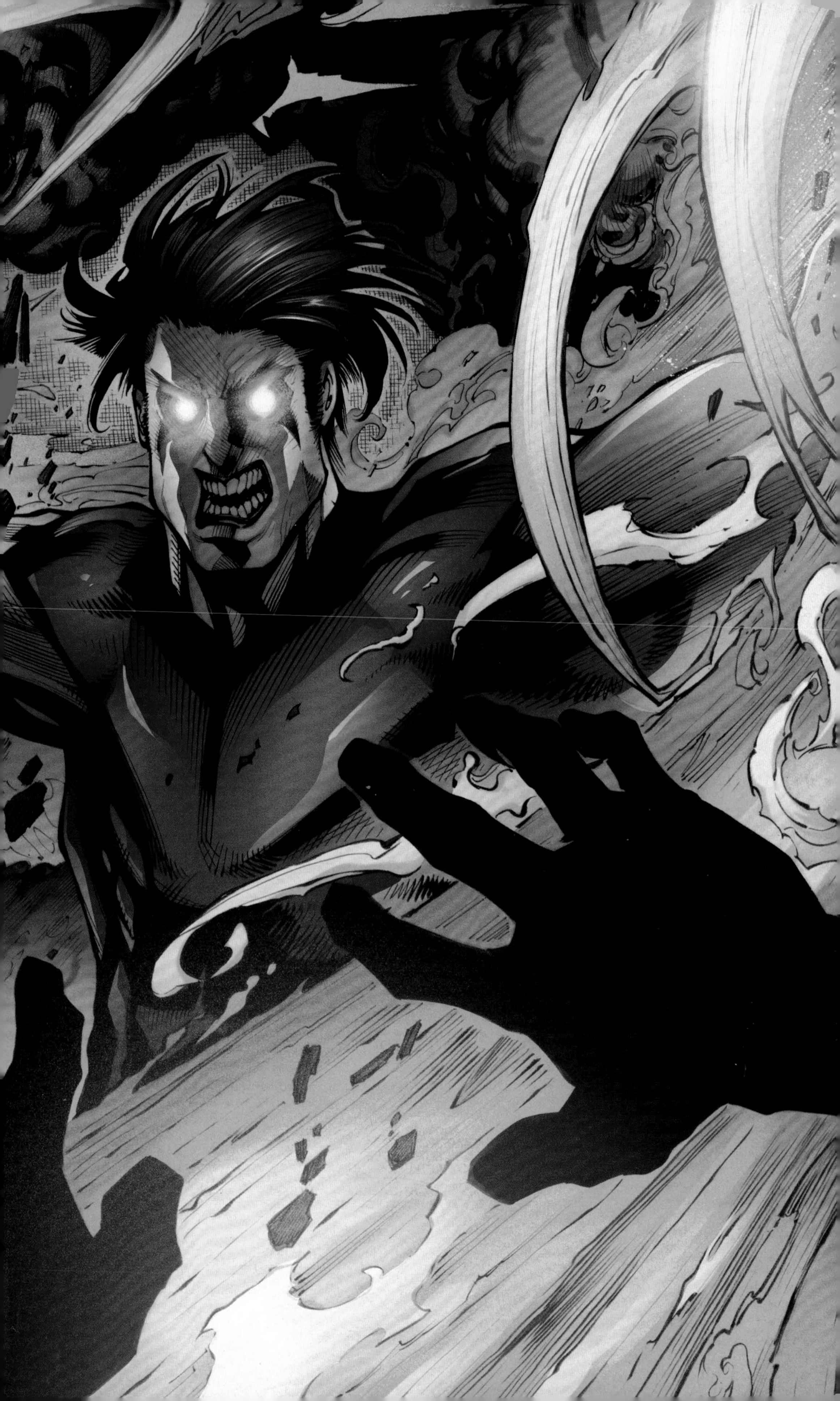

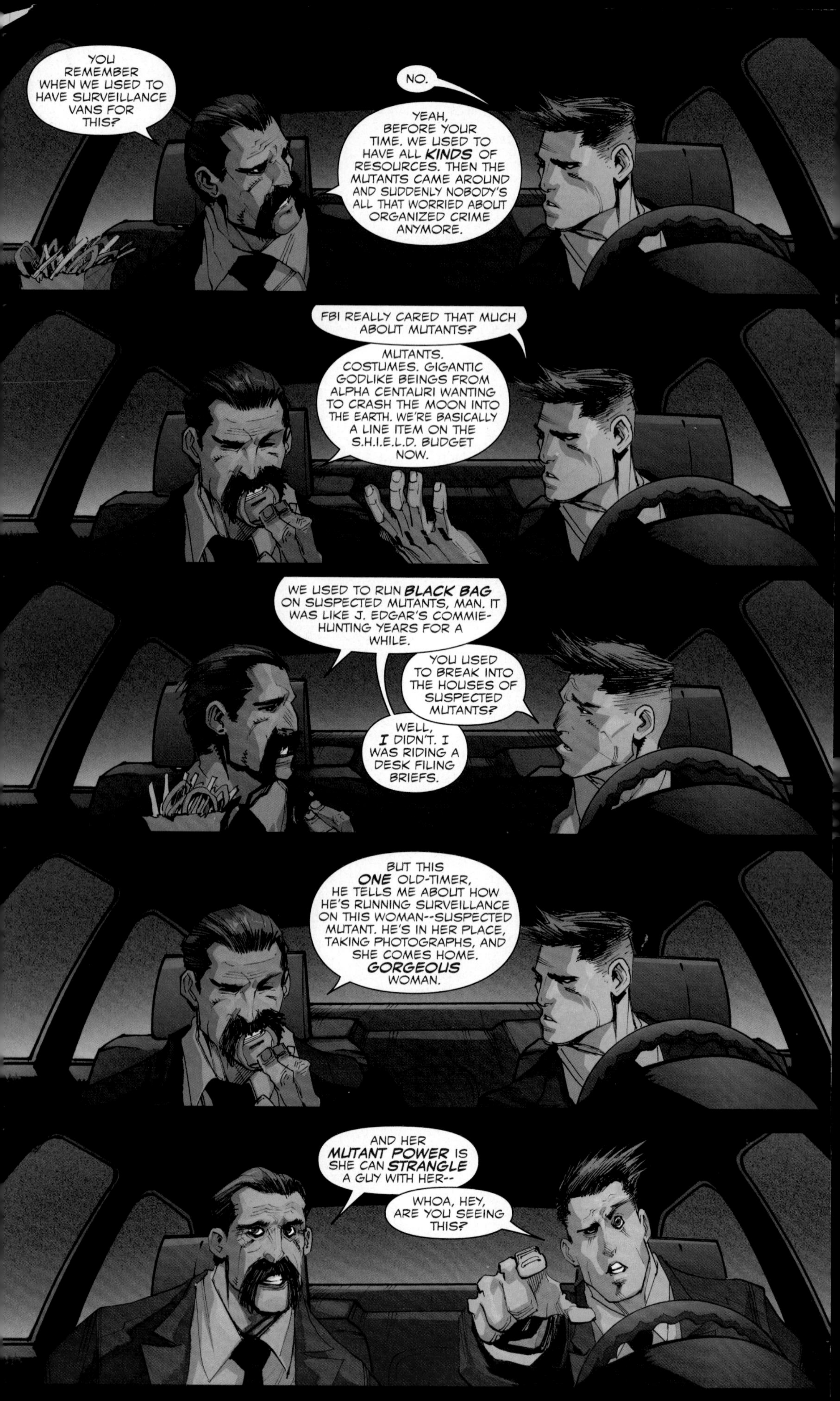

YOU REMEMBER WHEN WE USED TO HAVE SURVEILLANCE VANS FOR THIS?
NO.
YEAH, BEFORE YOUR TIME. WE USED TO HAVE ALL KINDS OF RESOURCES. THEN THE MUTANTS CAME AROUND AND SUDDENLY NOBODY'S ALL THAT WORRIED ABOUT ORGANIZED CRIME ANYMORE.
FBI REALLY CARED THAT MUCH ABOUT MUTANTS?
MUTANTS. COSTUMES. GIGANTIC GODLIKE BEINGS FROM ALPHA CENTAURI WANTING TO CRASH THE MOON INTO THE EARTH. WE'RE BASICALLY A LINE ITEM ON THE S.H.I.E.L.D. BUDGET NOW.
WE USED TO RUN BLACK BAG ON SUSPECTED MUTANTS, MAN. IT WAS LIKE J. EDGAR'S COMMIE-HUNTING YEARS FOR A WHILE.
YOU USED TO BREAK INTO THE HOUSES OF SUSPECTED MUTANTS?
WELL, I DIDN'T. I WAS RIDING A DESK FILING BRIEFS.
BUT THIS ONE OLD-TIMER, HE TELLS ME ABOUT HOW HE'S RUNNING SURVEILLANCE ON THIS WOMAN--SUSPECTED MUTANT. HE'S IN HER PLACE, TAKING PHOTOGRAPHS, AND SHE COMES HOME. GORGEOUS WOMAN.
AND HER MUTANT POWER IS SHE CAN STRANGLE A GUY WITH HER--
WHOA, HEY, ARE YOU SEEING THIS?

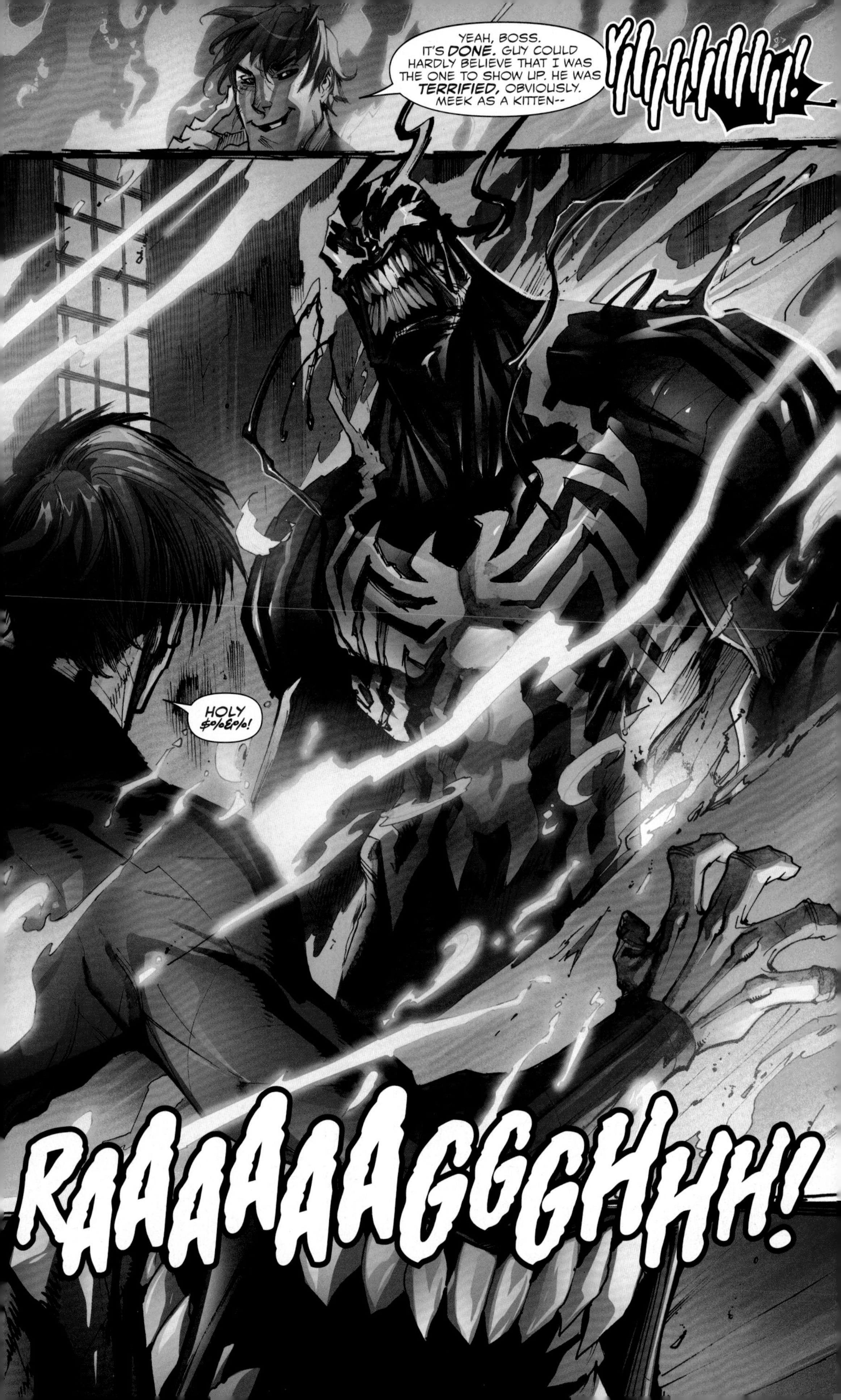
YEAH, BOSS. IT'S DONE. GUY COULD HARDLY BELIEVE THAT I WAS THE ONE TO SHOW UP. HE WAS TERRIFIED, OBVIOUSLY. MEEK AS A KITTEN--
HOLY $%&%!
RAAAAAAGGGHHH!

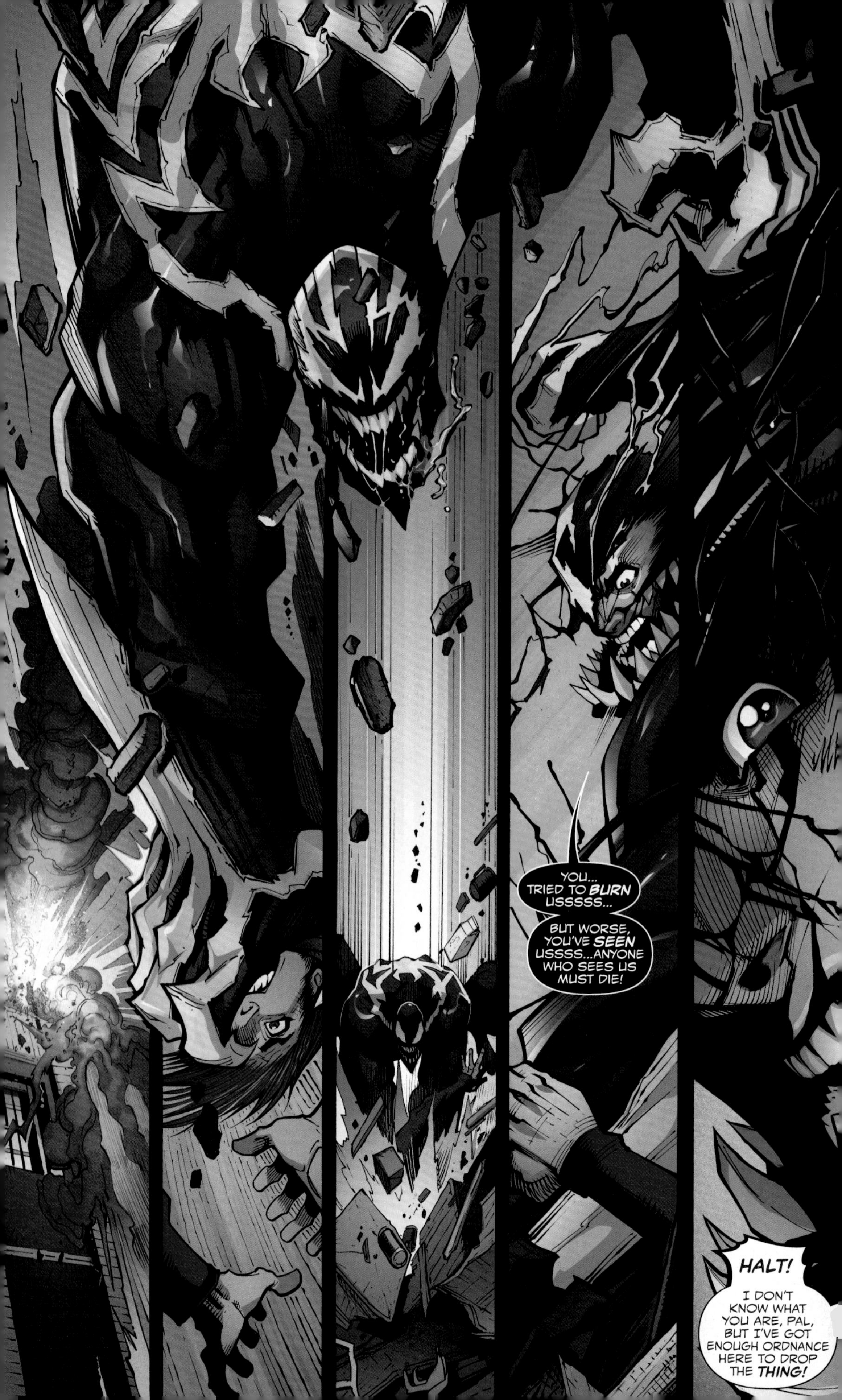
YOU... TRIED TO BURN USSSSS...
BUT WORSE, YOU'VE SEEN USSSS...ANYONE WHO SEES US MUST DIE!
HALT!
I DON'T KNOW WHAT YOU ARE, PAL, BUT I'VE GOT ENOUGH ORDNANCE HERE TO DROP THE THING!

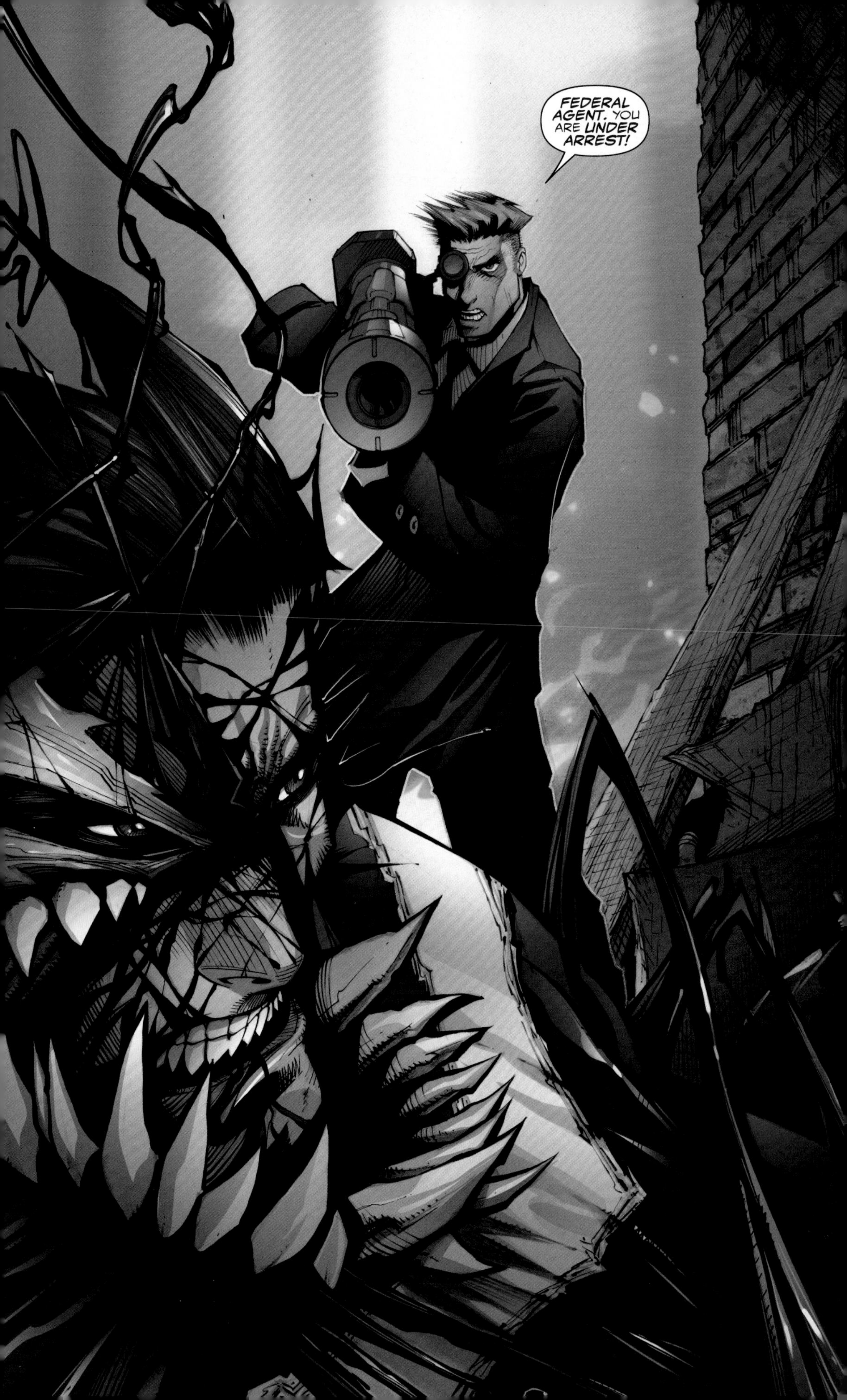
FEDERAL AGENT. YOU ARE UNDER ARREST!

3

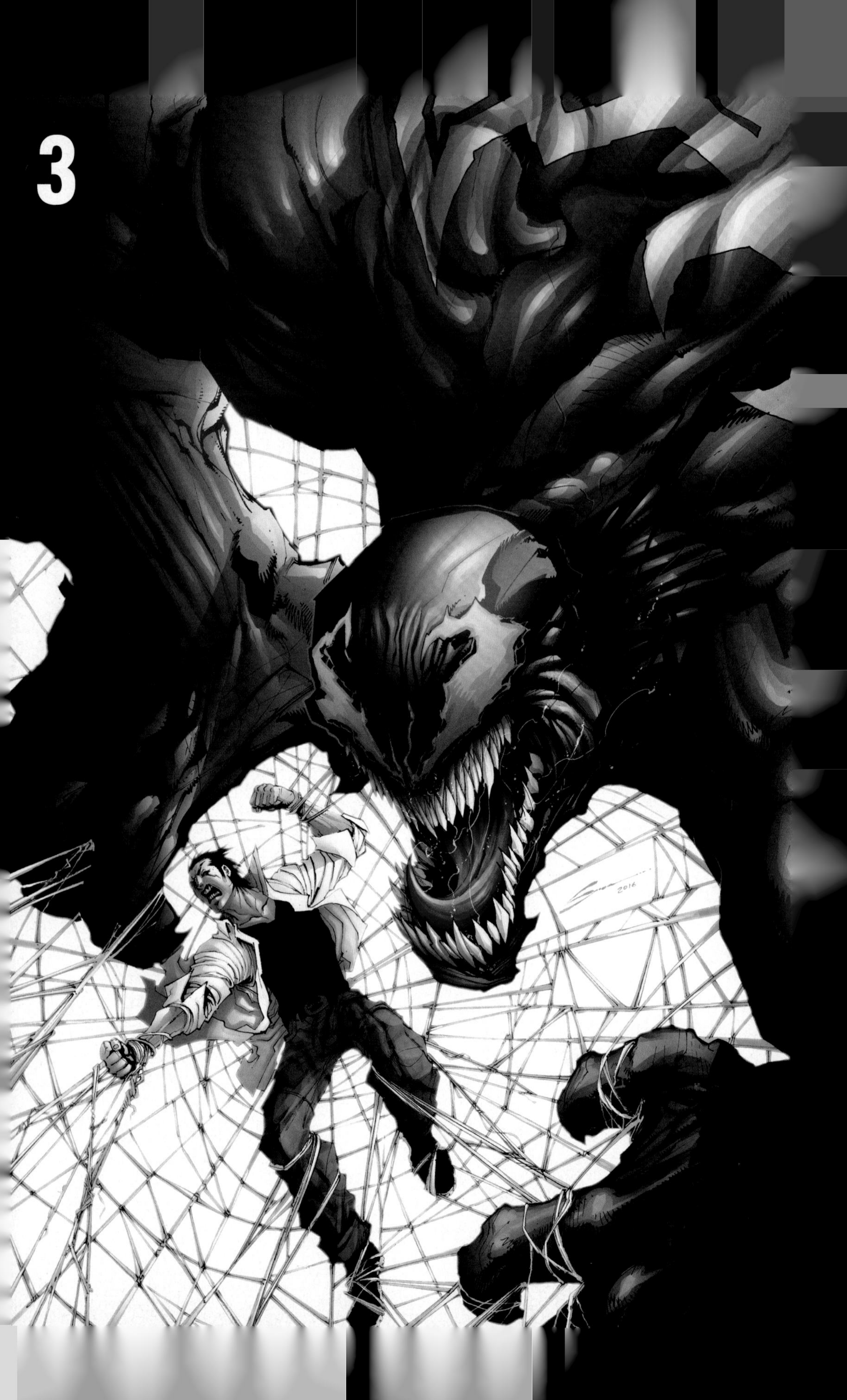

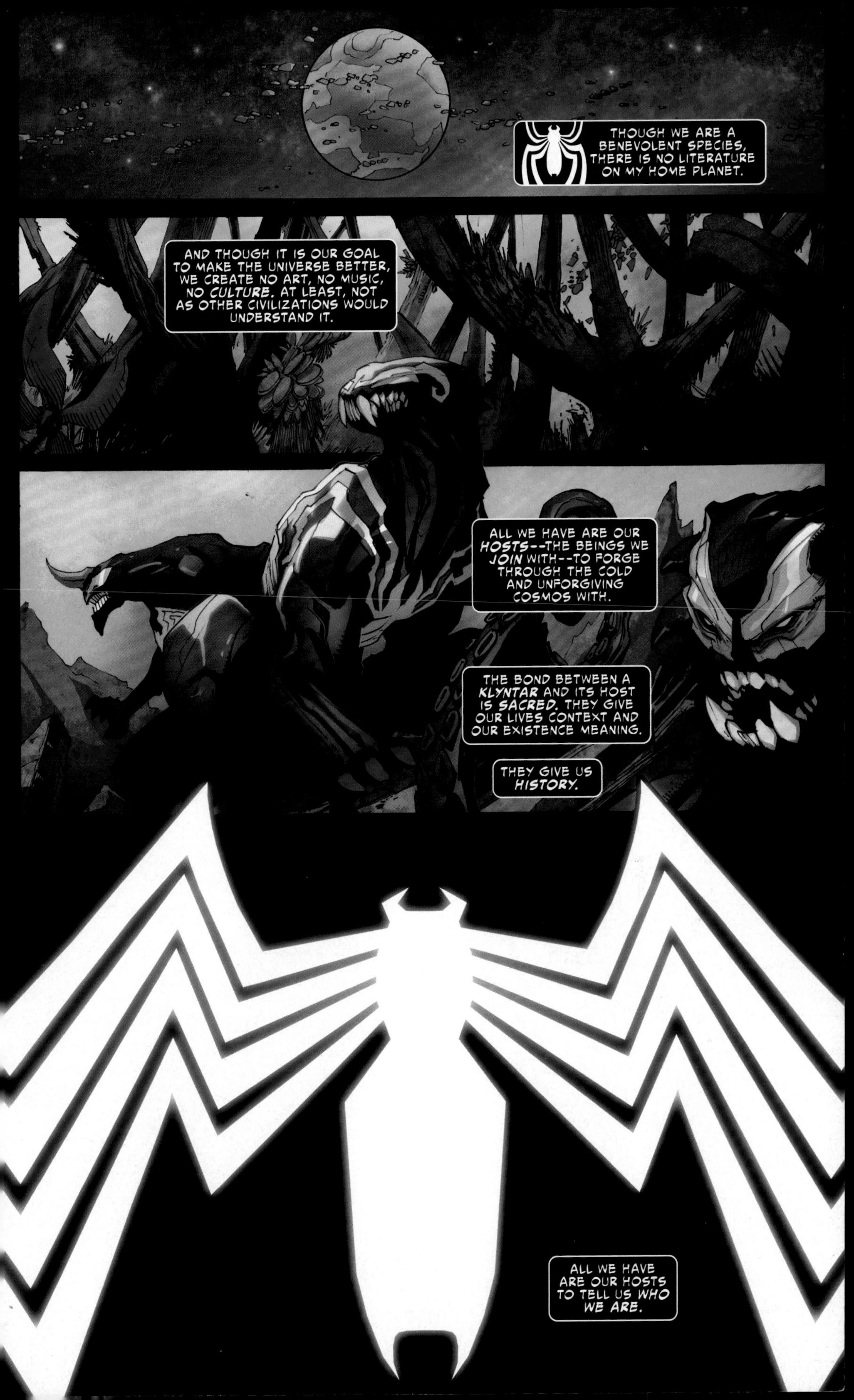
THOUGH WE ARE A BENEVOLENT SPECIES, THERE IS NO LITERATURE ON MY HOME PLANET.
AND THOUGH IT IS OUR GOAL TO MAKE THE UNIVERSE BETTER, WE CREATE NO ART, NO MUSIC, NO *CULTURE*. AT LEAST, NOT AS OTHER CIVILIZATIONS WOULD UNDERSTAND IT.
ALL WE HAVE ARE OUR *HOSTS*--THE BEINGS WE *JOIN* WITH--TO FORGE THROUGH THE COLD AND UNFORGIVING COSMOS WITH.
THE BOND BETWEEN A *KLYNTAR* AND ITS HOST IS *SACRED*. THEY GIVE OUR LIVES CONTEXT AND OUR EXISTENCE MEANING.
THEY GIVE US *HISTORY*.
ALL WE HAVE ARE OUR HOSTS TO TELL US *WHO WE ARE*.

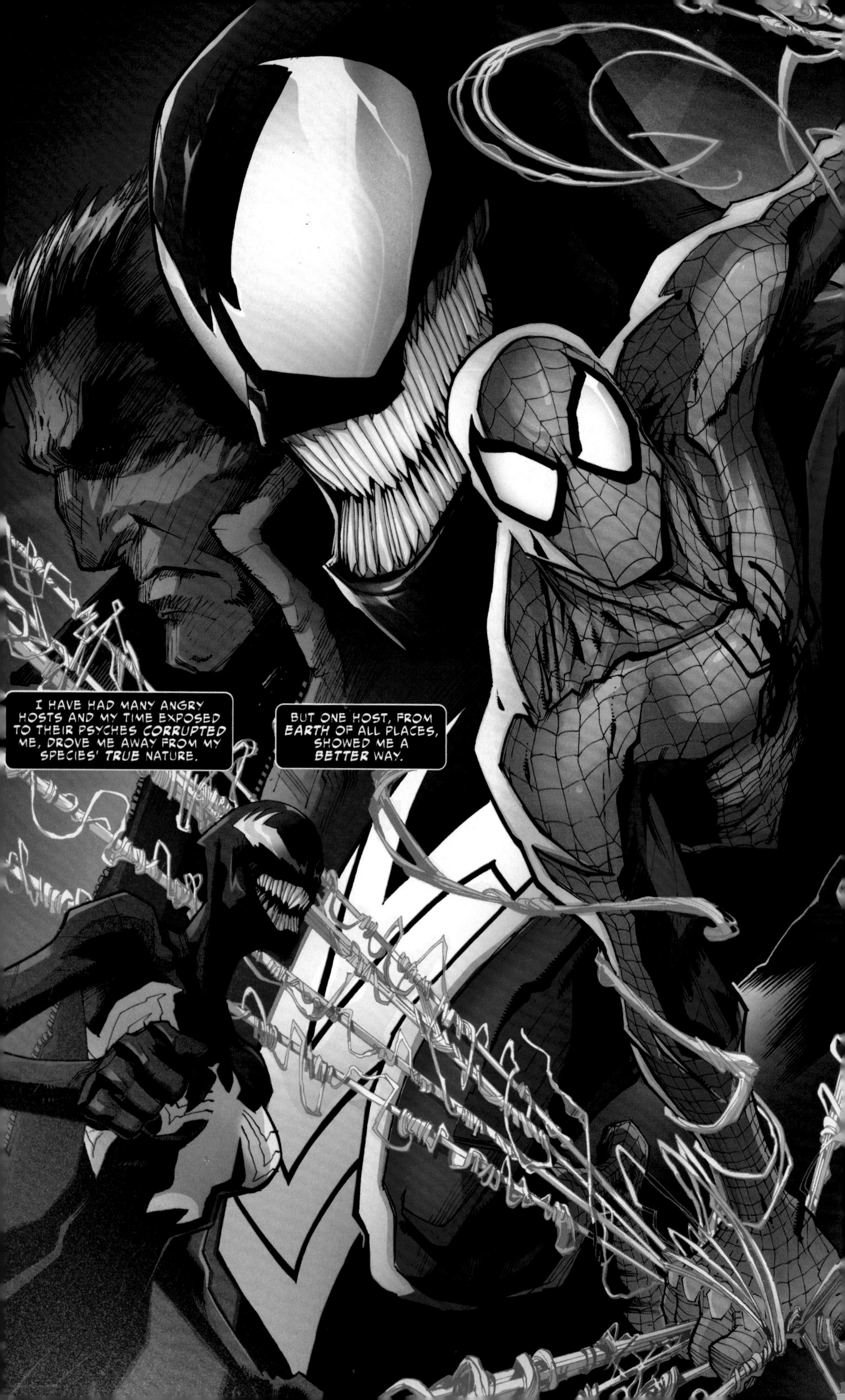
I HAVE HAD MANY ANGRY HOSTS AND MY TIME EXPOSED TO THEIR PSYCHES CORRUPTED ME, DROVE ME AWAY FROM MY SPECIES' TRUE NATURE.
BUT ONE HOST, FROM EARTH OF ALL PLACES, SHOWED ME A BETTER WAY.

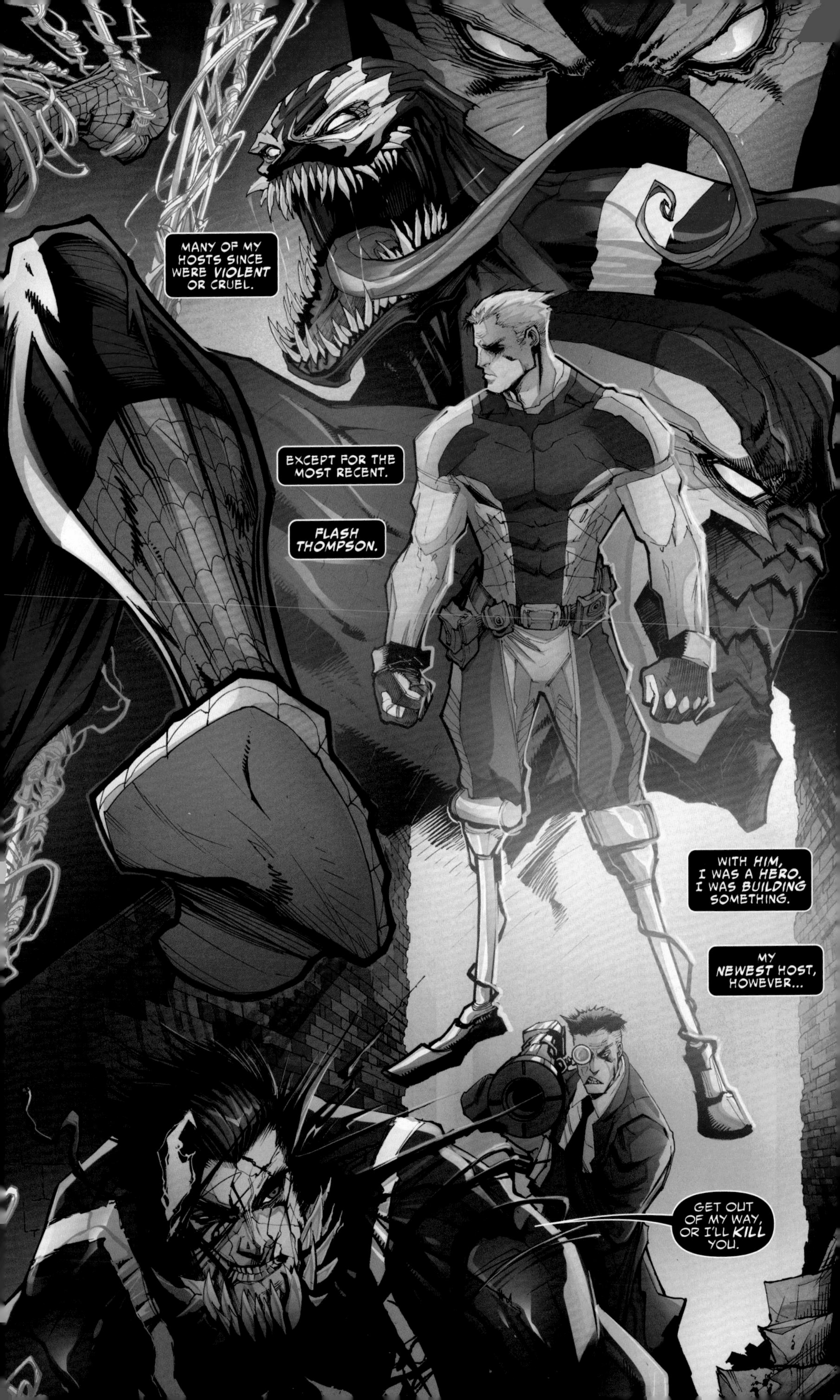
MANY OF MY HOSTS SINCE WERE VIOLENT OR CRUEL.
EXCEPT FOR THE MOST RECENT.
FLASH THOMPSON.
WITH HIM, I WAS A HERO. I WAS BUILDING SOMETHING.
MY NEWEST HOST, HOWEVER...
GET OUT OF MY WAY, OR I'LL KILL YOU.

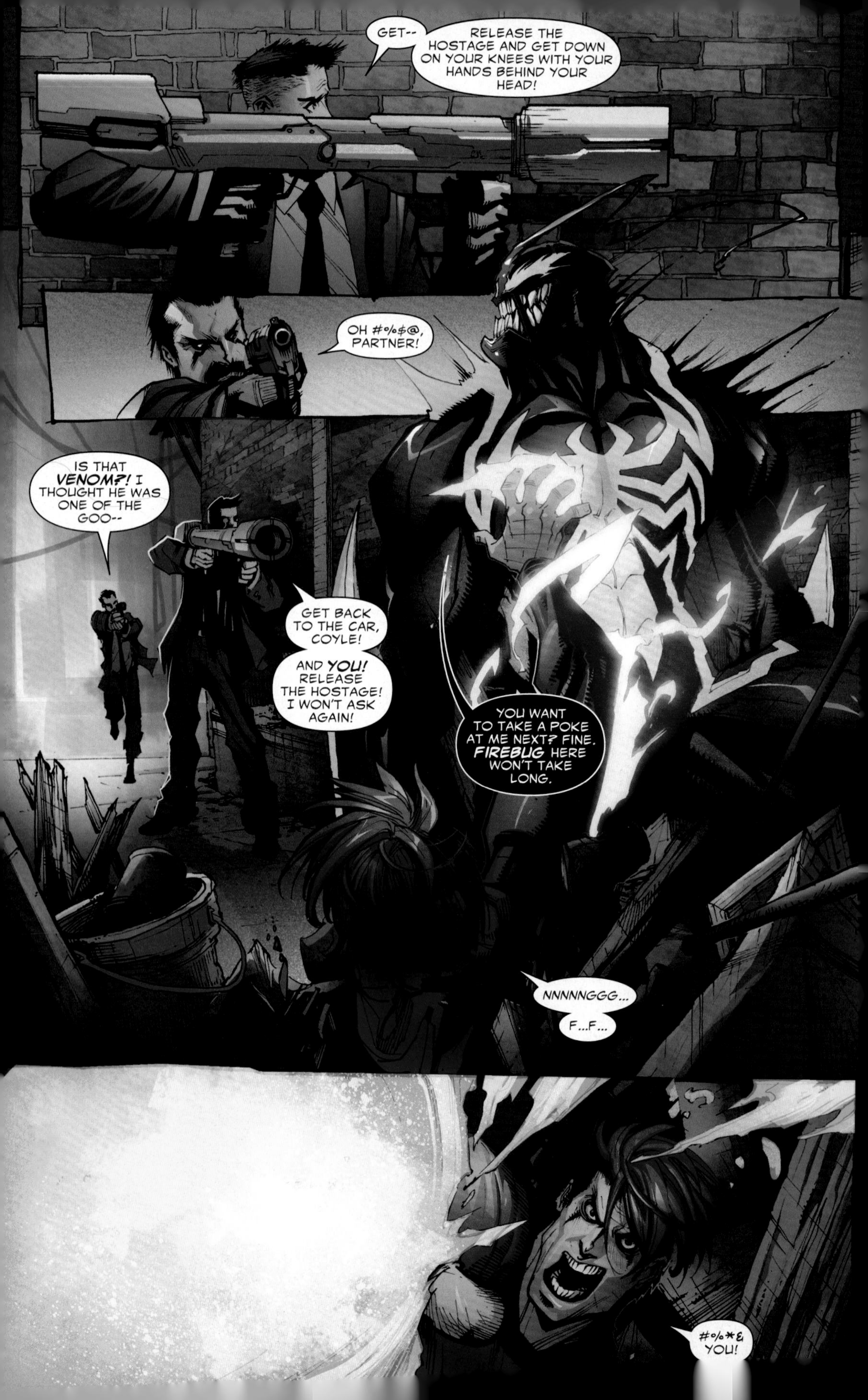
GET--
RELEASE THE HOSTAGE AND GET DOWN ON YOUR KNEES WITH YOUR HANDS BEHIND YOUR HEAD!
OH #%$@, PARTNER!
IS THAT VENOM?! I THOUGHT HE WAS ONE OF THE GOO--
GET BACK TO THE CAR, COYLE!
AND YOU! RELEASE THE HOSTAGE! I WON'T ASK AGAIN!
YOU WANT TO TAKE A POKE AT ME NEXT? FINE. FIREBUG HERE WON'T TAKE LONG.
NNNNNGGG...
F...F...
#%*& YOU!

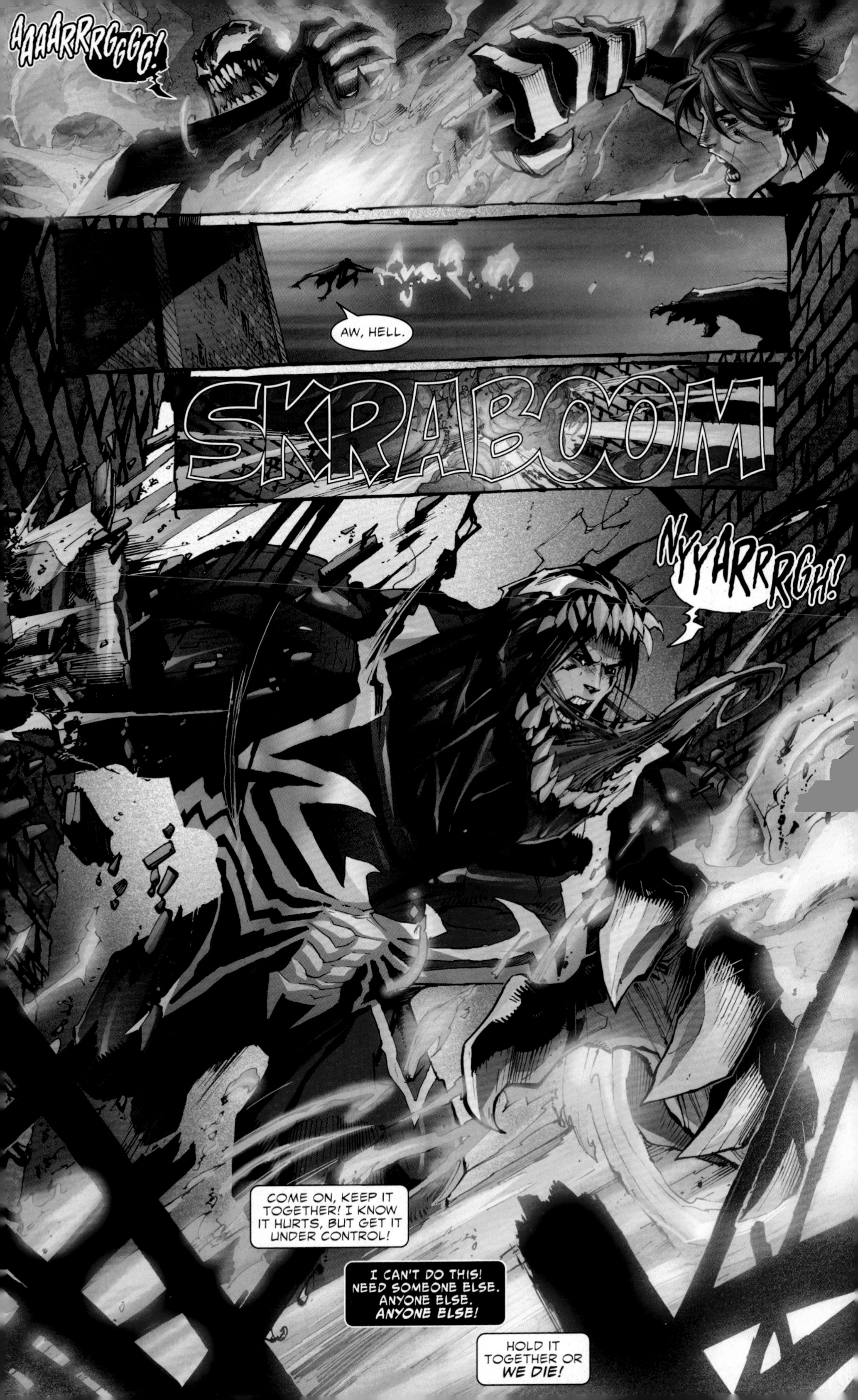
AAAARRRGGGG!
AW, HELL.
SKRABOOM
NYYARRRGH!
COME ON, KEEP IT TOGETHER! I KNOW IT HURTS, BUT GET IT UNDER CONTROL!
I CAN'T DO THIS! NEED SOMEONE ELSE. ANYONE ELSE. ANYONE ELSE!
HOLD IT TOGETHER OR WE DIE!

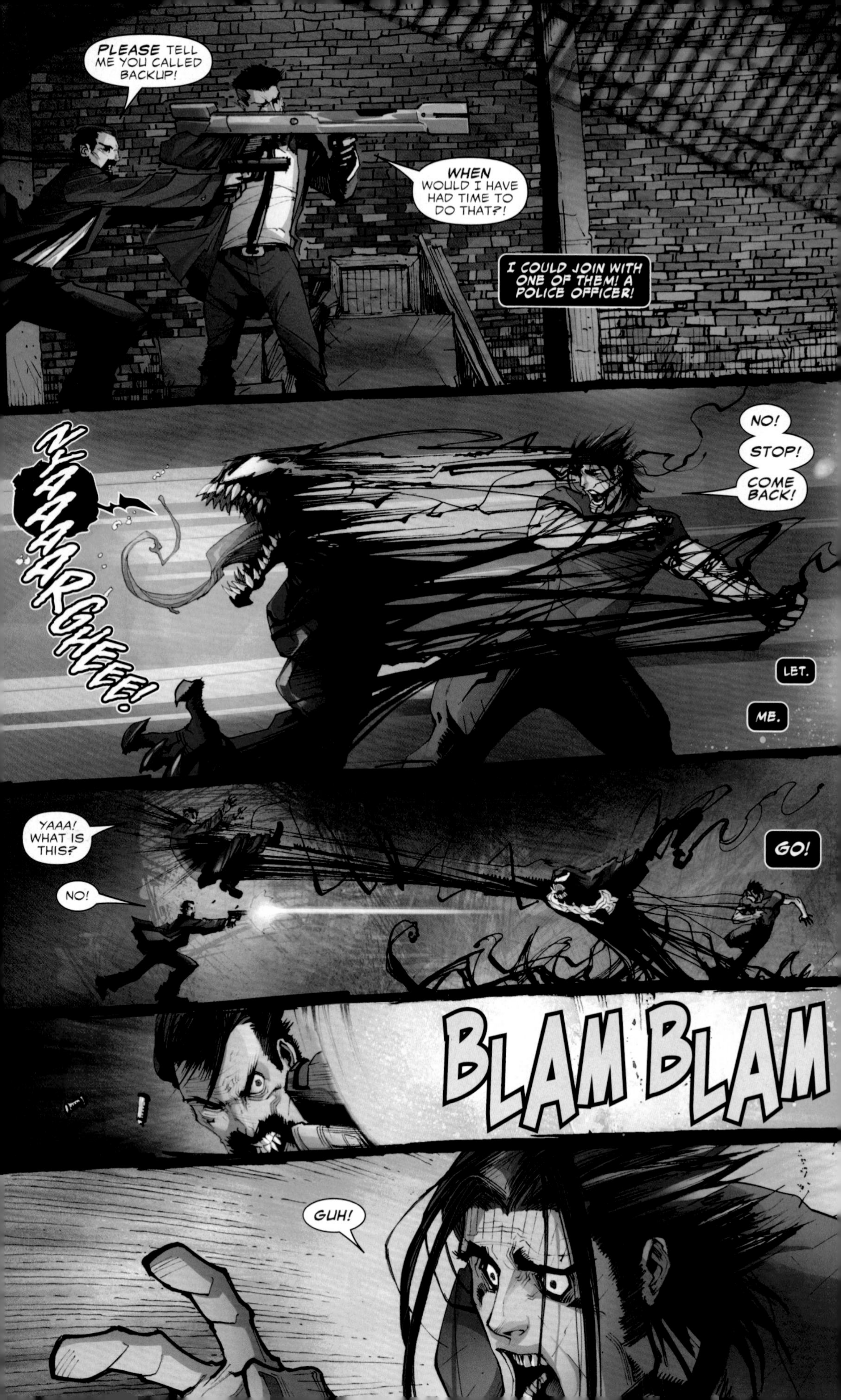
PLEASE TELL ME YOU CALLED BACKUP!
WHEN WOULD I HAVE HAD TIME TO DO THAT?!
I COULD JOIN WITH ONE OF THEM! A POLICE OFFICER!
NYAAAARGHEEE!
NO!
STOP!
COME BACK!
LET.
ME.
YAAA! WHAT IS THIS?
NO!
GO!
BLAM BLAM
GUH!

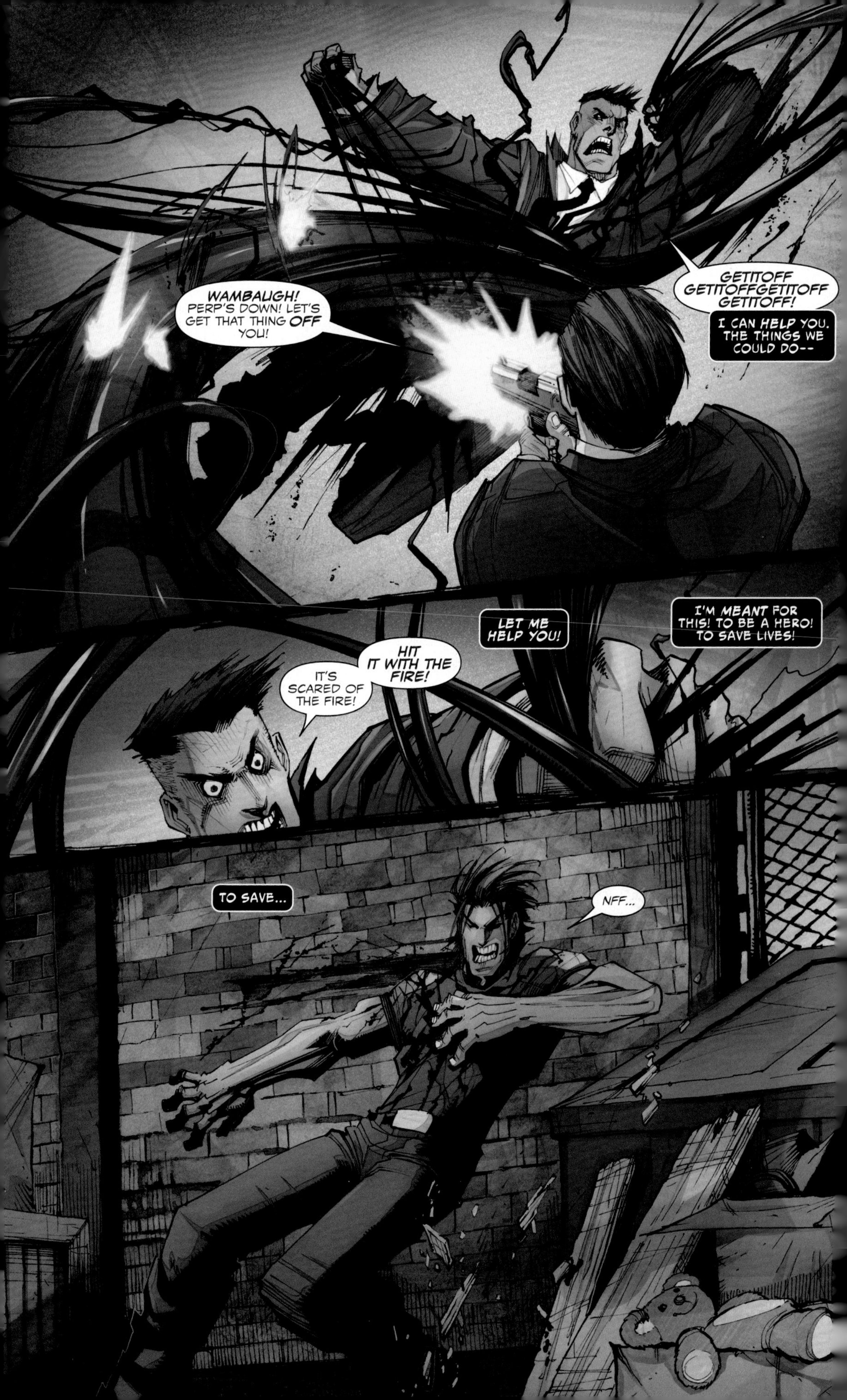
WAMBAUGH! PERP'S DOWN! LET'S GET THAT THING OFF YOU!
GETITOFF GETITOFFGETITOFF GETITOFF!
I CAN HELP YOU. THE THINGS WE COULD DO--
LET ME HELP YOU!
I'M MEANT FOR THIS! TO BE A HERO! TO SAVE LIVES!
HIT IT WITH THE FIRE!
IT'S SCARED OF THE FIRE!
TO SAVE...
NFF...

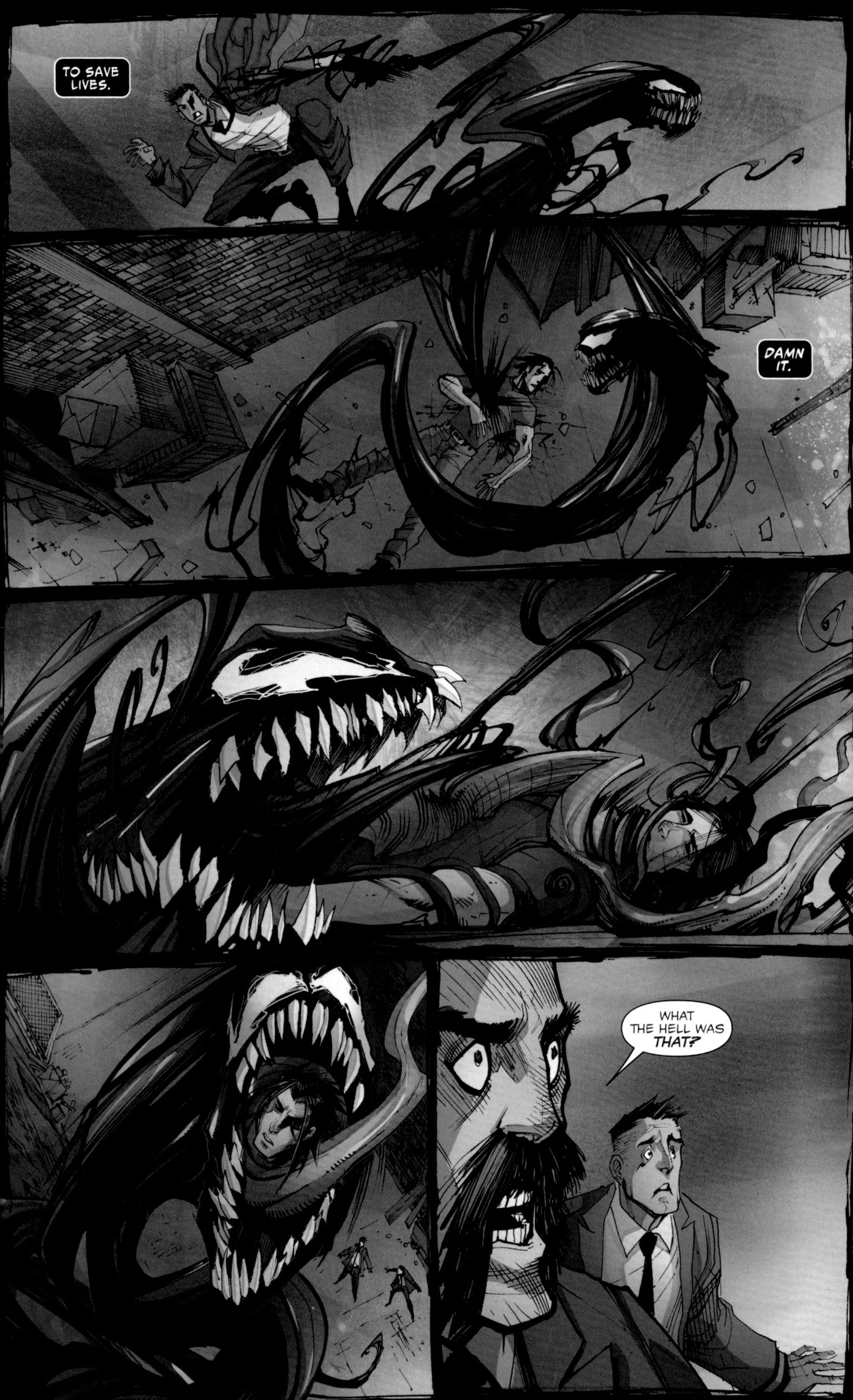
TO SAVE LIVES.
DAMN IT.
WHAT THE HELL WAS THAT?

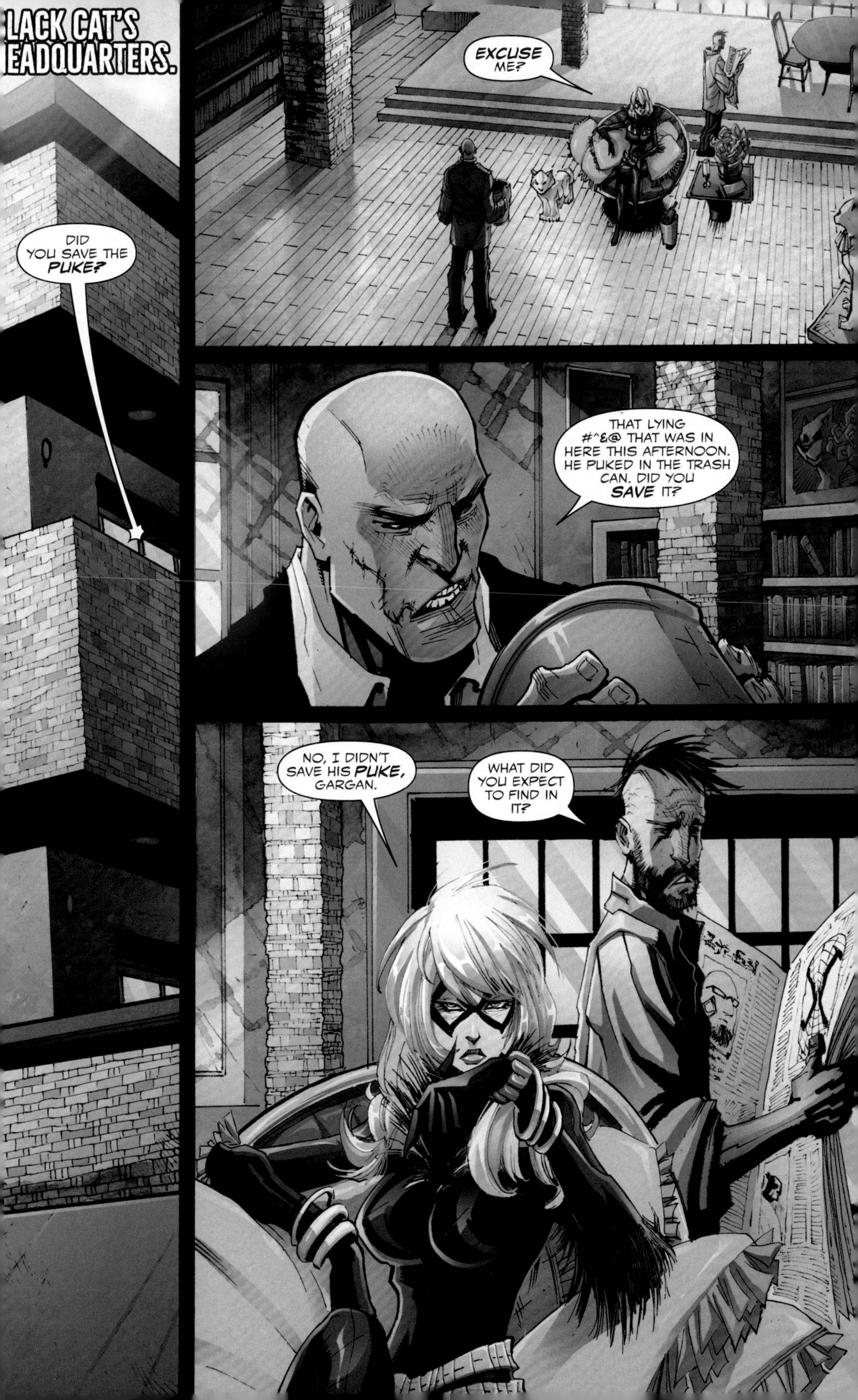
LACK CAT'S
EADQUARTERS.
DID YOU SAVE THE PUKE?
EXCUSE ME?
THAT LYING #^&@ THAT WAS IN HERE THIS AFTERNOON. HE PUKED IN THE TRASH CAN. DID YOU SAVE IT?
NO, I DIDN'T SAVE HIS PUKE, GARGAN.
WHAT DID YOU EXPECT TO FIND IN IT?

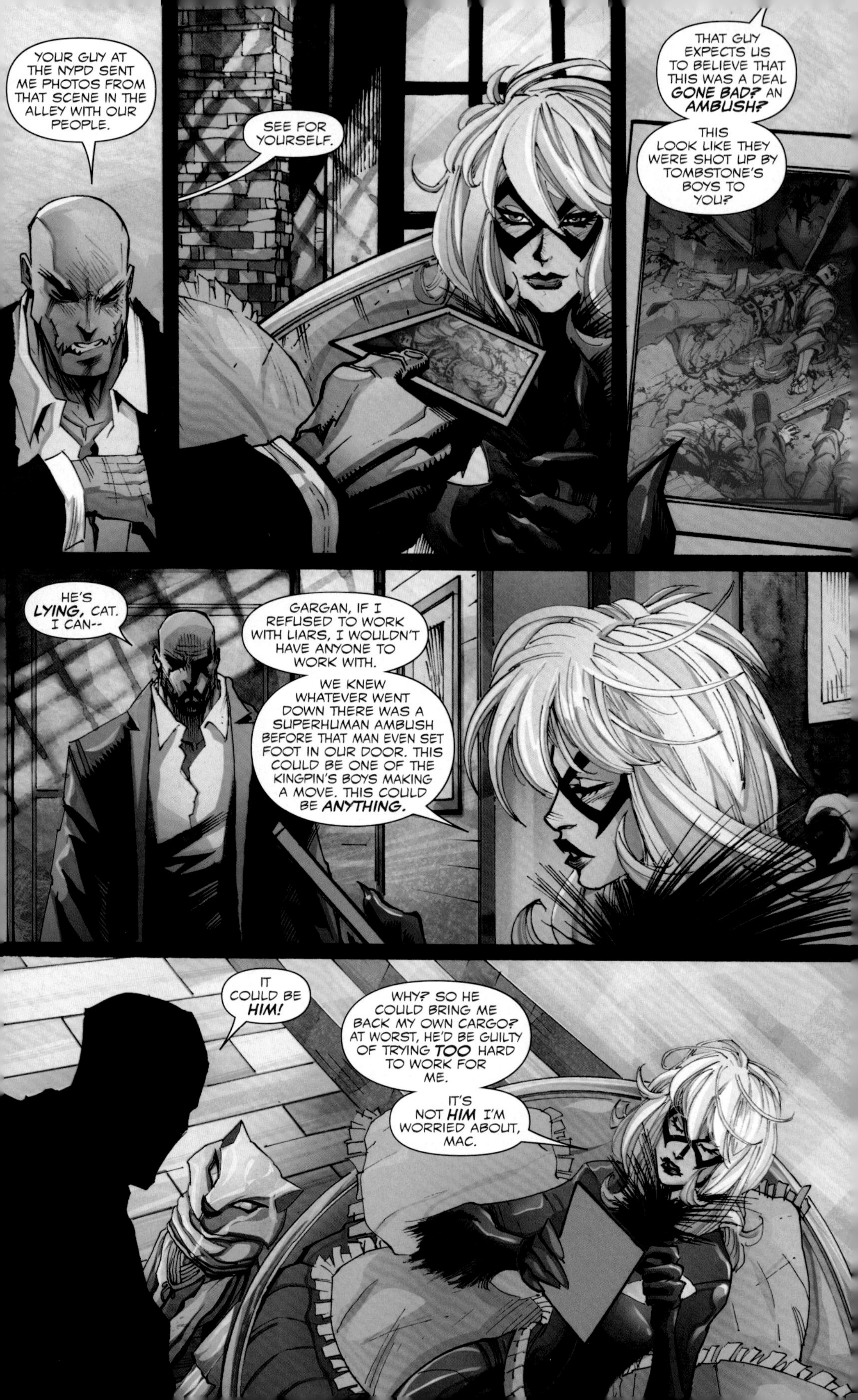
YOUR GUY AT THE NYPD SENT ME PHOTOS FROM THAT SCENE IN THE ALLEY WITH OUR PEOPLE.
SEE FOR YOURSELF.
THAT GUY EXPECTS US TO BELIEVE THAT THIS WAS A DEAL GONE BAD? AN AMBUSH?
THIS LOOK LIKE THEY WERE SHOT UP BY TOMBSTONE'S BOYS TO YOU?
HE'S LYING, CAT. I CAN--
GARGAN, IF I REFUSED TO WORK WITH LIARS, I WOULDN'T HAVE ANYONE TO WORK WITH.
WE KNEW WHATEVER WENT DOWN THERE WAS A SUPERHUMAN AMBUSH BEFORE THAT MAN EVEN SET FOOT IN OUR DOOR. THIS COULD BE ONE OF THE KINGPIN'S BOYS MAKING A MOVE. THIS COULD BE ANYTHING.
IT COULD BE HIM!
WHY? SO HE COULD BRING ME BACK MY OWN CARGO? AT WORST, HE'D BE GUILTY OF TRYING TOO HARD TO WORK FOR ME.
IT'S NOT HIM I'M WORRIED ABOUT, MAC.

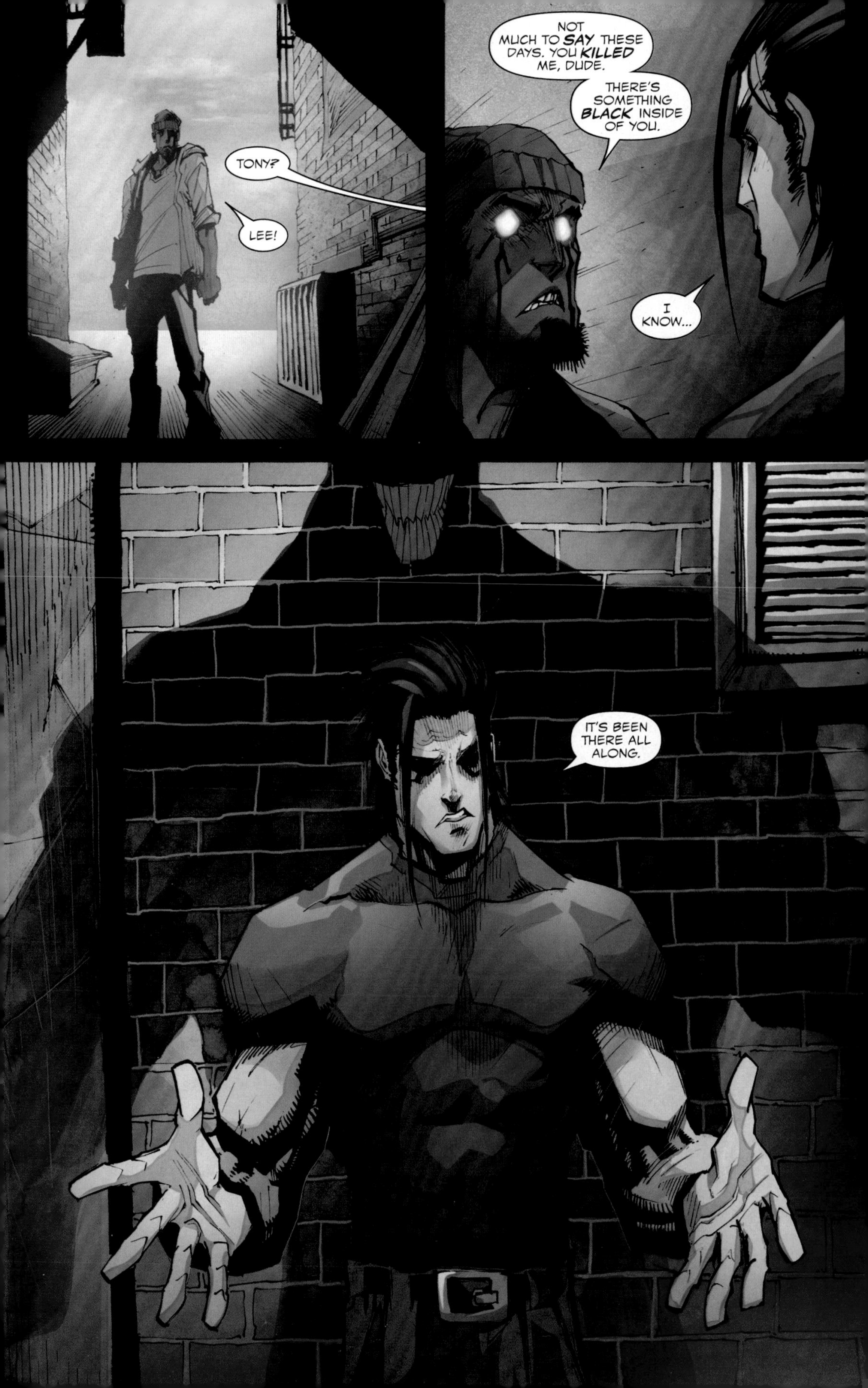
TONY?
LEE!
NOT MUCH TO SAY THESE DAYS. YOU KILLED ME, DUDE.
THERE'S SOMETHING BLACK INSIDE OF YOU.
I KNOW...
IT'S BEEN THERE ALL ALONG.

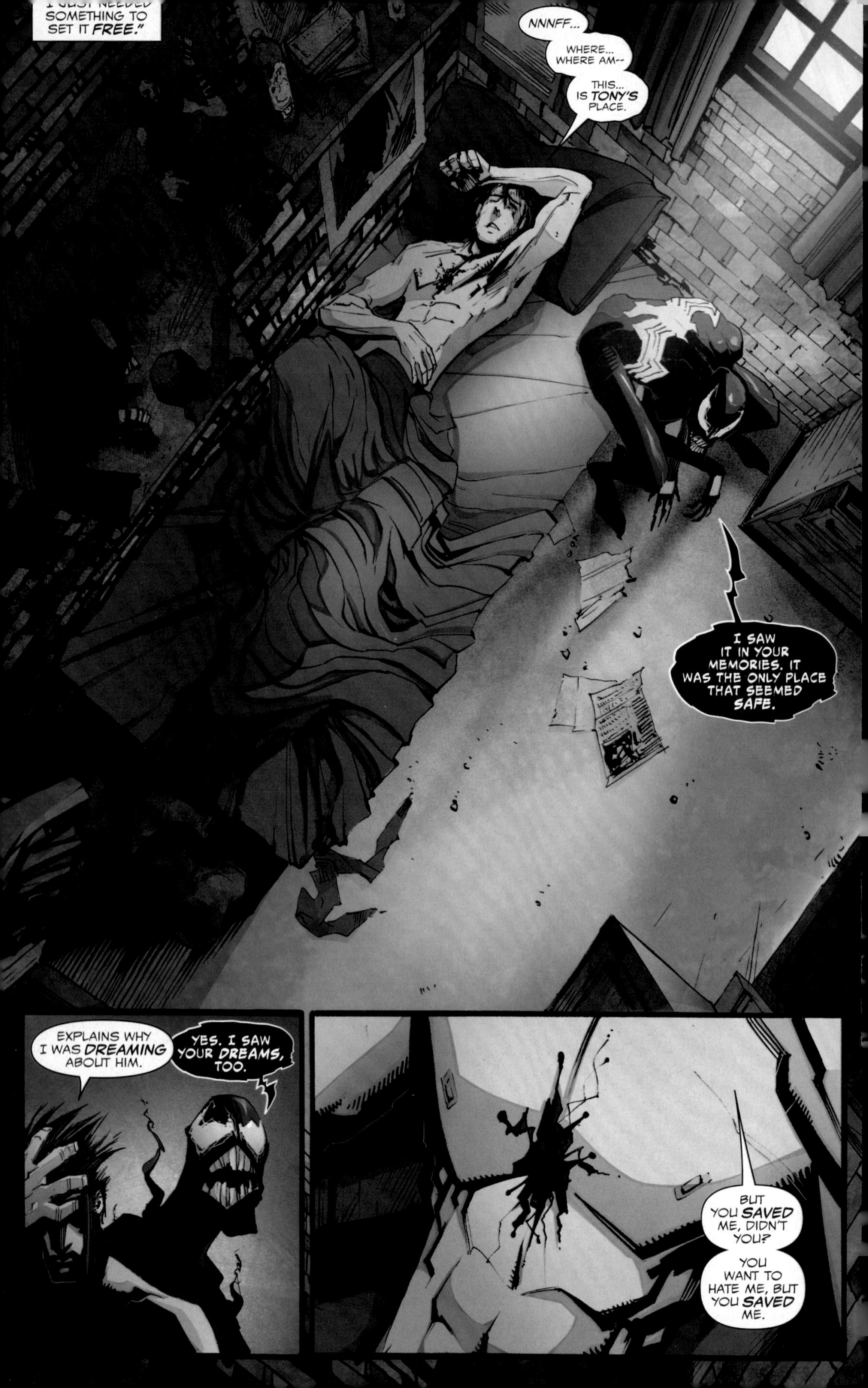

SOMETHING TO SET IT FREE."
NNNFF...
WHERE... WHERE AM--
THIS... IS TONY'S PLACE.
I SAW IT IN YOUR MEMORIES. IT WAS THE ONLY PLACE THAT SEEMED SAFE.
EXPLAINS WHY I WAS DREAMING ABOUT HIM.
YES. I SAW YOUR DREAMS, TOO.
BUT YOU SAVED ME, DIDN'T YOU?
YOU WANT TO HATE ME, BUT YOU SAVED ME.

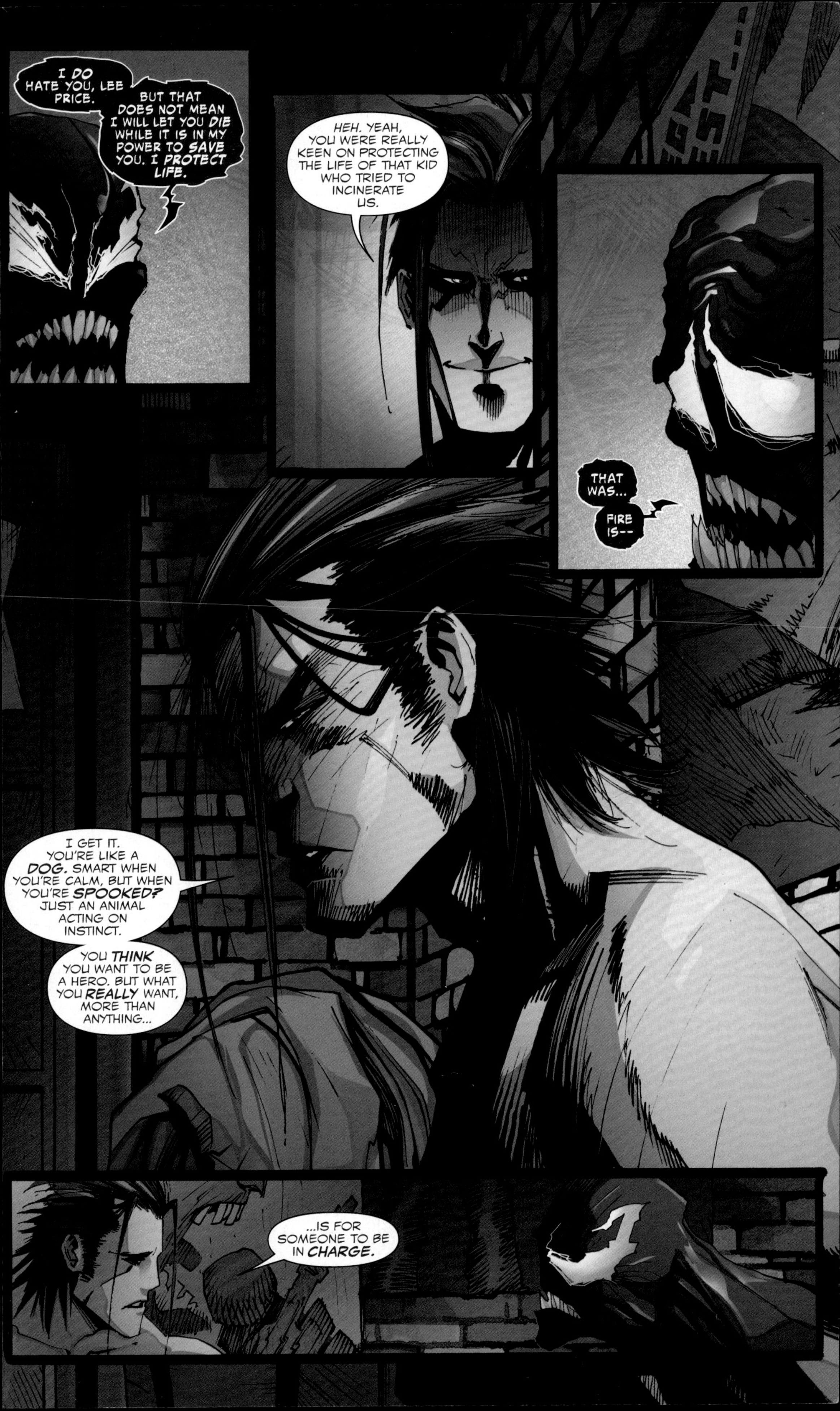
I DO HATE YOU, LEE PRICE.
BUT THAT DOES NOT MEAN I WILL LET YOU DIE WHILE IT IS IN MY POWER TO SAVE YOU. I PROTECT LIFE.
HEH. YEAH, YOU WERE REALLY KEEN ON PROTECTING THE LIFE OF THAT KID WHO TRIED TO INCINERATE US.
THAT WAS...
FIRE IS--
I GET IT. YOU'RE LIKE A DOG. SMART WHEN YOU'RE CALM, BUT WHEN YOU'RE SPOOKED? JUST AN ANIMAL ACTING ON INSTINCT.
YOU THINK YOU WANT TO BE A HERO. BUT WHAT YOU REALLY WANT, MORE THAN ANYTHING...
...IS FOR SOMEONE TO BE IN CHARGE.

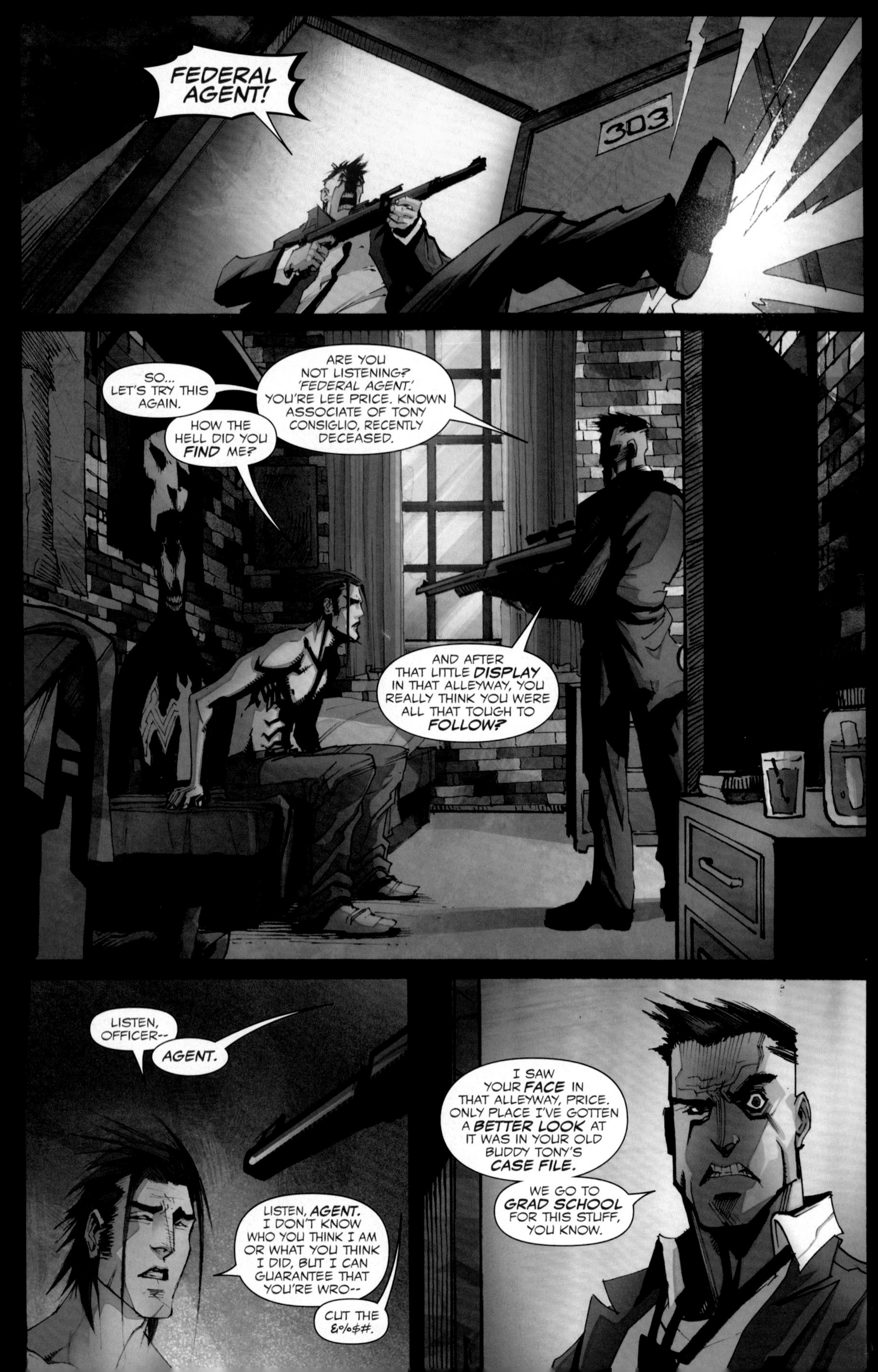

FEDERAL AGENT!
303
SO... LET'S TRY THIS AGAIN.
HOW THE HELL DID YOU FIND ME?
ARE YOU NOT LISTENING? 'FEDERAL AGENT.' YOU'RE LEE PRICE. KNOWN ASSOCIATE OF TONY CONSIGLIO, RECENTLY DECEASED.
AND AFTER THAT LITTLE DISPLAY IN THAT ALLEYWAY, YOU REALLY THINK YOU WERE ALL THAT TOUGH TO FOLLOW?
LISTEN, OFFICER--
AGENT.
LISTEN, AGENT. I DON'T KNOW WHO YOU THINK I AM OR WHAT YOU THINK I DID, BUT I CAN GUARANTEE THAT YOU'RE WRO--
CUT THE &%$#.
I SAW YOUR FACE IN THAT ALLEYWAY, PRICE. ONLY PLACE I'VE GOTTEN A BETTER LOOK AT IT WAS IN YOUR OLD BUDDY TONY'S CASE FILE.
WE GO TO GRAD SCHOOL FOR THIS STUFF, YOU KNOW.

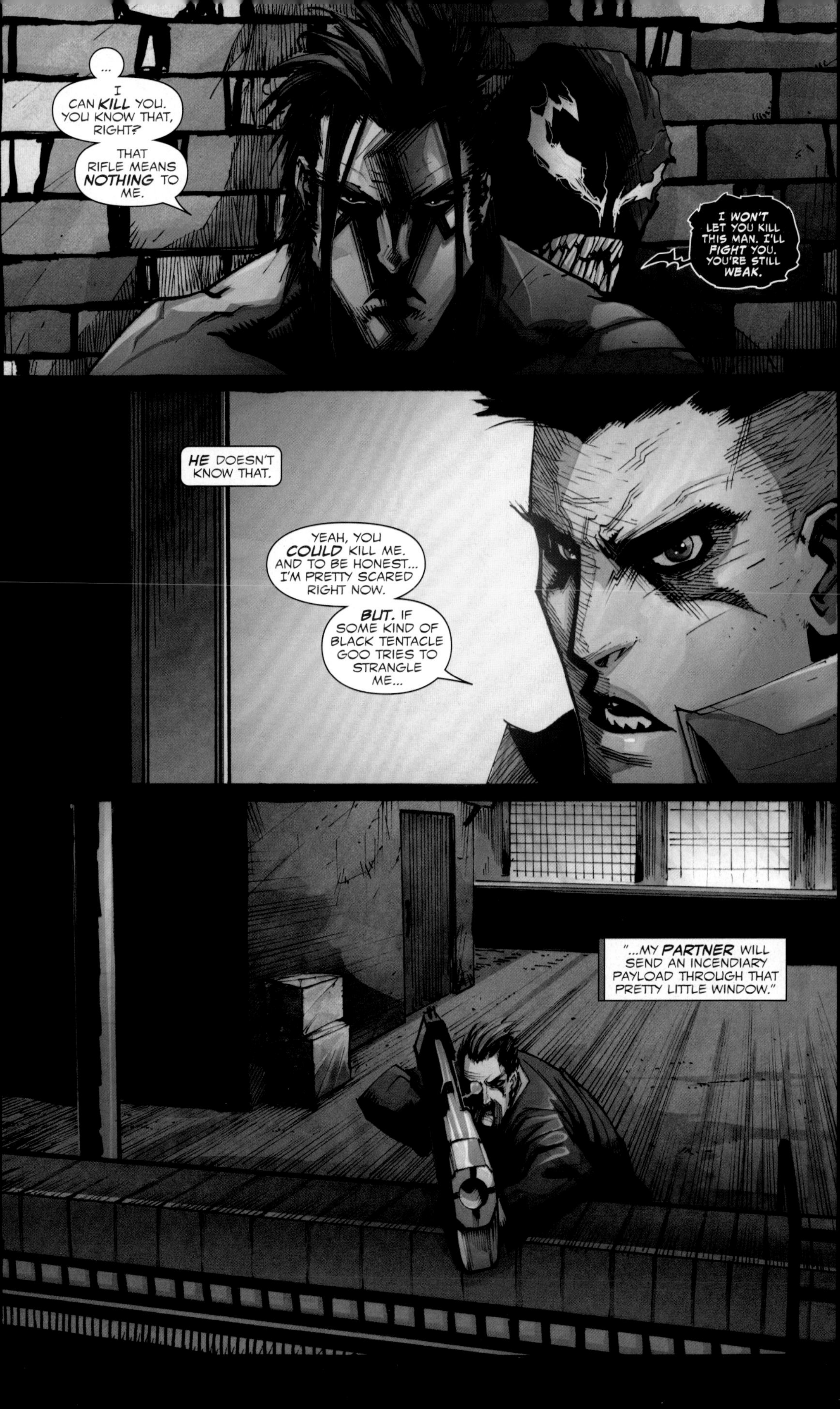
...
I CAN KILL YOU. YOU KNOW THAT, RIGHT?
THAT RIFLE MEANS NOTHING TO ME.
I WON'T LET YOU KILL THIS MAN. I'LL FIGHT YOU. YOU'RE STILL WEAK.
HE DOESN'T KNOW THAT.
YEAH, YOU COULD KILL ME. AND TO BE HONEST... I'M PRETTY SCARED RIGHT NOW.
BUT. IF SOME KIND OF BLACK TENTACLE GOO TRIES TO STRANGLE ME...
"...MY PARTNER WILL SEND AN INCENDIARY PAYLOAD THROUGH THAT PRETTY LITTLE WINDOW."

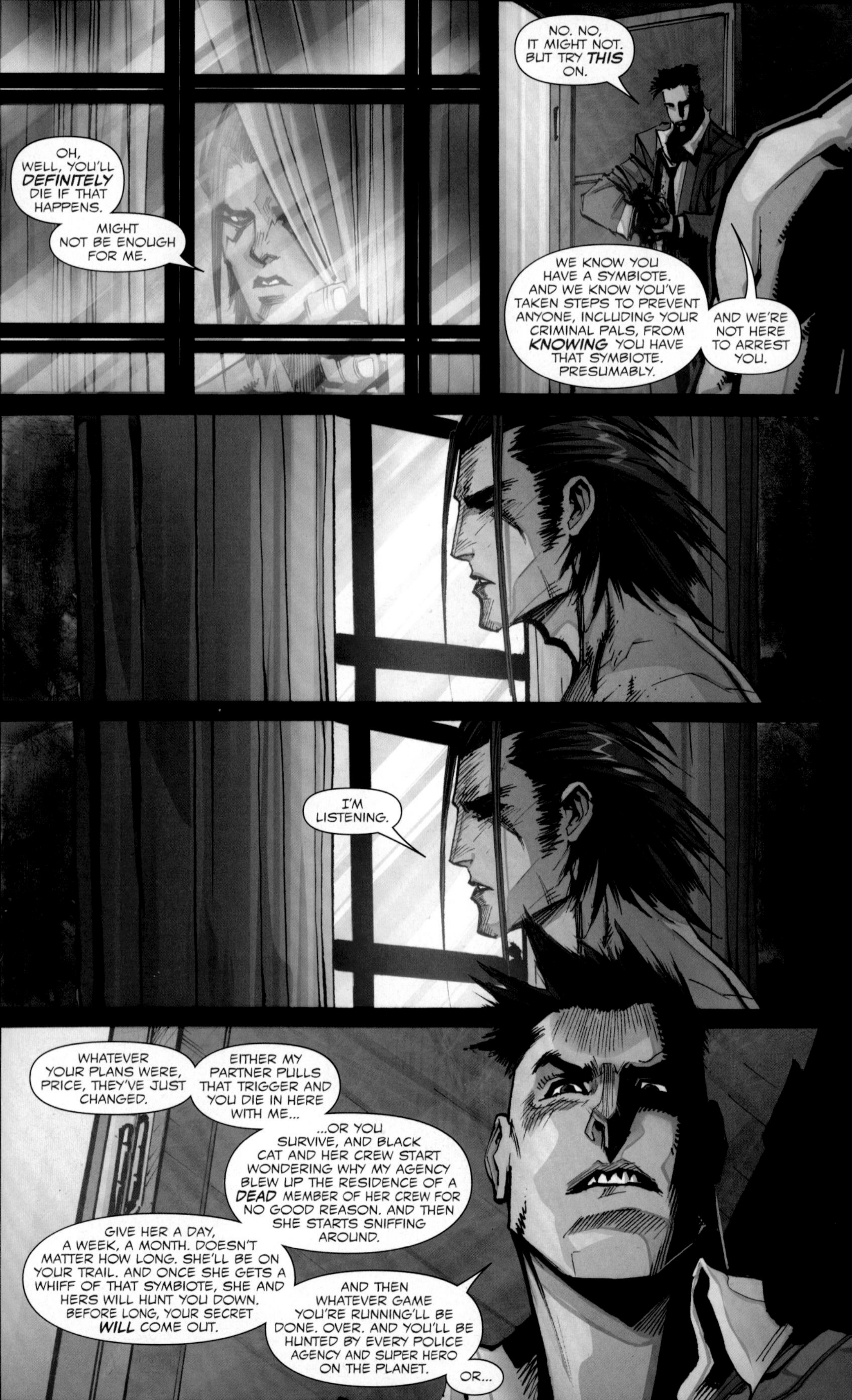

OH, WELL, YOU'LL ***DEFINITELY*** DIE IF THAT HAPPENS.
MIGHT NOT BE ENOUGH FOR ME.
NO. NO, IT MIGHT NOT. BUT TRY ***THIS*** ON.
WE KNOW YOU HAVE A SYMBIOTE. AND WE KNOW YOU'VE TAKEN STEPS TO PREVENT ANYONE, INCLUDING YOUR CRIMINAL PALS, FROM ***KNOWING*** YOU HAVE THAT SYMBIOTE. PRESUMABLY.
AND WE'RE NOT HERE TO ARREST YOU.
I'M LISTENING.
WHATEVER YOUR PLANS WERE, PRICE, THEY'VE JUST CHANGED.
EITHER MY PARTNER PULLS THAT TRIGGER AND YOU DIE IN HERE WITH ME...
...OR YOU SURVIVE, AND BLACK CAT AND HER CREW START WONDERING WHY MY AGENCY BLEW UP THE RESIDENCE OF A ***DEAD*** MEMBER OF HER CREW FOR NO GOOD REASON. AND THEN SHE STARTS SNIFFING AROUND.
GIVE HER A DAY, A WEEK, A MONTH. DOESN'T MATTER HOW LONG. SHE'LL BE ON YOUR TRAIL. AND ONCE SHE GETS A WHIFF OF THAT SYMBIOTE, SHE AND HERS WILL HUNT YOU DOWN. BEFORE LONG, YOUR SECRET ***WILL*** COME OUT.
AND THEN WHATEVER GAME YOU'RE RUNNING'LL BE DONE. OVER. AND YOU'LL BE HUNTED BY EVERY POLICE AGENCY AND SUPER HERO ON THE PLANET.
OR...

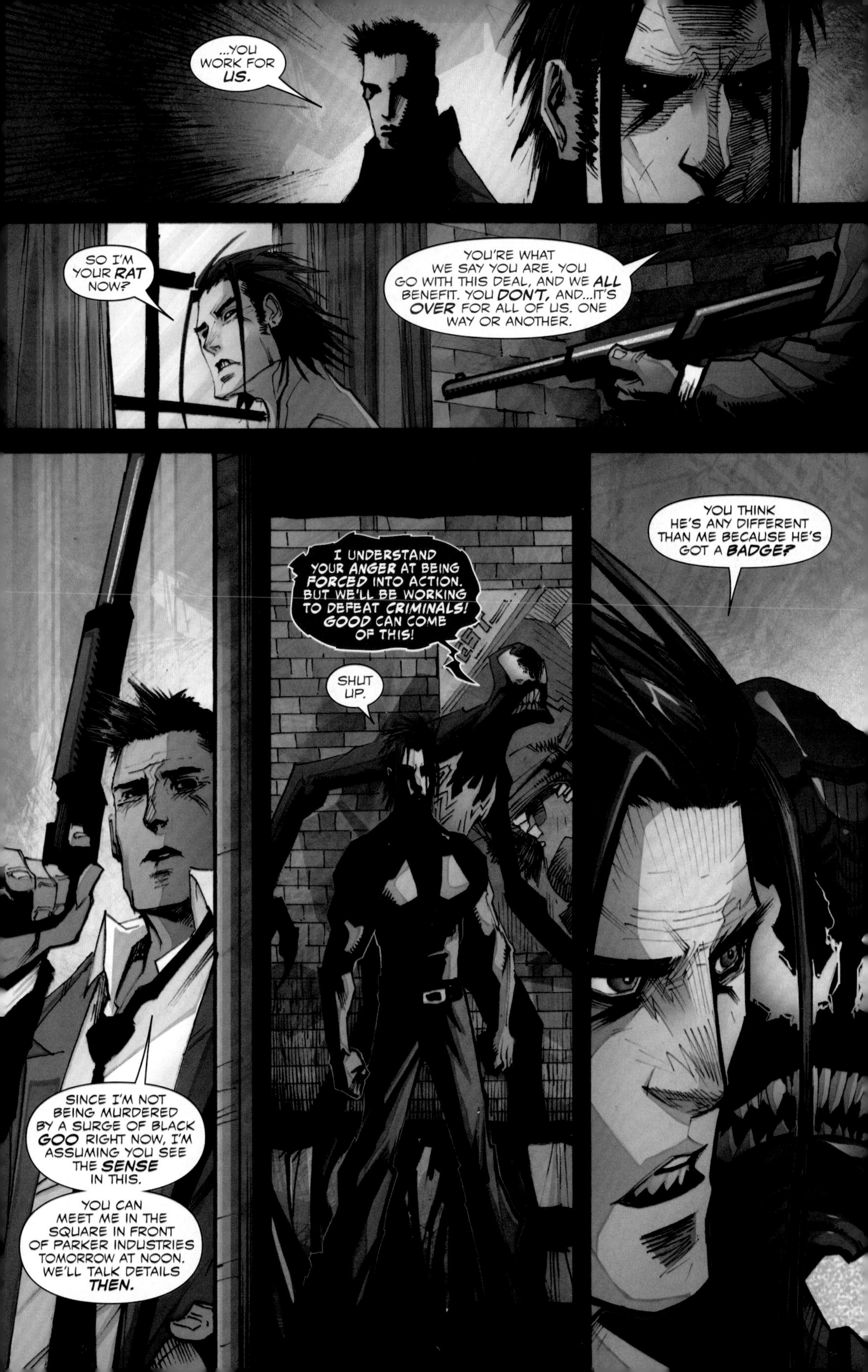
...YOU WORK FOR US.
SO I'M YOUR RAT NOW?
YOU'RE WHAT WE SAY YOU ARE. YOU GO WITH THIS DEAL, AND WE ALL BENEFIT. YOU DON'T, AND...IT'S OVER FOR ALL OF US. ONE WAY OR ANOTHER.
YOU THINK HE'S ANY DIFFERENT THAN ME BECAUSE HE'S GOT A BADGE?
I UNDERSTAND YOUR ANGER AT BEING FORCED INTO ACTION. BUT WE'LL BE WORKING TO DEFEAT CRIMINALS! GOOD CAN COME OF THIS!
SHUT UP.
SINCE I'M NOT BEING MURDERED BY A SURGE OF BLACK GOO RIGHT NOW, I'M ASSUMING YOU SEE THE SENSE IN THIS.
YOU CAN MEET ME IN THE SQUARE IN FRONT OF PARKER INDUSTRIES TOMORROW AT NOON. WE'LL TALK DETAILS THEN.

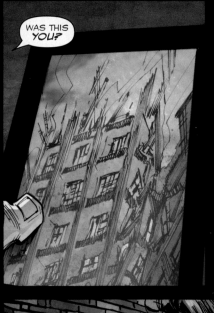

WAS THIS *YOU?*

WHAT? I'M BURNING BUILDINGS NOW? WHO DO YOU THINK I AM? THE *MOLTEN MAN?*

THAT'S *LEE PRICE'S* APARTMENT.

IT IS? WHAT THE HELL IS THIS? IS HE *DEAD?*

NO. NO BODIES IN THE APARTMENT.

I'D JUST ASSUMED YOU'D TAKEN MATTERS INTO YOUR OWN HANDS.

OH, YOU *"ASSUMED,"* HUH? THAT I'D GO BEHIND THE CAT'S BACK?

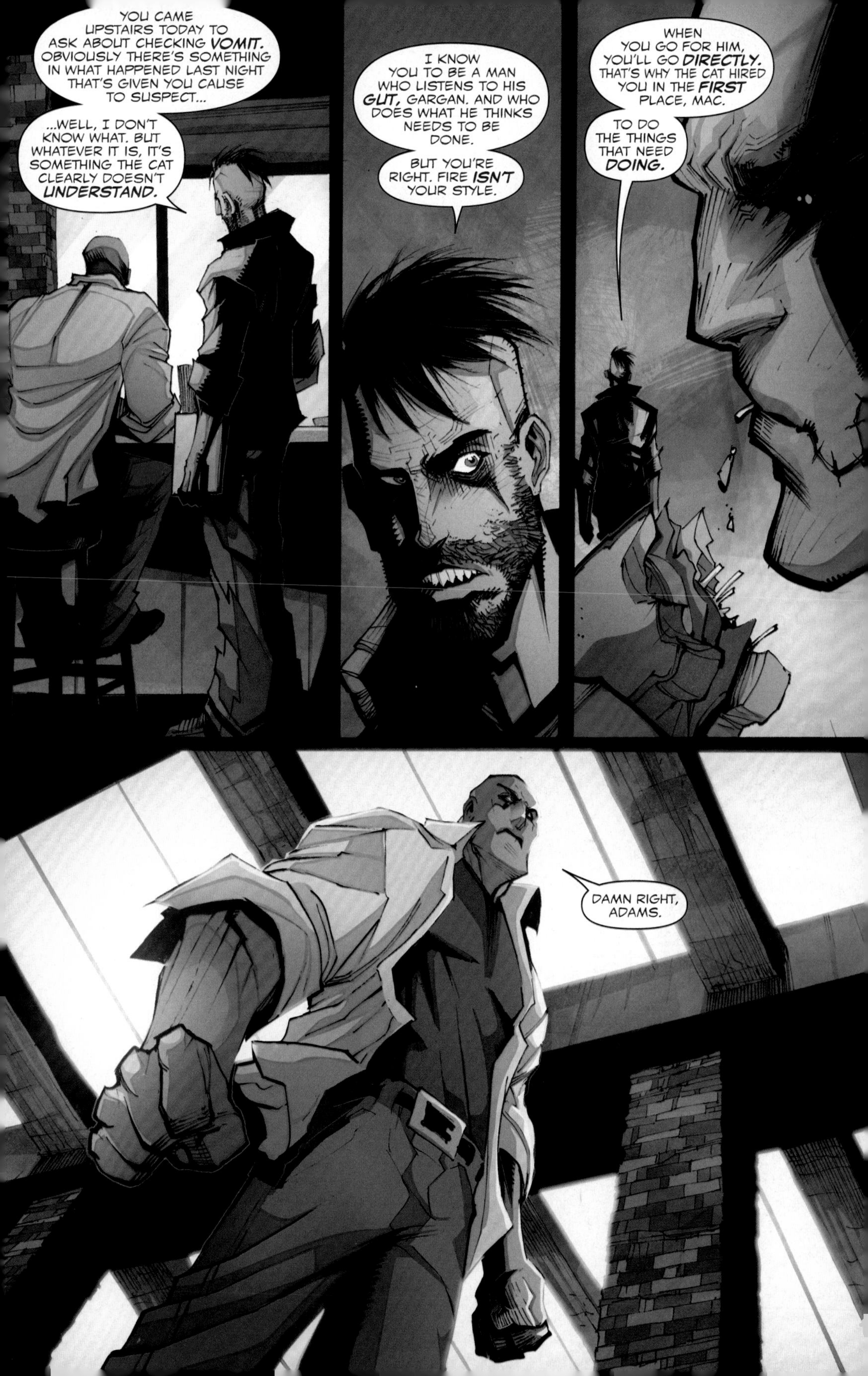
YOU CAME UPSTAIRS TODAY TO ASK ABOUT CHECKING VOMIT. OBVIOUSLY THERE'S SOMETHING IN WHAT HAPPENED LAST NIGHT THAT'S GIVEN YOU CAUSE TO SUSPECT...
...WELL, I DON'T KNOW WHAT. BUT WHATEVER IT IS, IT'S SOMETHING THE CAT CLEARLY DOESN'T UNDERSTAND.
I KNOW YOU TO BE A MAN WHO LISTENS TO HIS GUT, GARGAN. AND WHO DOES WHAT HE THINKS NEEDS TO BE DONE.
BUT YOU'RE RIGHT. FIRE ISN'T YOUR STYLE.
WHEN YOU GO FOR HIM, YOU'LL GO DIRECTLY. THAT'S WHY THE CAT HIRED YOU IN THE FIRST PLACE, MAC.
TO DO THE THINGS THAT NEED DOING.
DAMN RIGHT, ADAMS.

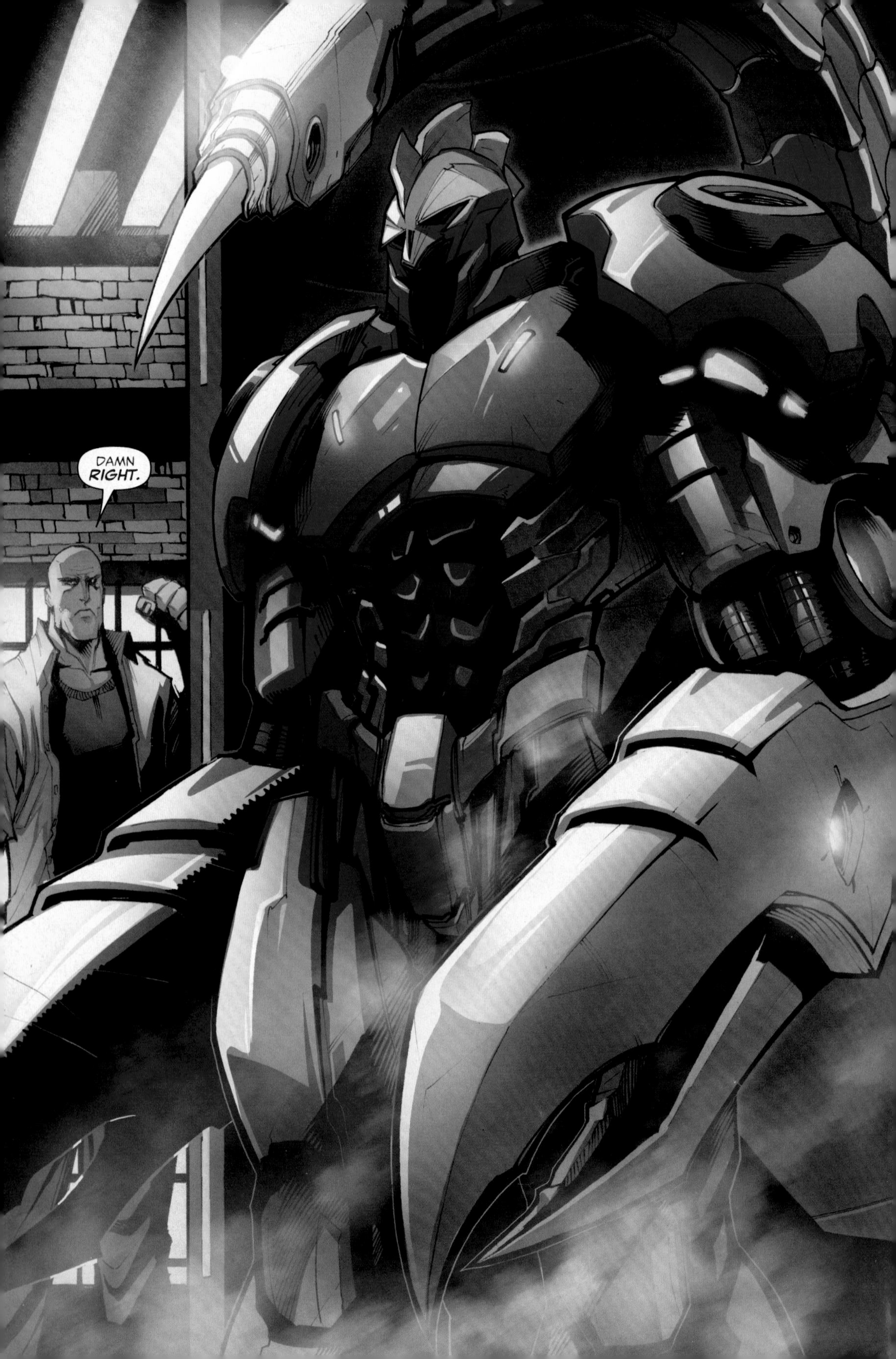
DAMN RIGHT.

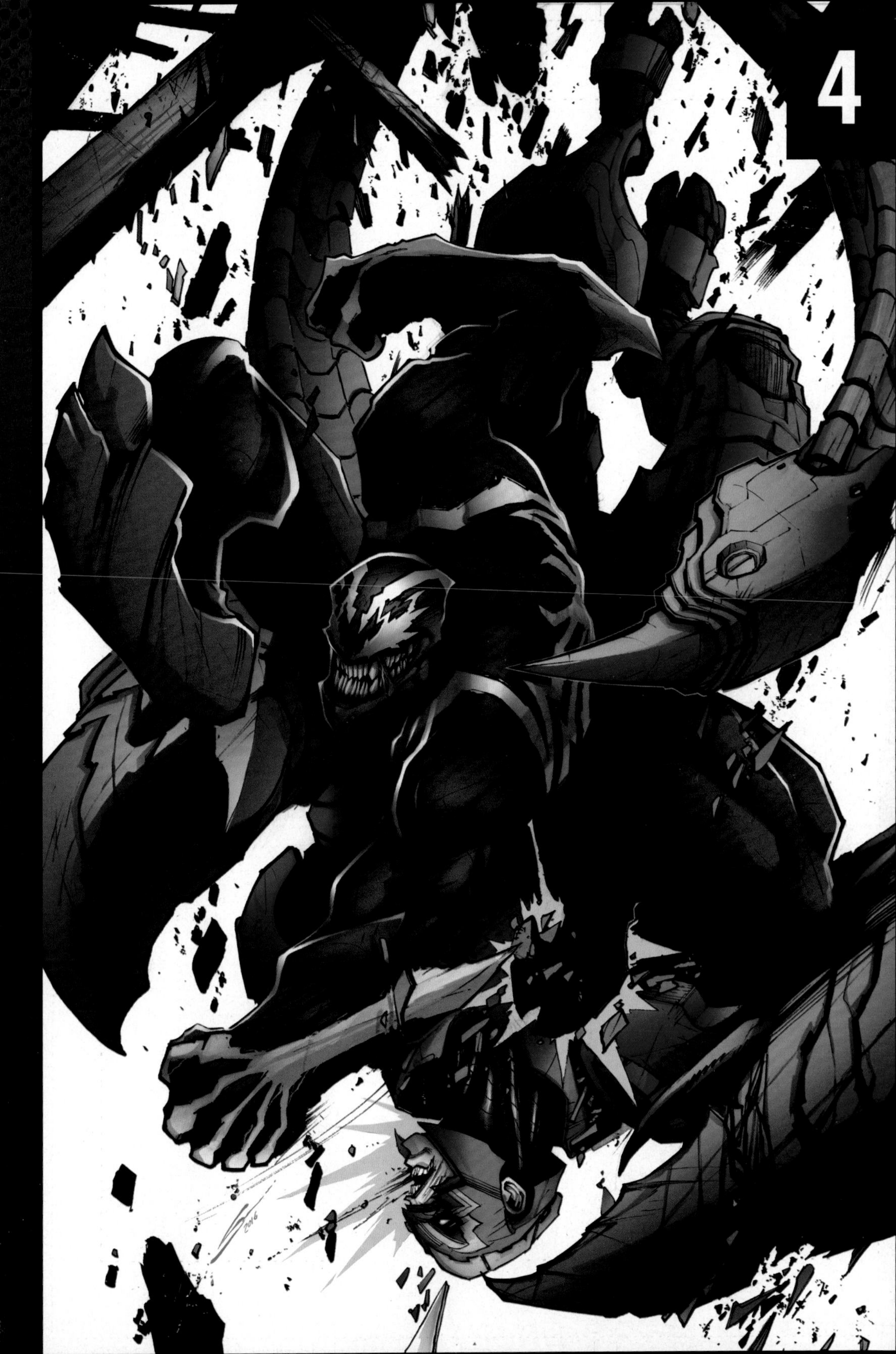
4

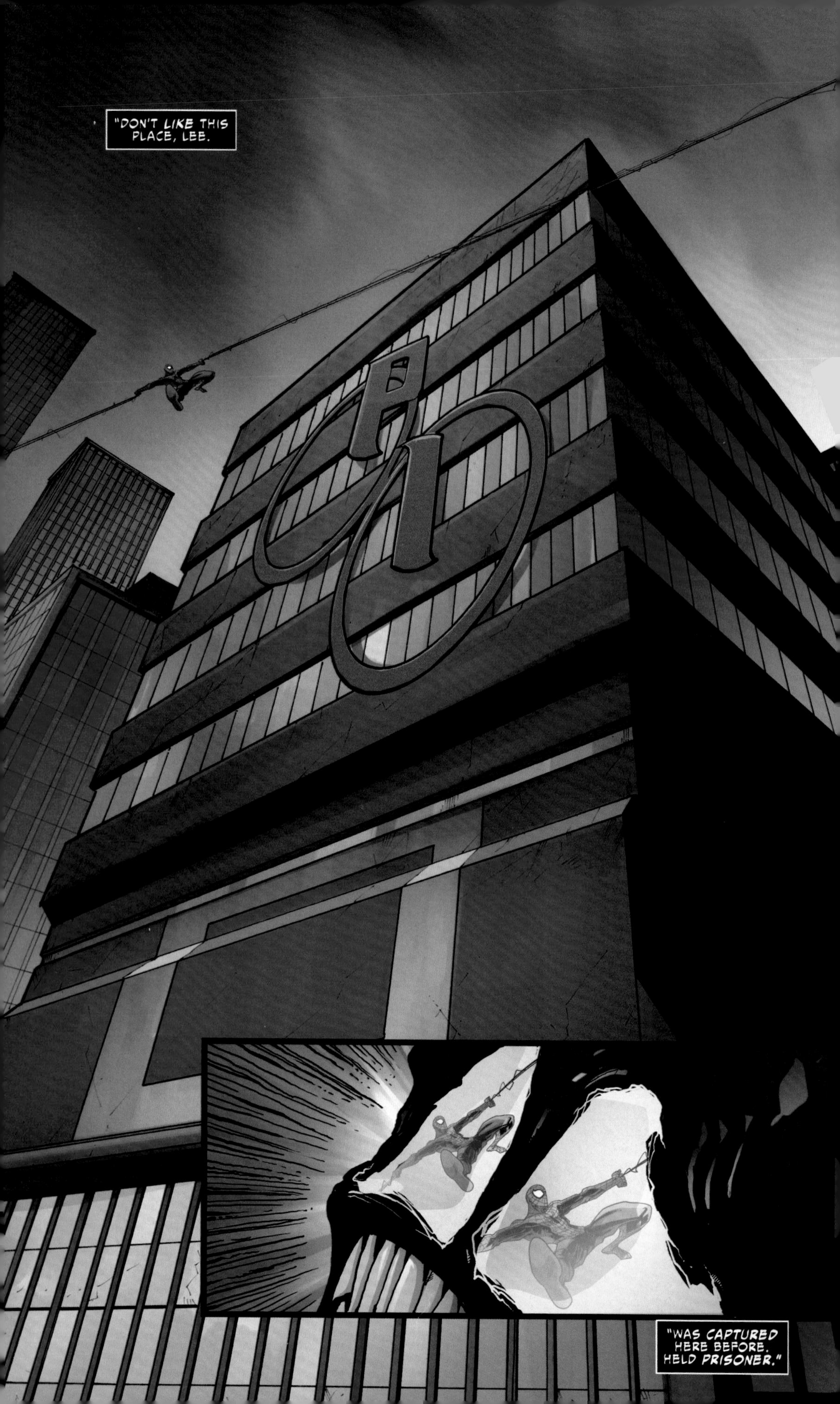
"DON'T LIKE THIS PLACE, LEE.
"WAS CAPTURED HERE BEFORE. HELD PRISONER."

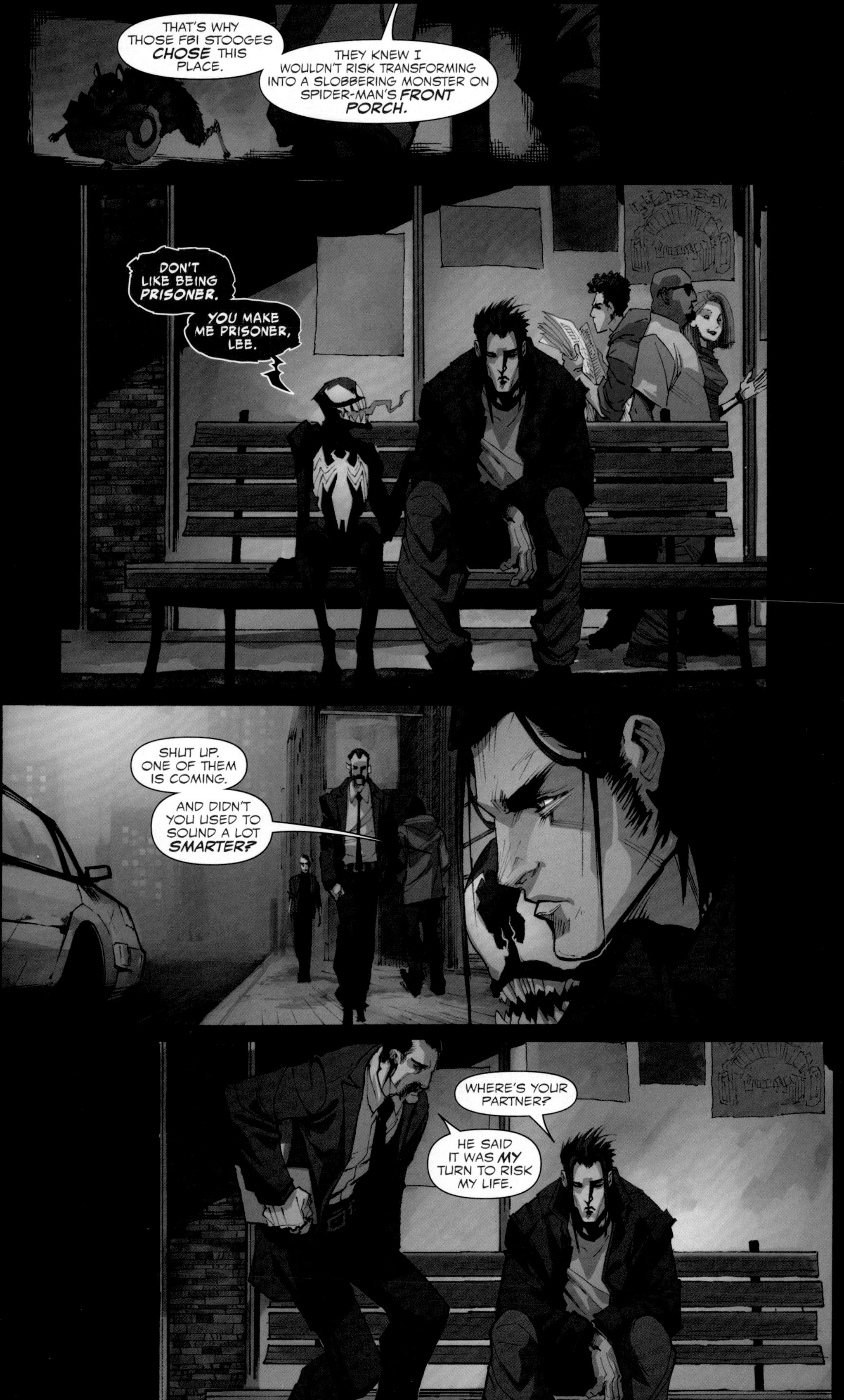
THAT'S WHY THOSE FBI STOOGES CHOSE THIS PLACE.
THEY KNEW I WOULDN'T RISK TRANSFORMING INTO A SLOBBERING MONSTER ON SPIDER-MAN'S FRONT PORCH.
DON'T LIKE BEING PRISONER.
YOU MAKE ME PRISONER, LEE.
SHUT UP. ONE OF THEM IS COMING.
AND DIDN'T YOU USED TO SOUND A LOT SMARTER?
WHERE'S YOUR PARTNER?
HE SAID IT WAS MY TURN TO RISK MY LIFE.

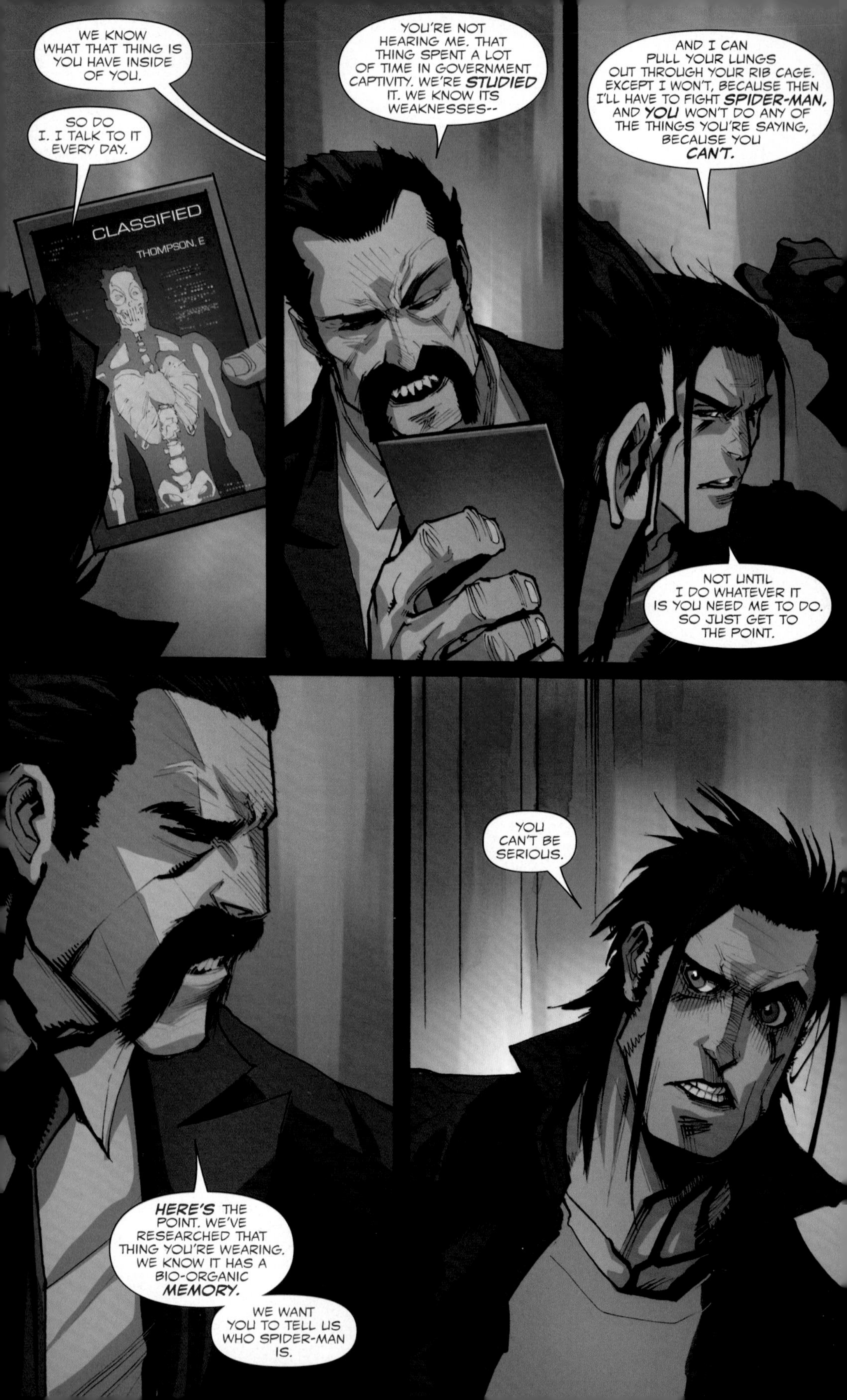
WE KNOW WHAT THAT THING IS YOU HAVE INSIDE OF YOU.
SO DO I. I TALK TO IT EVERY DAY.
CLASSIFIED
THOMPSON, E
YOU'RE NOT HEARING ME. THAT THING SPENT A LOT OF TIME IN GOVERNMENT CAPTIVITY. WE'RE STUDIED IT. WE KNOW ITS WEAKNESSES--
AND I CAN PULL YOUR LUNGS OUT THROUGH YOUR RIB CAGE. EXCEPT I WON'T, BECAUSE THEN I'LL HAVE TO FIGHT SPIDER-MAN, AND YOU WON'T DO ANY OF THE THINGS YOU'RE SAYING, BECAUSE YOU CAN'T.
NOT UNTIL I DO WHATEVER IT IS YOU NEED ME TO DO. SO JUST GET TO THE POINT.
HERE'S THE POINT. WE'VE RESEARCHED THAT THING YOU'RE WEARING. WE KNOW IT HAS A BIO-ORGANIC MEMORY.
WE WANT YOU TO TELL US WHO SPIDER-MAN IS.
YOU CAN'T BE SERIOUS.

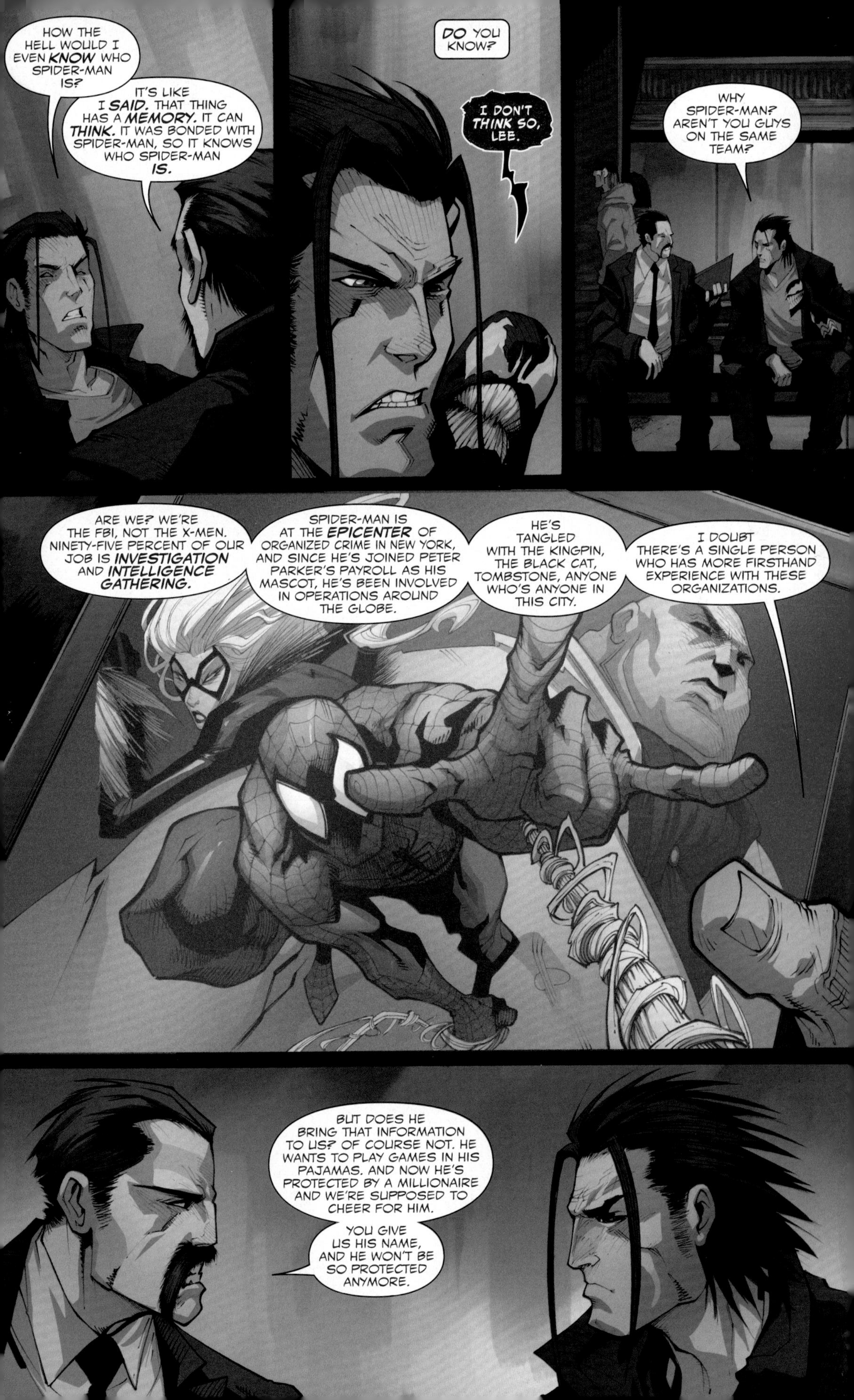
HOW THE HELL WOULD I EVEN KNOW WHO SPIDER-MAN IS?
IT'S LIKE I SAID. THAT THING HAS A MEMORY. IT CAN THINK. IT WAS BONDED WITH SPIDER-MAN, SO IT KNOWS WHO SPIDER-MAN IS.
DO YOU KNOW?
I DON'T THINK SO, LEE.
WHY SPIDER-MAN? AREN'T YOU GUYS ON THE SAME TEAM?
ARE WE? WE'RE THE FBI, NOT THE X-MEN. NINETY-FIVE PERCENT OF OUR JOB IS INVESTIGATION AND INTELLIGENCE GATHERING.
SPIDER-MAN IS AT THE EPICENTER OF ORGANIZED CRIME IN NEW YORK, AND SINCE HE'S JOINED PETER PARKER'S PAYROLL AS HIS MASCOT, HE'S BEEN INVOLVED IN OPERATIONS AROUND THE GLOBE.
HE'S TANGLED WITH THE KINGPIN, THE BLACK CAT, TOMBSTONE, ANYONE WHO'S ANYONE IN THIS CITY.
I DOUBT THERE'S A SINGLE PERSON WHO HAS MORE FIRSTHAND EXPERIENCE WITH THESE ORGANIZATIONS.
BUT DOES HE BRING THAT INFORMATION TO US? OF COURSE NOT. HE WANTS TO PLAY GAMES IN HIS PAJAMAS. AND NOW HE'S PROTECTED BY A MILLIONAIRE AND WE'RE SUPPOSED TO CHEER FOR HIM.
YOU GIVE US HIS NAME, AND HE WON'T BE SO PROTECTED ANYMORE.

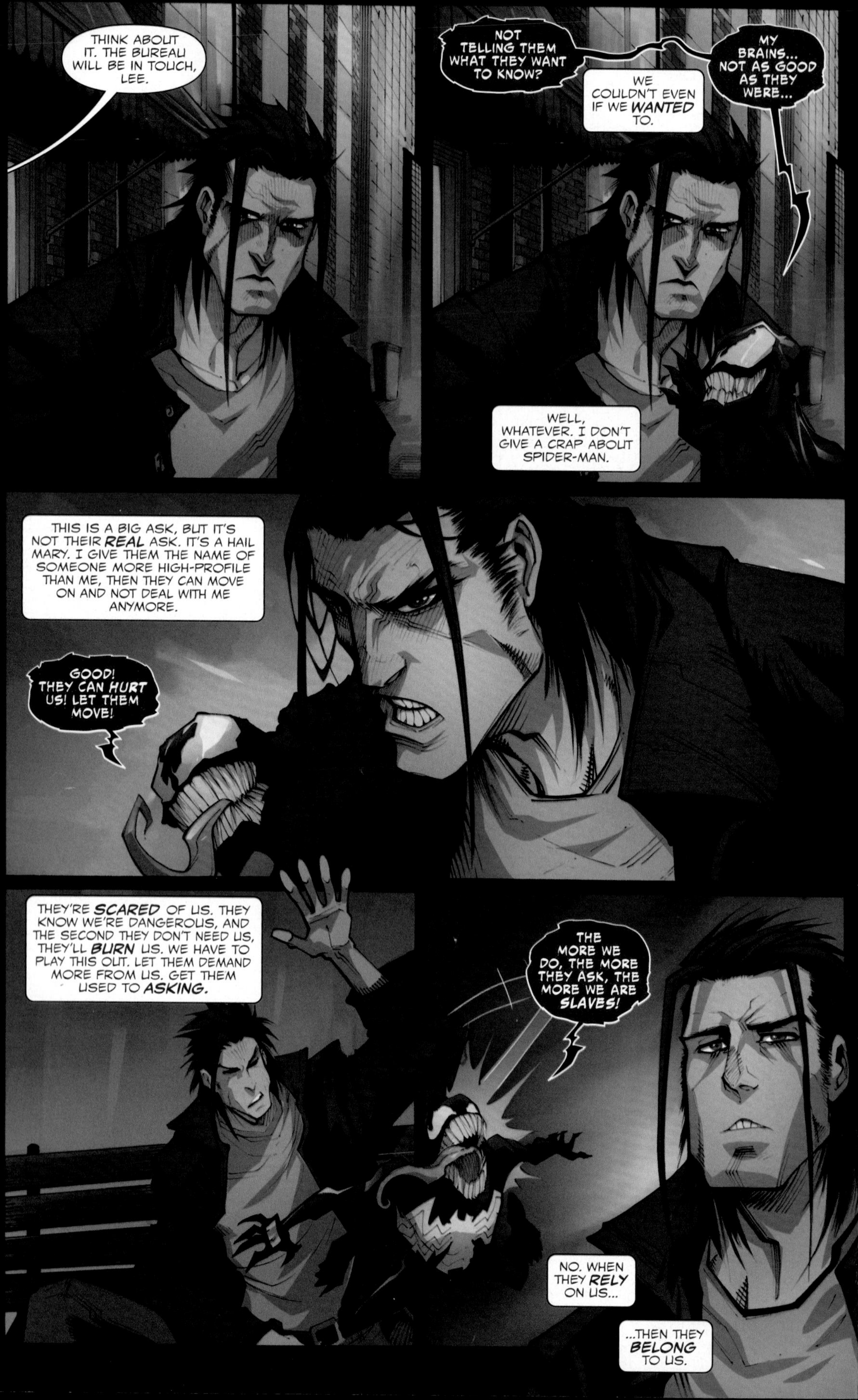
THINK ABOUT IT. THE BUREAU WILL BE IN TOUCH, LEE.
NOT TELLING THEM WHAT THEY WANT TO KNOW?
MY BRAINS... NOT AS GOOD AS THEY WERE...
WE COULDN'T EVEN IF WE WANTED TO.
WELL, WHATEVER. I DON'T GIVE A CRAP ABOUT SPIDER-MAN.
THIS IS A BIG ASK, BUT IT'S NOT THEIR REAL ASK. IT'S A HAIL MARY. I GIVE THEM THE NAME OF SOMEONE MORE HIGH-PROFILE THAN ME, THEN THEY CAN MOVE ON AND NOT DEAL WITH ME ANYMORE.
GOOD! THEY CAN HURT US! LET THEM MOVE!
THEY'RE SCARED OF US. THEY KNOW WE'RE DANGEROUS, AND THE SECOND THEY DON'T NEED US, THEY'LL BURN US. WE HAVE TO PLAY THIS OUT. LET THEM DEMAND MORE FROM US. GET THEM USED TO ASKING.
THE MORE WE DO, THE MORE THEY ASK, THE MORE WE ARE SLAVES!
NO. WHEN THEY RELY ON US...
...THEN THEY BELONG TO US.

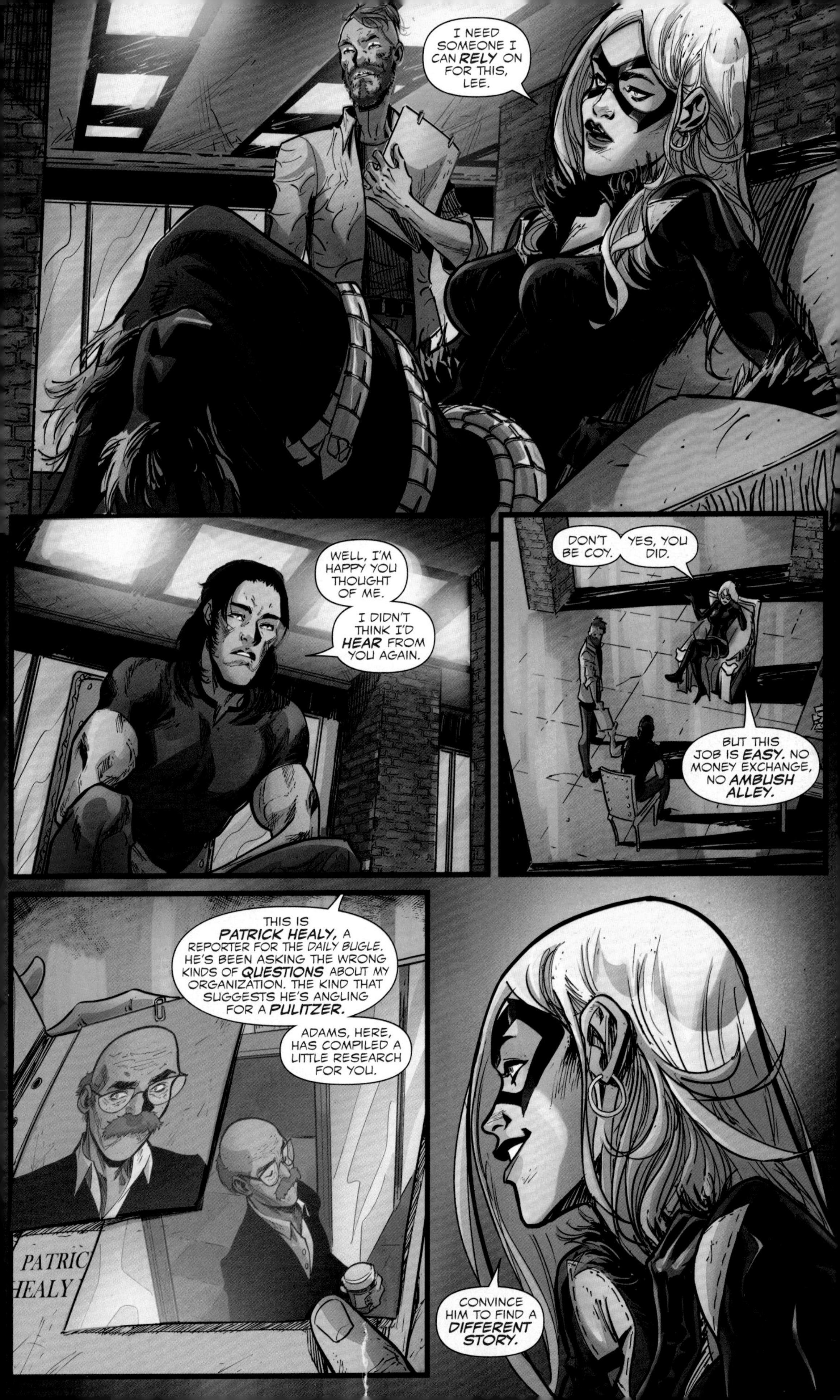
I NEED SOMEONE I CAN **RELY** ON FOR THIS, LEE.
WELL, I'M HAPPY YOU THOUGHT OF ME.
I DIDN'T THINK I'D **HEAR** FROM YOU AGAIN.
DON'T BE COY.
YES, YOU DID.
BUT THIS JOB IS **EASY.** NO MONEY EXCHANGE, NO **AMBUSH ALLEY.**
THIS IS **PATRICK HEALY,** A REPORTER FOR THE *DAILY BUGLE.* HE'S BEEN ASKING THE WRONG KINDS OF **QUESTIONS** ABOUT MY ORGANIZATION. THE KIND THAT SUGGESTS HE'S ANGLING FOR A **PULITZER.**
ADAMS, HERE, HAS COMPILED A LITTLE RESEARCH FOR YOU.
PATRIC
HEALY
CONVINCE HIM TO FIND A **DIFFERENT STORY.**

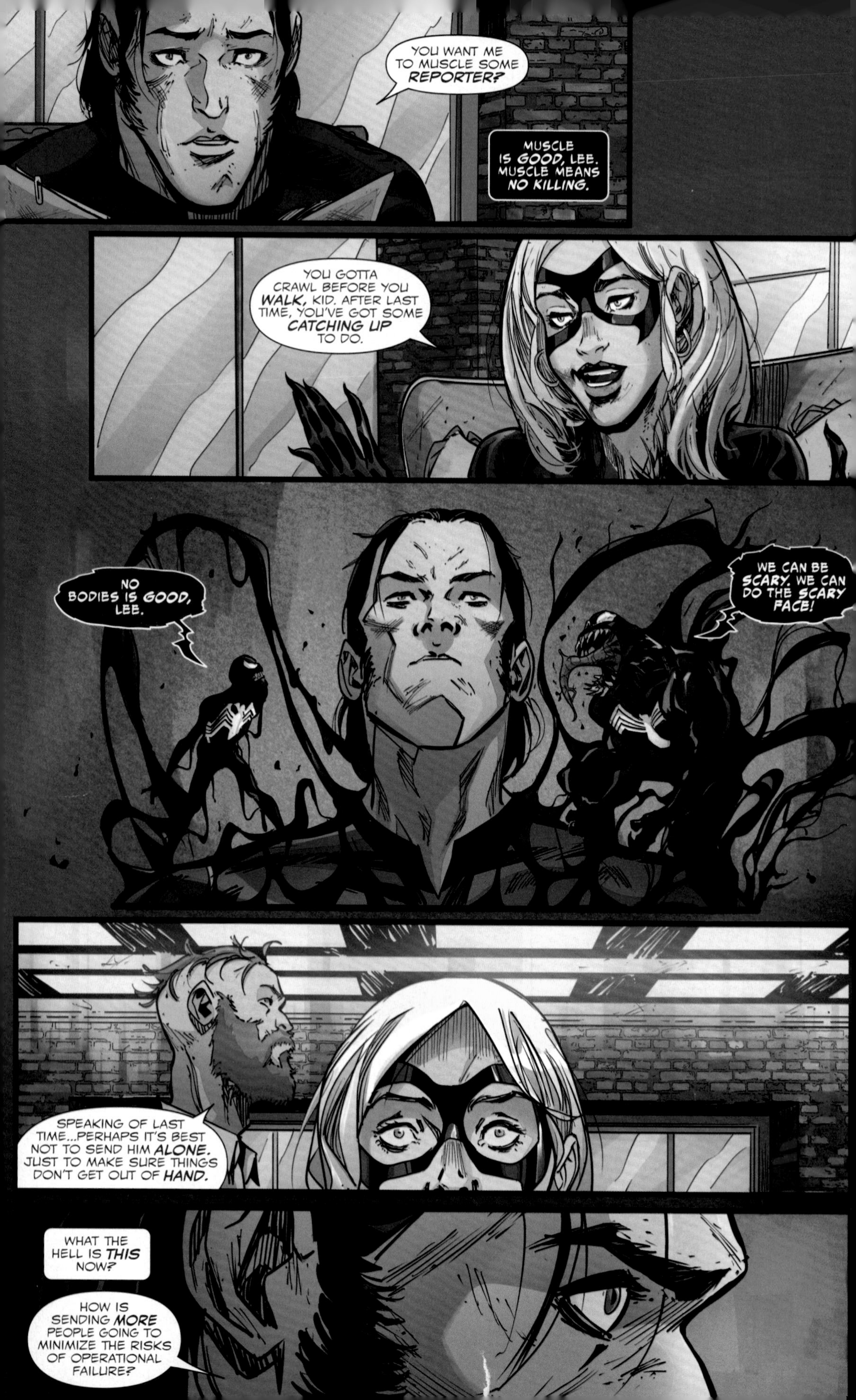
YOU WANT ME TO MUSCLE SOME REPORTER?
MUSCLE IS GOOD, LEE. MUSCLE MEANS NO KILLING.
YOU GOTTA CRAWL BEFORE YOU WALK, KID. AFTER LAST TIME, YOU'VE GOT SOME CATCHING UP TO DO.
NO BODIES IS GOOD, LEE.
WE CAN BE SCARY. WE CAN DO THE SCARY FACE!
SPEAKING OF LAST TIME...PERHAPS IT'S BEST NOT TO SEND HIM ALONE. JUST TO MAKE SURE THINGS DON'T GET OUT OF HAND.
WHAT THE HELL IS THIS NOW?
HOW IS SENDING MORE PEOPLE GOING TO MINIMIZE THE RISKS OF OPERATIONAL FAILURE?

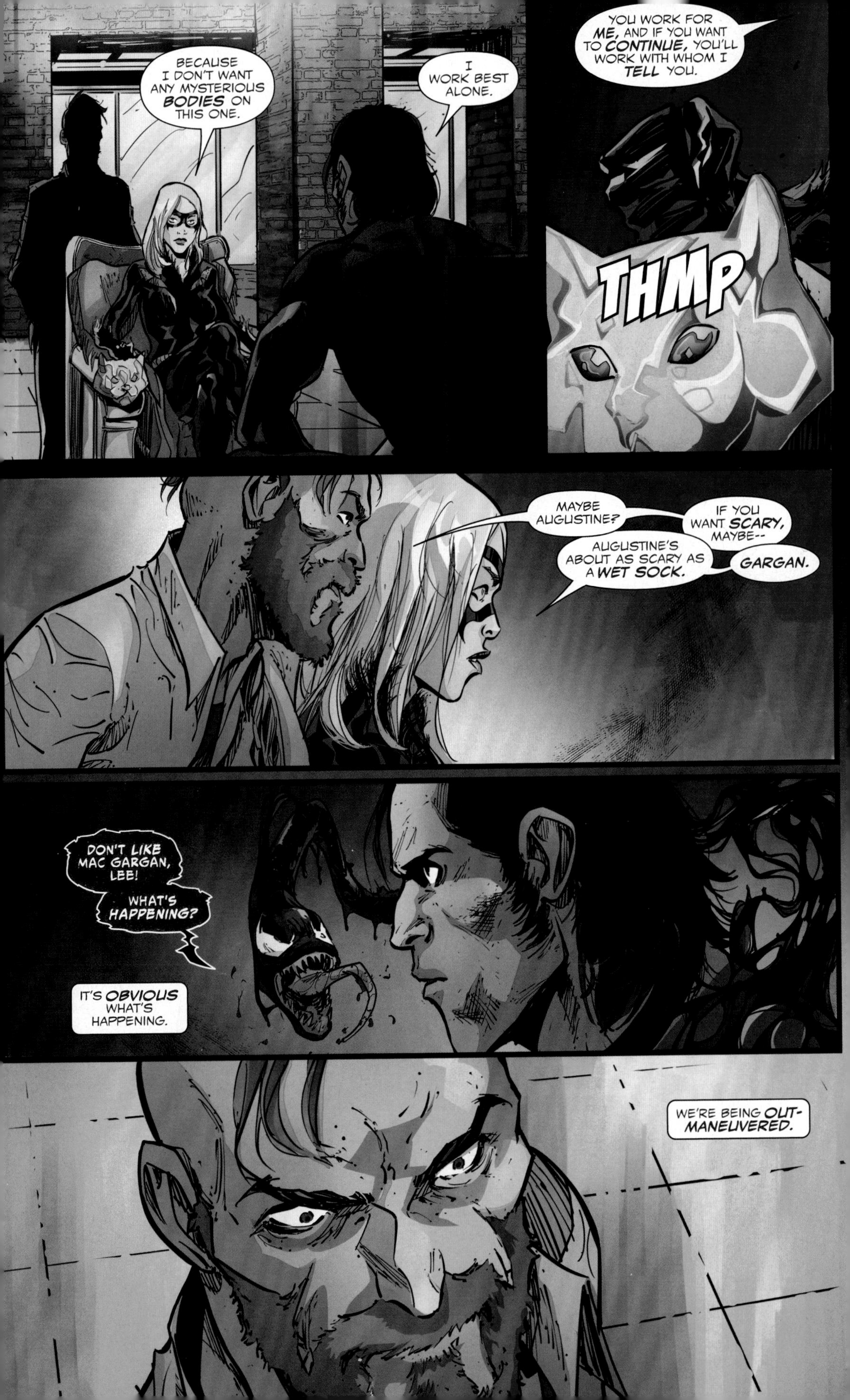
BECAUSE I DON'T WANT ANY MYSTERIOUS BODIES ON THIS ONE.
I WORK BEST ALONE.
YOU WORK FOR ME, AND IF YOU WANT TO CONTINUE, YOU'LL WORK WITH WHOM I TELL YOU.
THMP
MAYBE AUGUSTINE?
IF YOU WANT SCARY, MAYBE--
AUGUSTINE'S ABOUT AS SCARY AS A WET SOCK.
GARGAN.
DON'T LIKE MAC GARGAN, LEE!
WHAT'S HAPPENING?
IT'S OBVIOUS WHAT'S HAPPENING.
WE'RE BEING OUT-MANEUVERED.

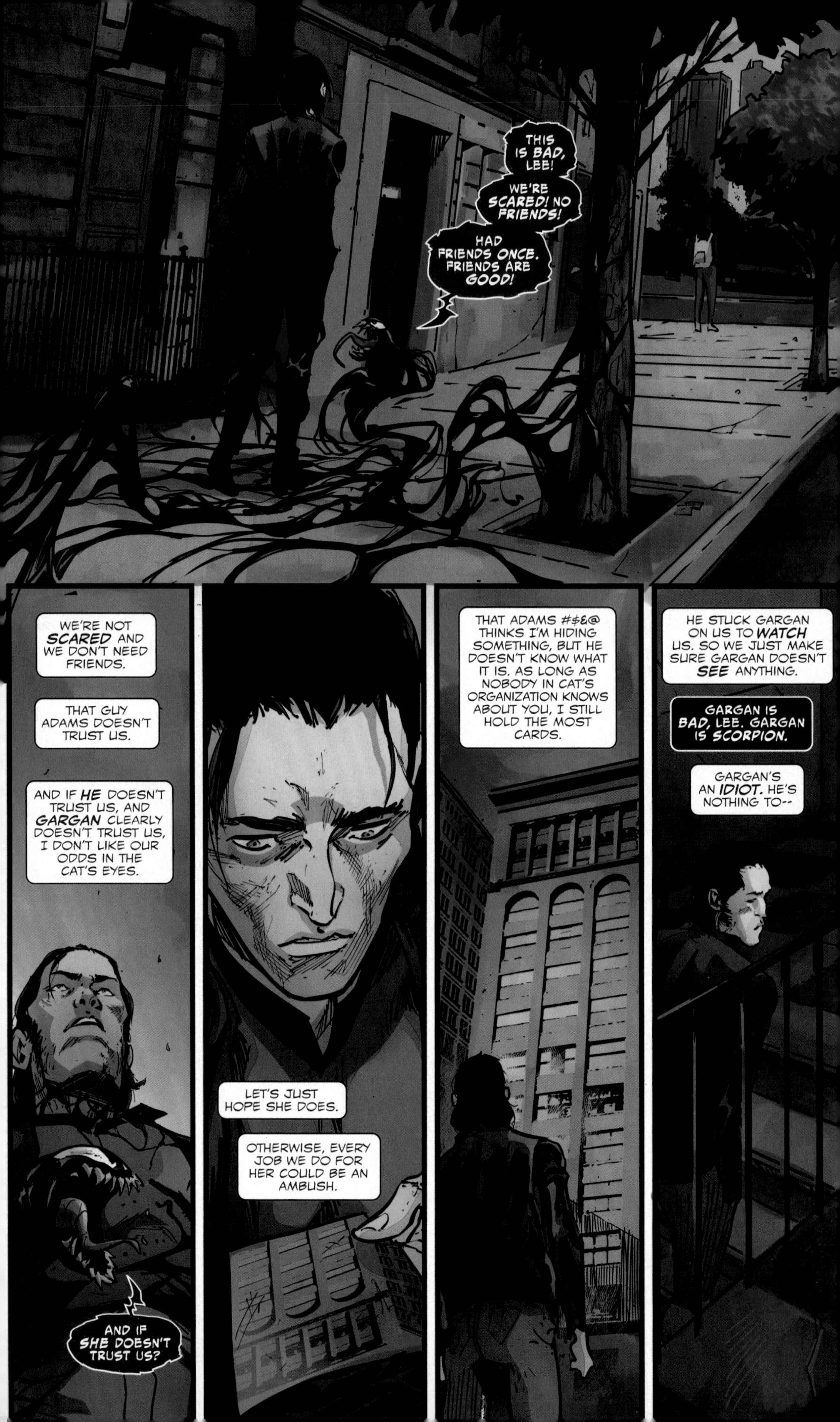
THIS IS BAD, LEE!
WE'RE SCARED! NO FRIENDS!
HAD FRIENDS ONCE. FRIENDS ARE GOOD!
WE'RE NOT SCARED AND WE DON'T NEED FRIENDS.
THAT GUY ADAMS DOESN'T TRUST US.
AND IF HE DOESN'T TRUST US, AND GARGAN CLEARLY DOESN'T TRUST US, I DON'T LIKE OUR ODDS IN THE CAT'S EYES.
AND IF SHE DOESN'T TRUST US?
LET'S JUST HOPE SHE DOES.
OTHERWISE, EVERY JOB WE DO FOR HER COULD BE AN AMBUSH.
THAT ADAMS #$&@ THINKS I'M HIDING SOMETHING, BUT HE DOESN'T KNOW WHAT IT IS. AS LONG AS NOBODY IN CAT'S ORGANIZATION KNOWS ABOUT YOU, I STILL HOLD THE MOST CARDS.
HE STUCK GARGAN ON US TO WATCH US. SO WE JUST MAKE SURE GARGAN DOESN'T SEE ANYTHING.
GARGAN IS BAD, LEE. GARGAN IS SCORPION.
GARGAN'S AN IDIOT. HE'S NOTHING TO--

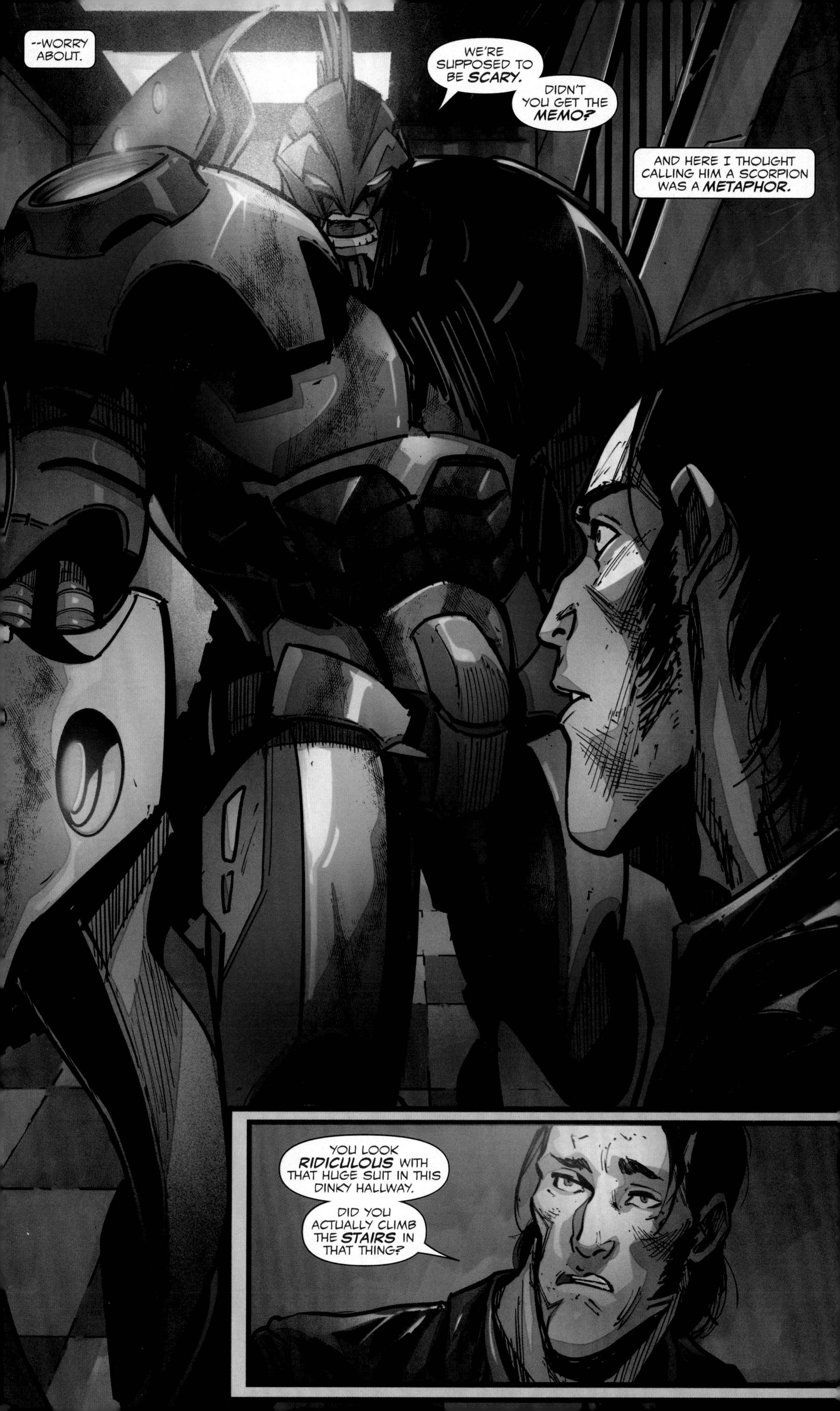
--WORRY ABOUT.
WE'RE SUPPOSED TO BE SCARY.
DIDN'T YOU GET THE MEMO?
AND HERE I THOUGHT CALLING HIM A SCORPION WAS A METAPHOR.
YOU LOOK RIDICULOUS WITH THAT HUGE SUIT IN THIS DINKY HALLWAY.
DID YOU ACTUALLY CLIMB THE STAIRS IN THAT THING?

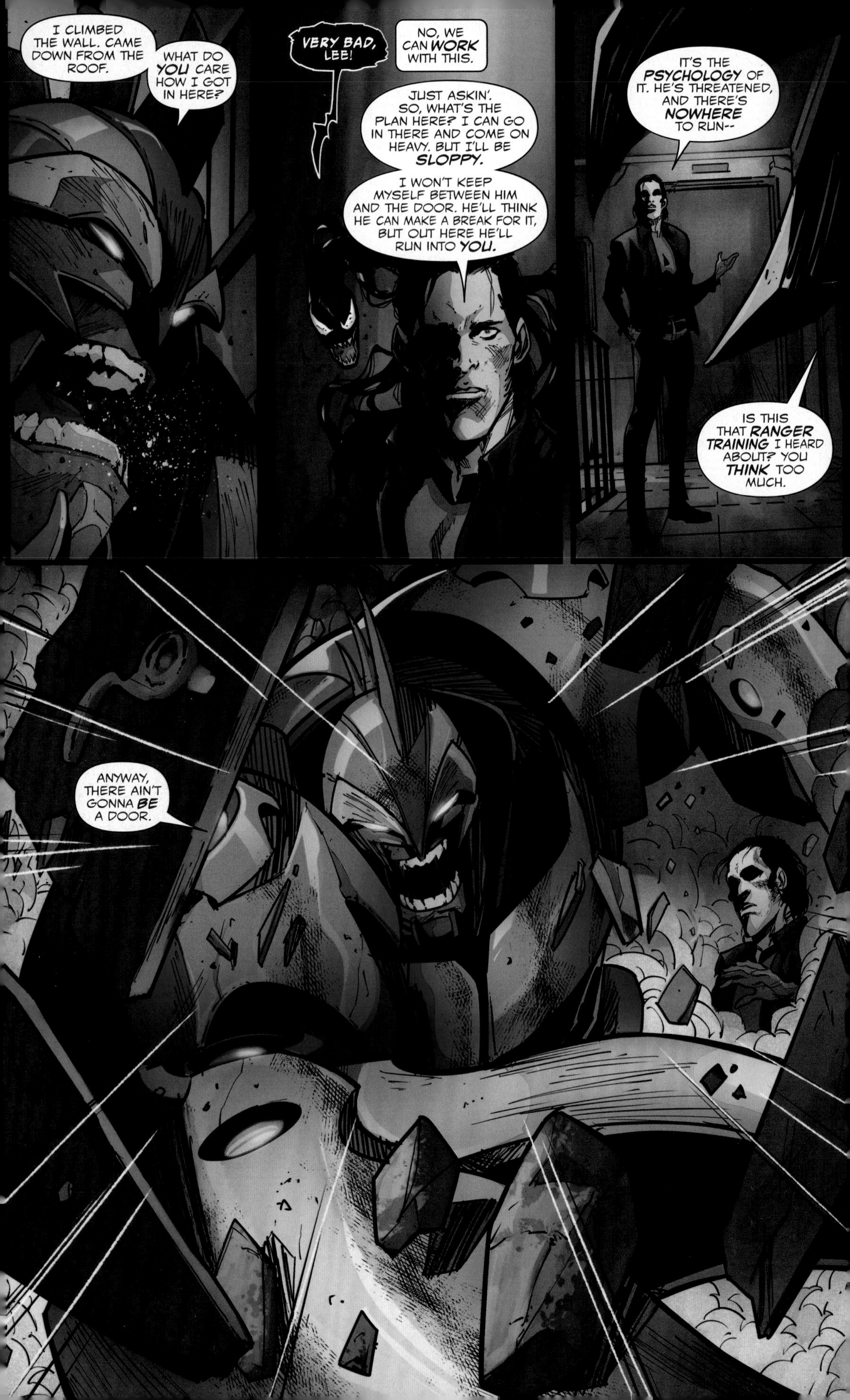
I CLIMBED THE WALL. CAME DOWN FROM THE ROOF.
WHAT DO YOU CARE HOW I GOT IN HERE?
VERY BAD, LEE!
NO, WE CAN WORK WITH THIS.
JUST ASKIN'. SO, WHAT'S THE PLAN HERE? I CAN GO IN THERE AND COME ON HEAVY. BUT I'LL BE SLOPPY.
I WON'T KEEP MYSELF BETWEEN HIM AND THE DOOR. HE'LL THINK HE CAN MAKE A BREAK FOR IT, BUT OUT HERE HE'LL RUN INTO YOU.
IT'S THE PSYCHOLOGY OF IT. HE'S THREATENED, AND THERE'S NOWHERE TO RUN--
IS THIS THAT RANGER TRAINING I HEARD ABOUT? YOU THINK TOO MUCH.
ANYWAY, THERE AIN'T GONNA BE A DOOR.

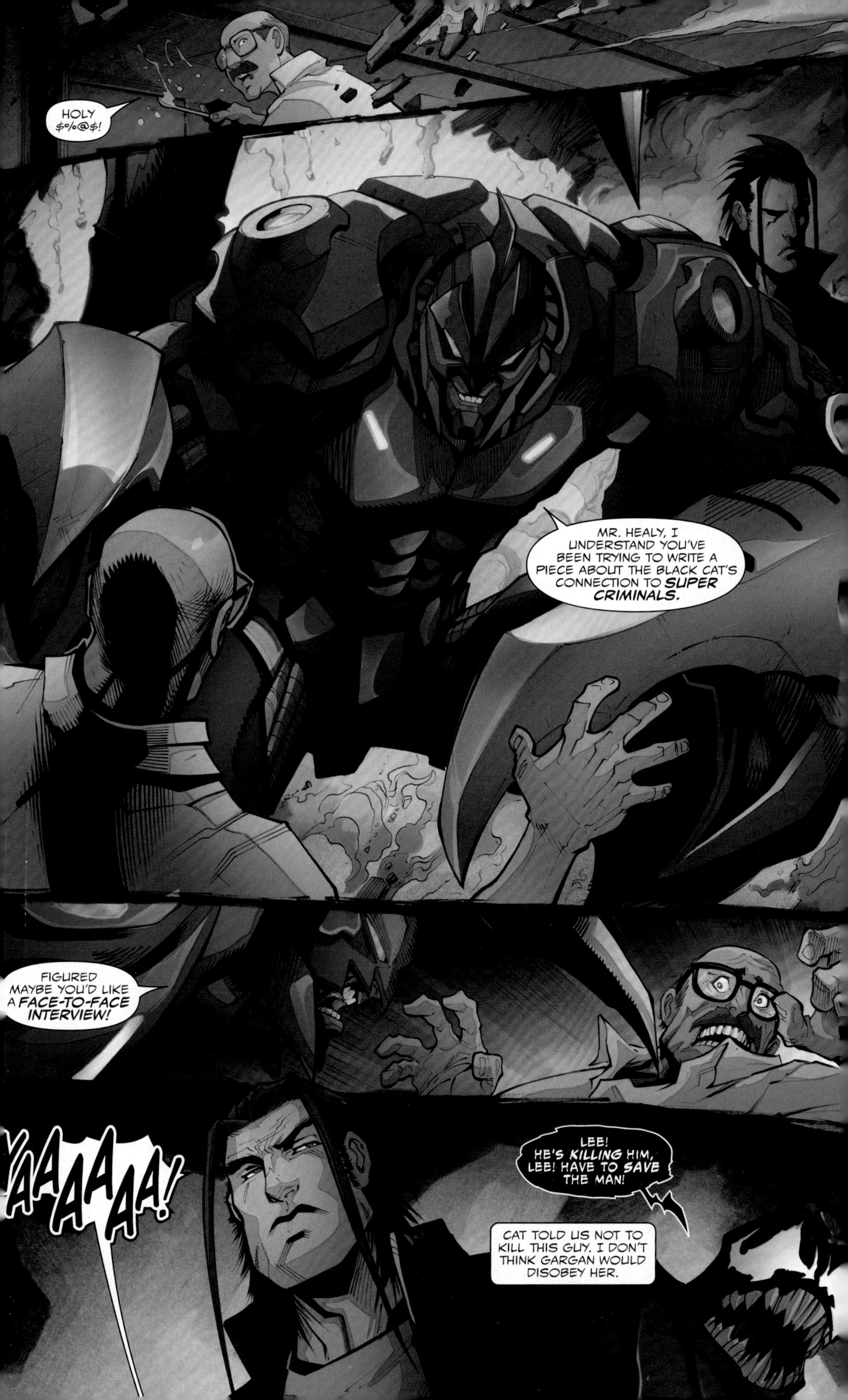
HOLY $%@$!
MR. HEALY, I UNDERSTAND YOU'VE BEEN TRYING TO WRITE A PIECE ABOUT THE BLACK CAT'S CONNECTION TO SUPER CRIMINALS.
FIGURED MAYBE YOU'D LIKE A FACE-TO-FACE INTERVIEW!
YAAAAAAA!
LEE! HE'S KILLING HIM, LEE! HAVE TO SAVE THE MAN!
CAT TOLD US NOT TO KILL THIS GUY. I DON'T THINK GARGAN WOULD DISOBEY HER.

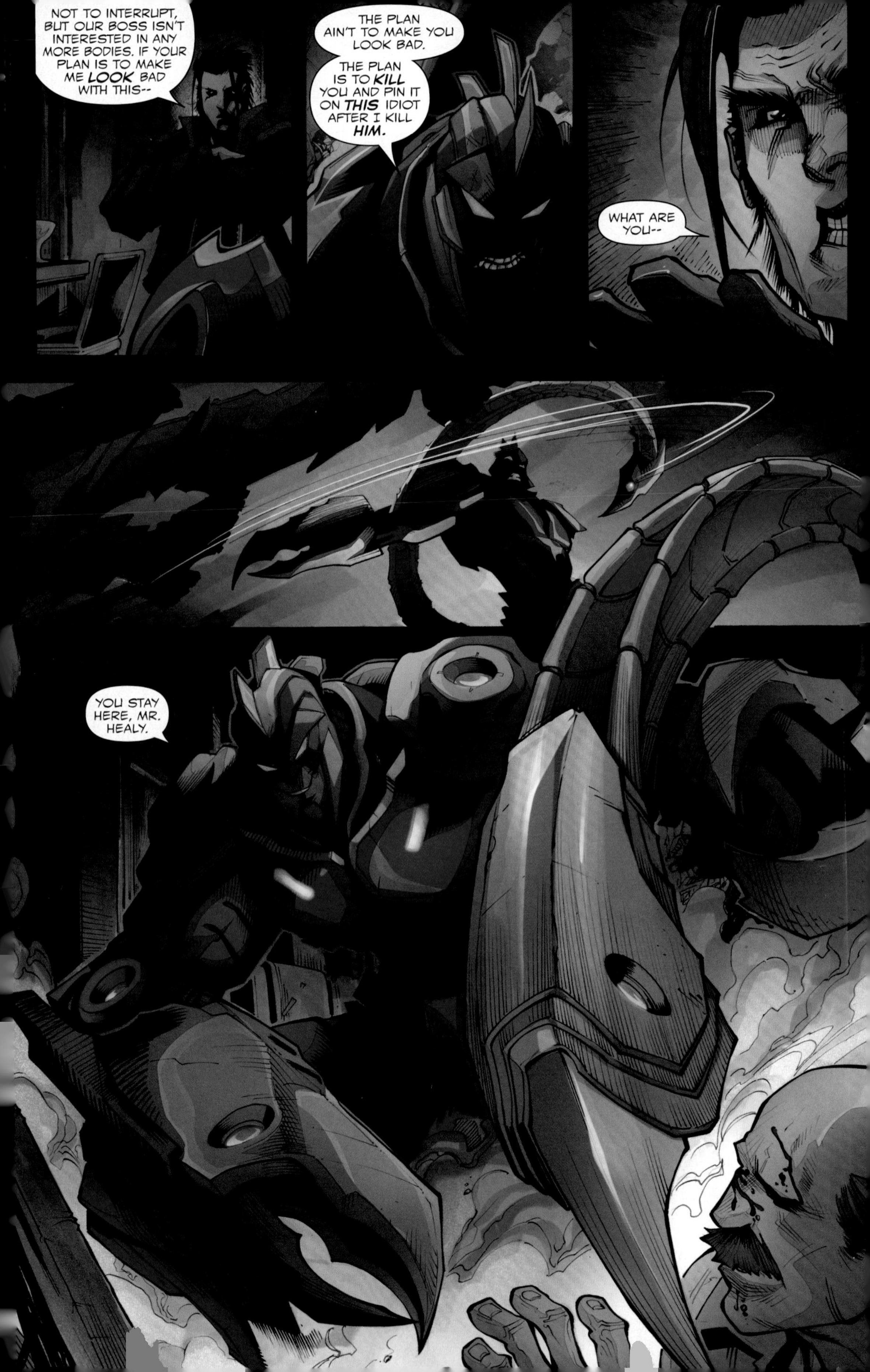
NOT TO INTERRUPT, BUT OUR BOSS ISN'T INTERESTED IN ANY MORE BODIES. IF YOUR PLAN IS TO MAKE ME LOOK BAD WITH THIS--
THE PLAN AIN'T TO MAKE YOU LOOK BAD.
THE PLAN IS TO KILL YOU AND PIN IT ON THIS IDIOT AFTER I KILL HIM.
WHAT ARE YOU--
YOU STAY HERE, MR. HEALY.

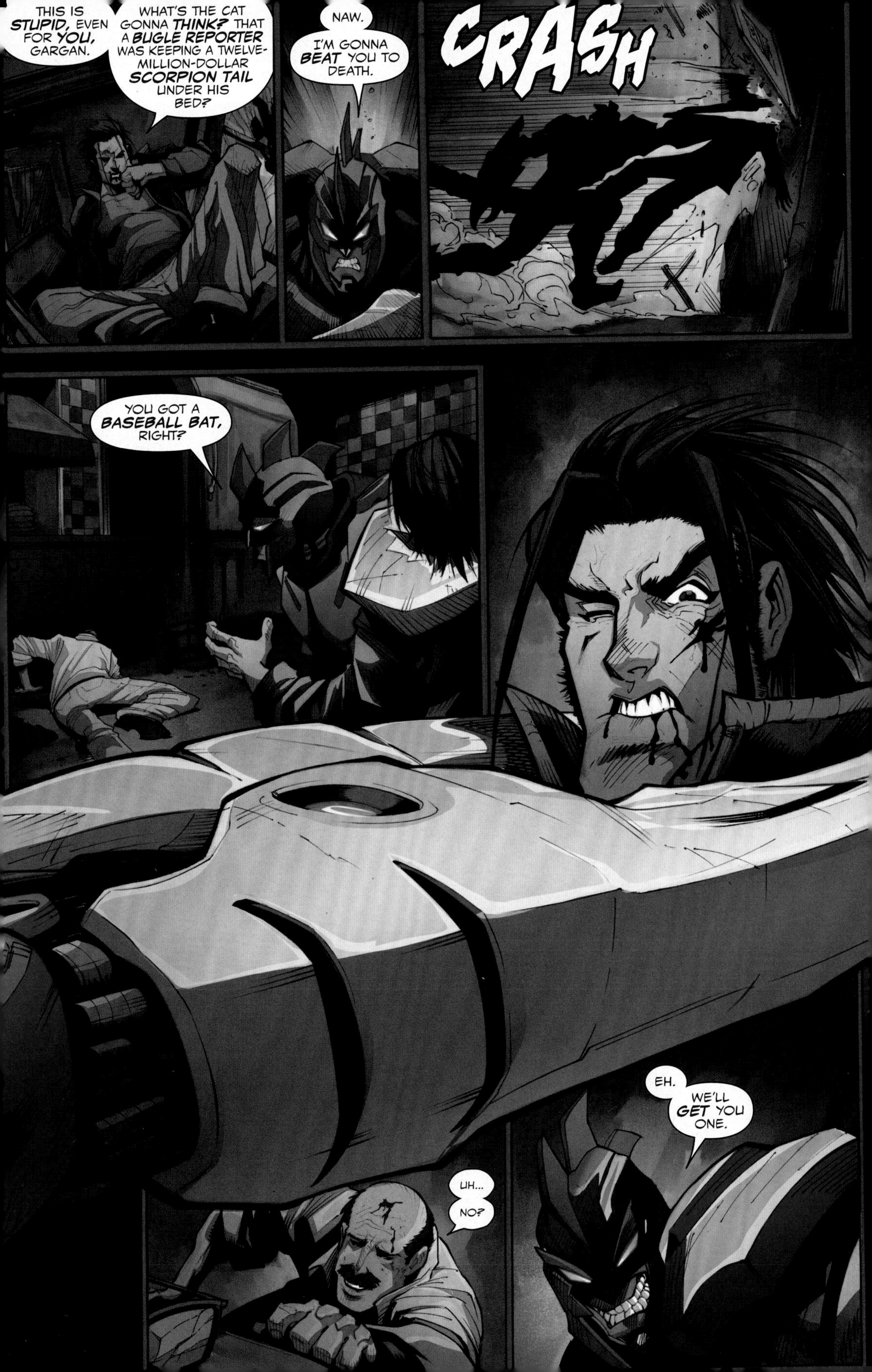
THIS IS STUPID, EVEN FOR YOU, GARGAN.
WHAT'S THE CAT GONNA THINK? THAT A BUGLE REPORTER WAS KEEPING A TWELVE-MILLION-DOLLAR SCORPION TAIL UNDER HIS BED?
NAW.
I'M GONNA BEAT YOU TO DEATH.
CRASH
YOU GOT A BASEBALL BAT, RIGHT?
EH.
WE'LL GET YOU ONE.
UH...
NO?

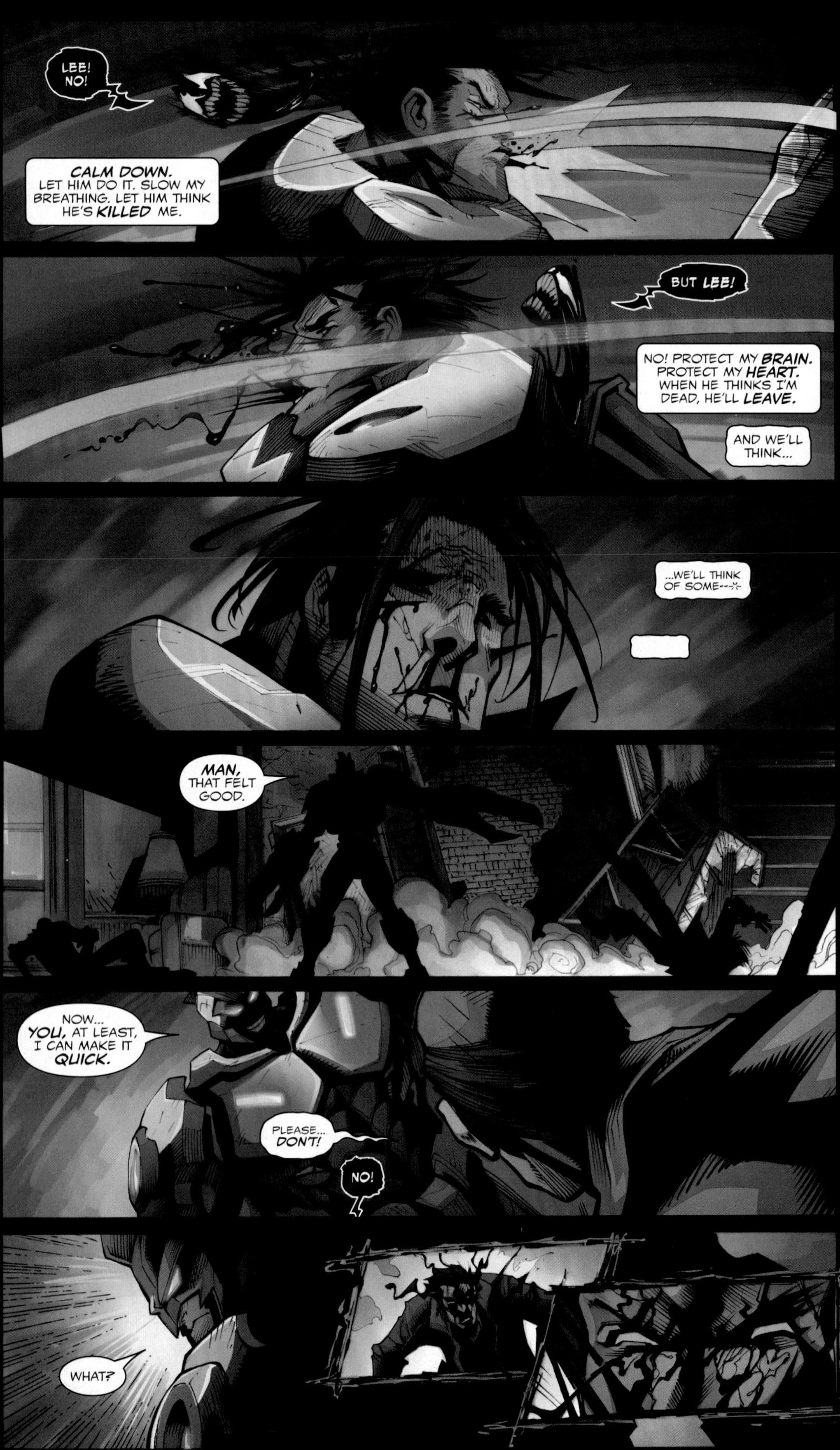
LEE! NO!
CALM DOWN. LET HIM DO IT. SLOW MY BREATHING. LET HIM THINK HE'S KILLED ME.
BUT LEE!
NO! PROTECT MY BRAIN. PROTECT MY HEART. WHEN HE THINKS I'M DEAD, HE'LL LEAVE.
AND WE'LL THINK...
...WE'LL THINK OF SOME---
MAN, THAT FELT GOOD.
NOW... YOU, AT LEAST, I CAN MAKE IT QUICK.
PLEASE... DON'T!
NO!
WHAT?

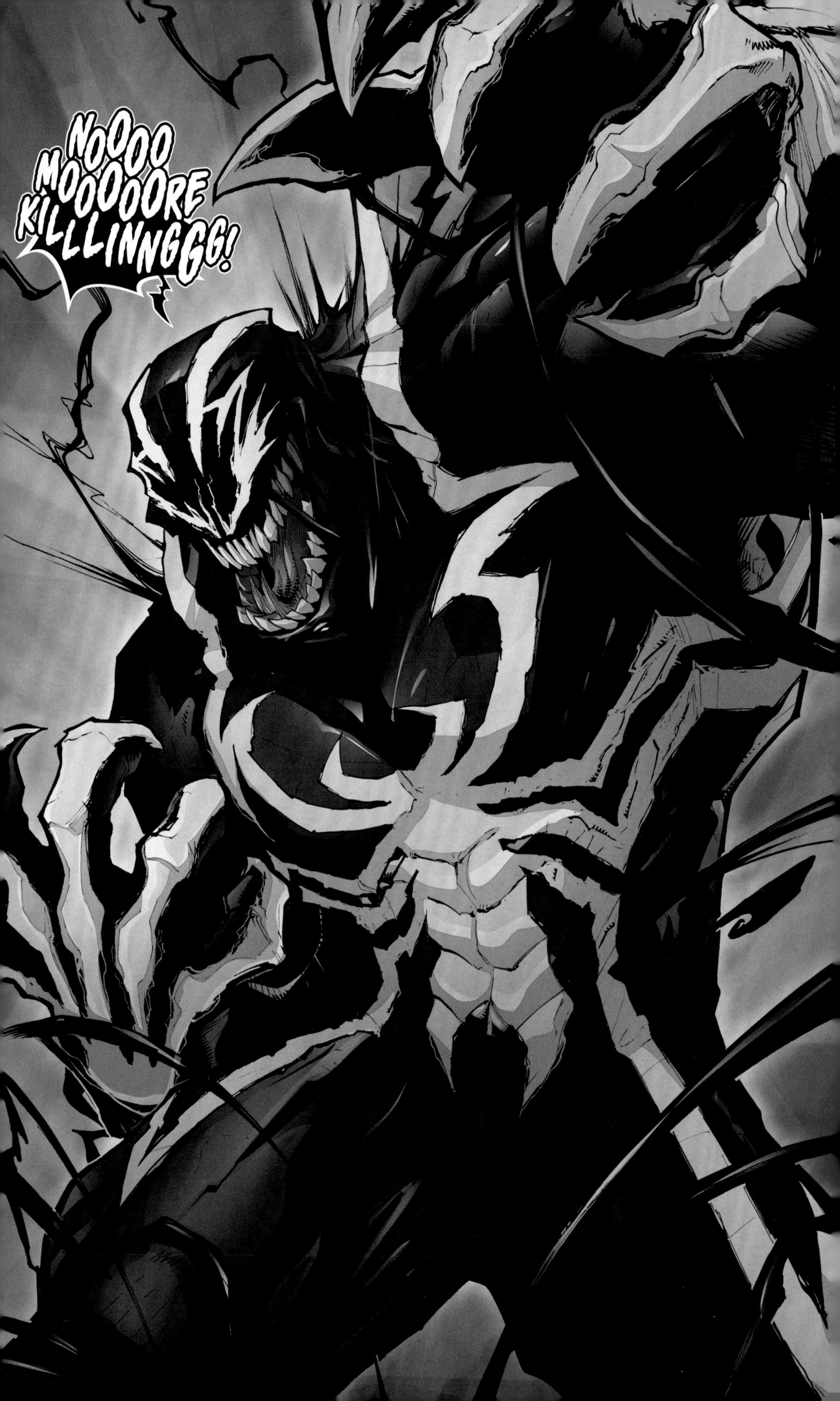
NOOOO MOOOOOORE KILLLINNGGG!

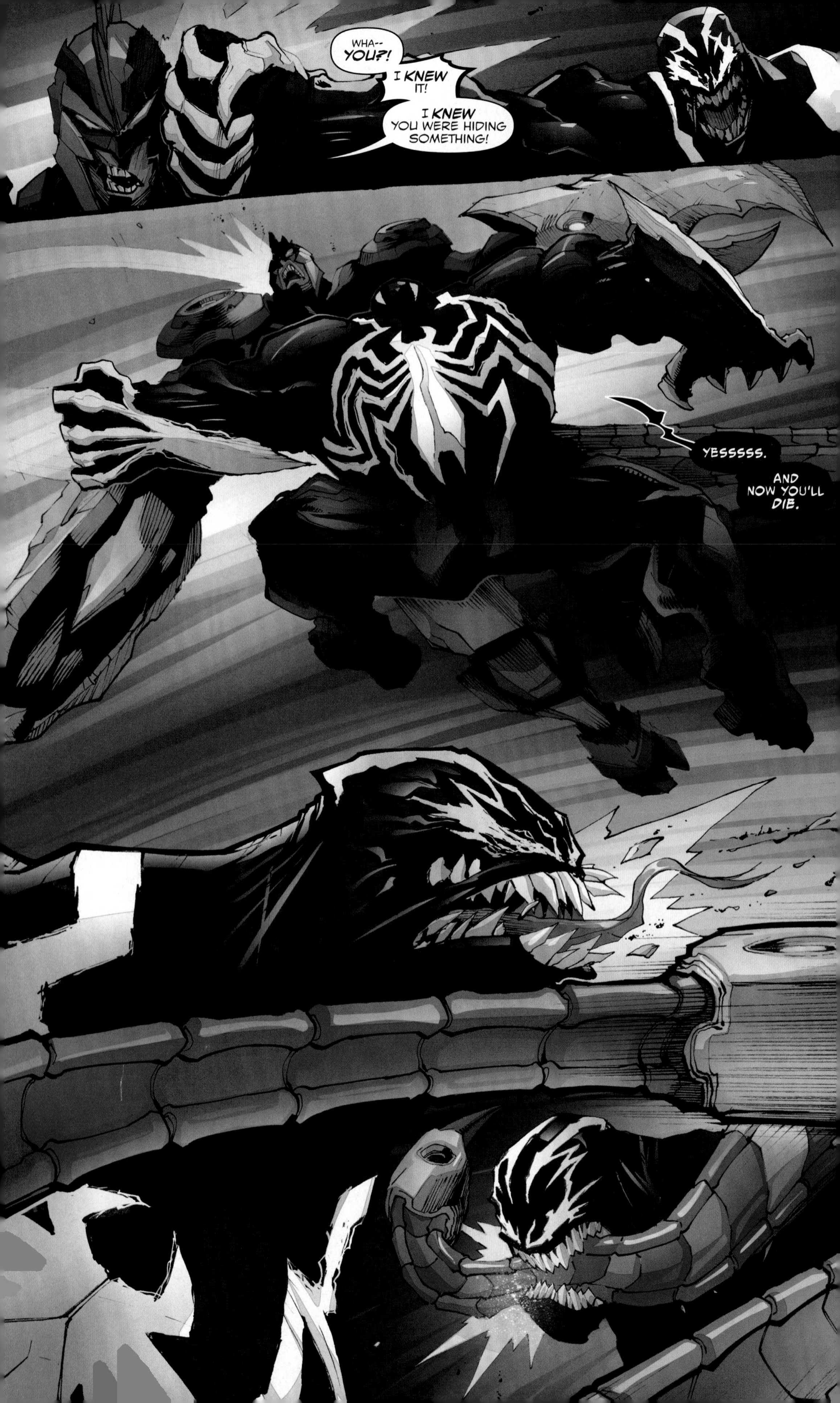
WHA-- YOU?!
I KNEW IT!
I KNEW YOU WERE HIDING SOMETHING!
YESSSSS.
AND NOW YOU'LL DIE.

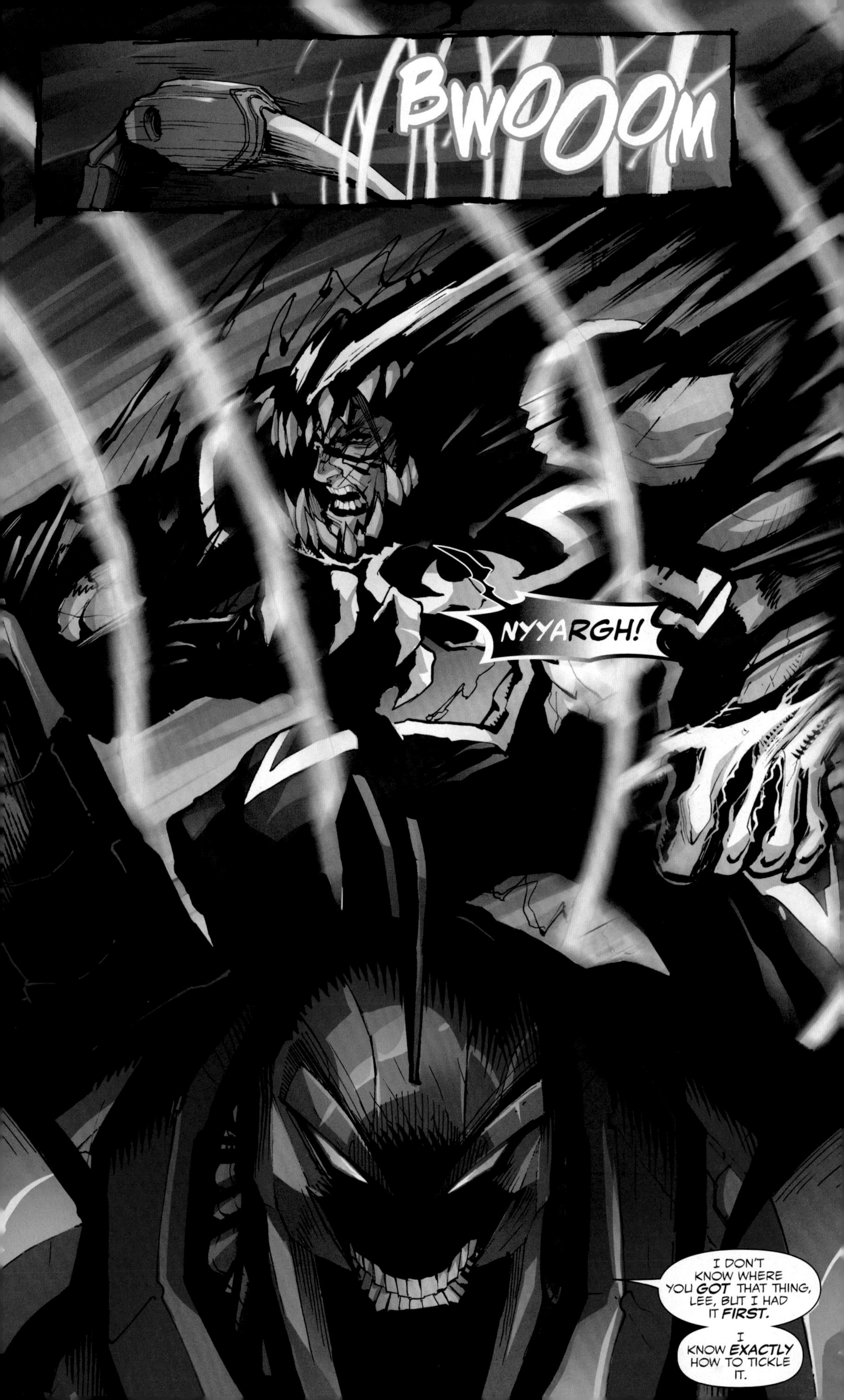
BWOOOM
NYYARGH!
I DON'T KNOW WHERE YOU GOT THAT THING, LEE, BUT I HAD IT FIRST.
I KNOW EXACTLY HOW TO TICKLE IT.

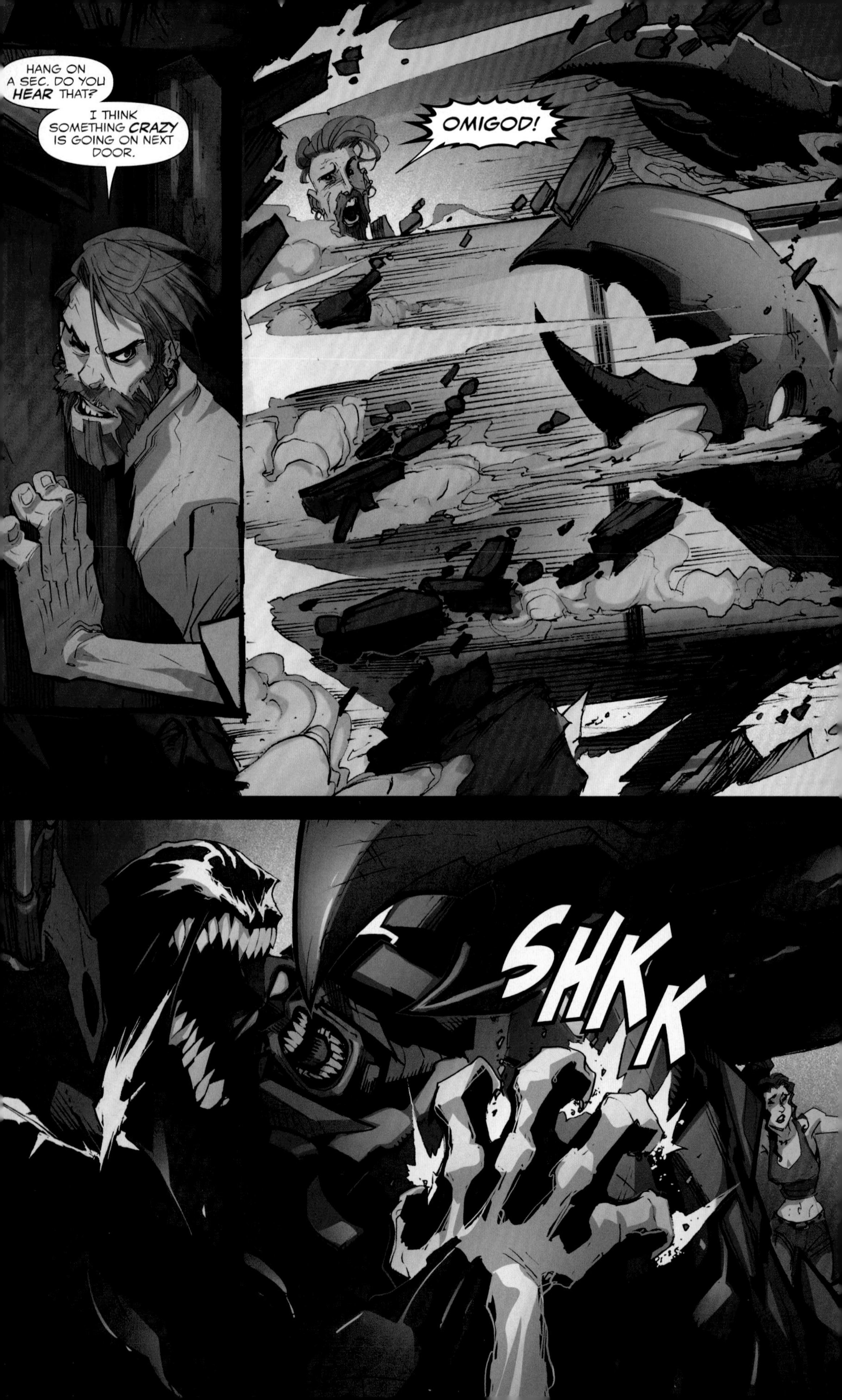
HANG ON A SEC. DO YOU HEAR THAT?
I THINK SOMETHING CRAZY IS GOING ON NEXT DOOR.
OMIGOD!
SHKK

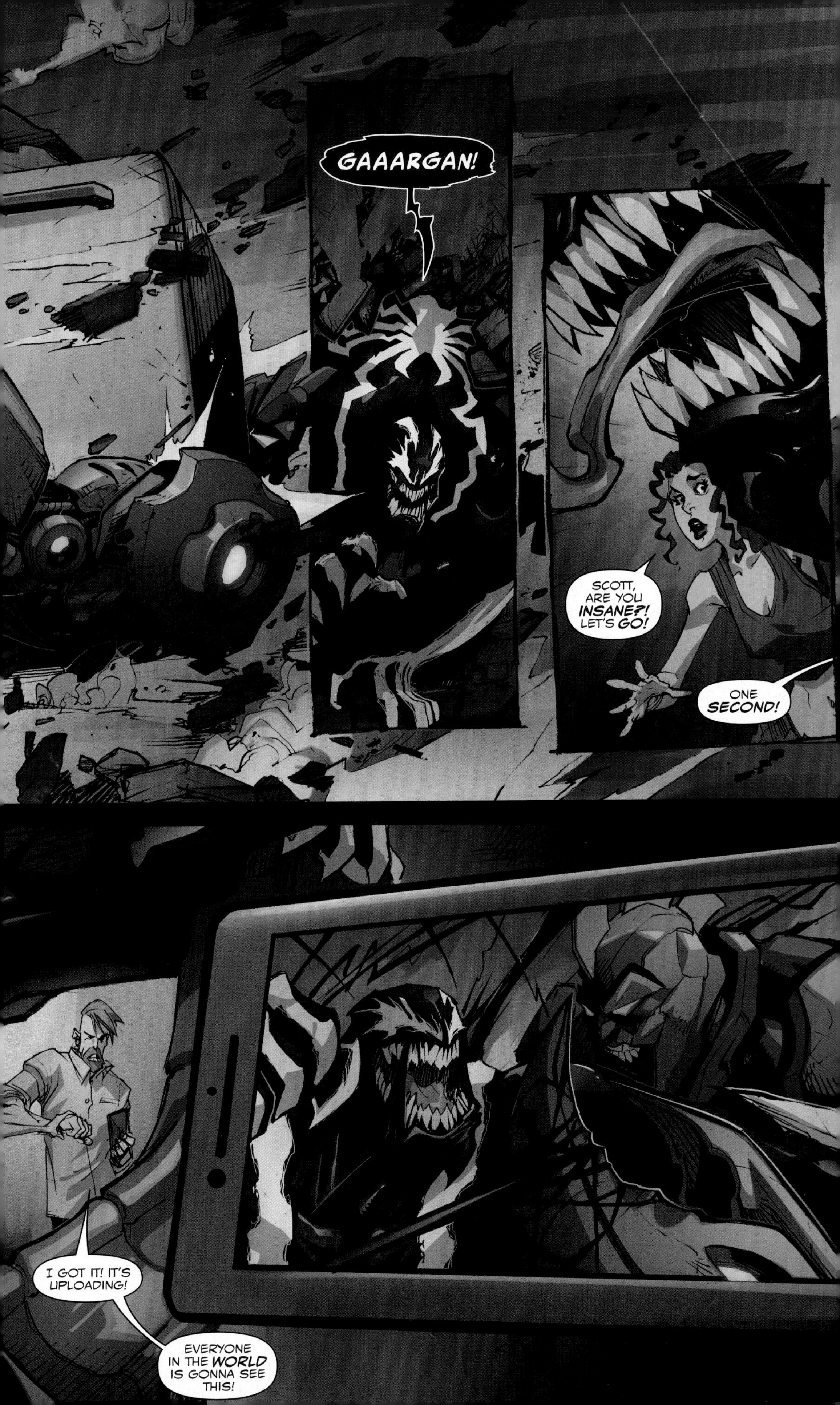
GAAARGAN!
SCOTT, ARE YOU INSANE?! LET'S GO!
ONE SECOND!
I GOT IT! IT'S UPLOADING!
EVERYONE IN THE WORLD IS GONNA SEE THIS!

5

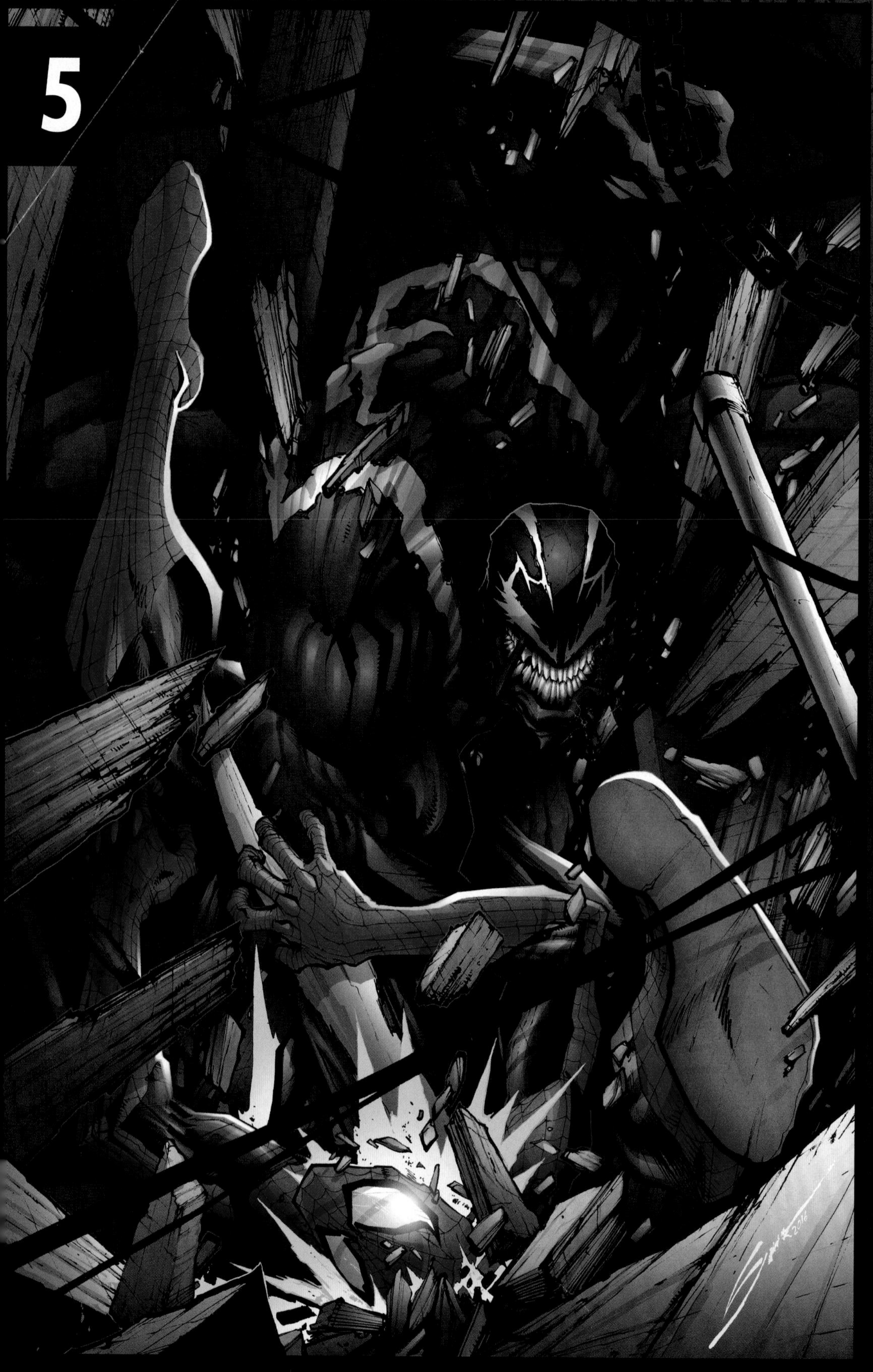

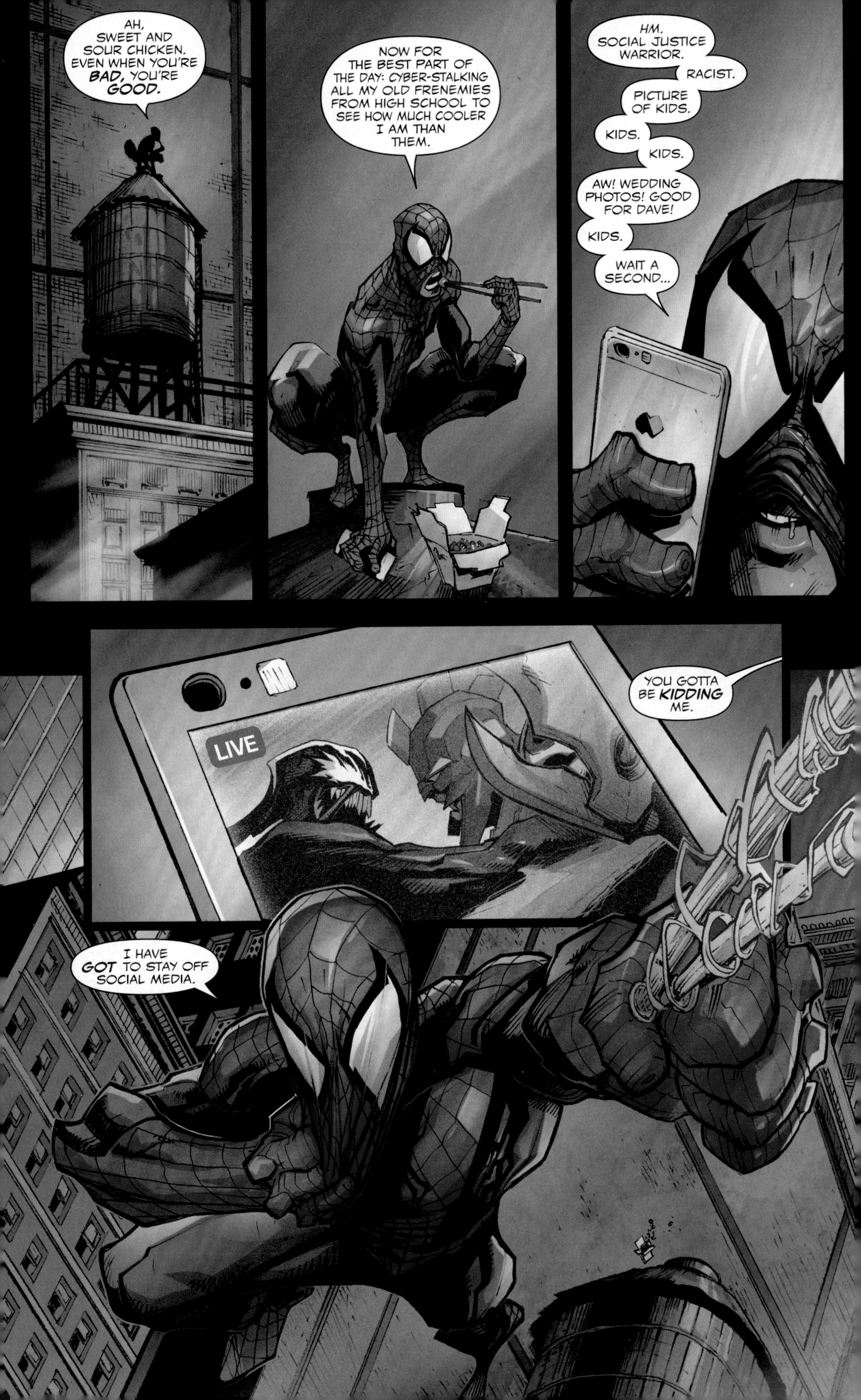
AH, SWEET AND SOUR CHICKEN. EVEN WHEN YOU'RE BAD, YOU'RE GOOD.
NOW FOR THE BEST PART OF THE DAY: CYBER-STALKING ALL MY OLD FRENEMIES FROM HIGH SCHOOL TO SEE HOW MUCH COOLER I AM THAN THEM.
HM. SOCIAL JUSTICE WARRIOR.
RACIST.
PICTURE OF KIDS.
KIDS.
KIDS.
AW! WEDDING PHOTOS! GOOD FOR DAVE!
KIDS.
WAIT A SECOND...
LIVE
YOU GOTTA BE KIDDING ME.
I HAVE GOT TO STAY OFF SOCIAL MEDIA.

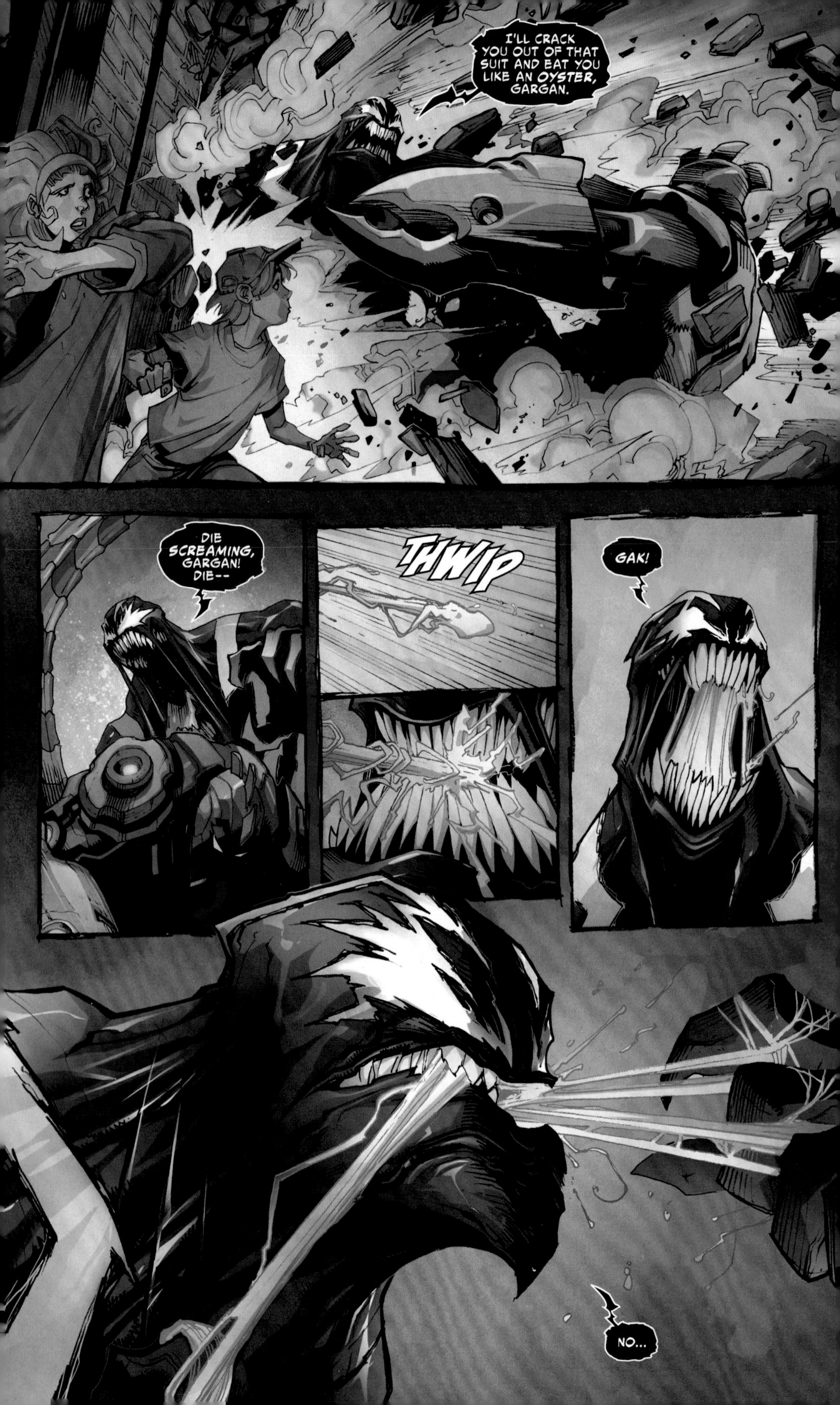
I'LL CRACK YOU OUT OF THAT SUIT AND EAT YOU LIKE AN OYSTER, GARGAN.
DIE SCREAMING, GARGAN! DIE--
THWIP
GAK!
NO...

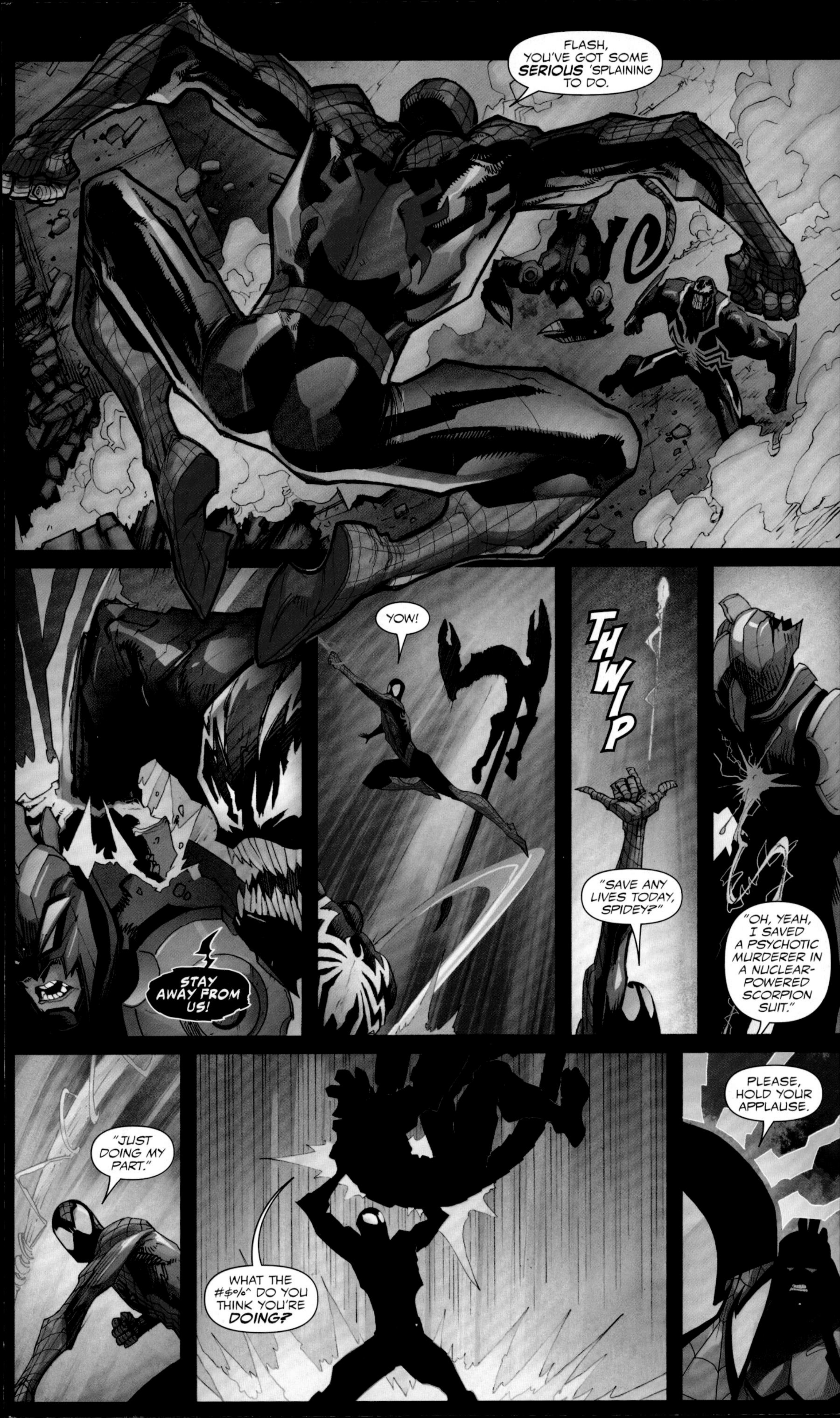
FLASH, YOU'VE GOT SOME SERIOUS 'SPLAINING TO DO.
STAY AWAY FROM US!
YOW!
THWIP
"SAVE ANY LIVES TODAY, SPIDEY?"
"OH, YEAH, I SAVED A PSYCHOTIC MURDERER IN A NUCLEAR-POWERED SCORPION SUIT."
"JUST DOING MY PART."
WHAT THE #$%^ DO YOU THINK YOU'RE DOING?
PLEASE, HOLD YOUR APPLAUSE.

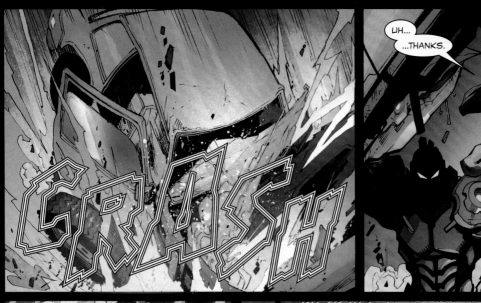

UH...

...THANKS.

I WANT THAT SUIT!

WHAT ARE YOU DOING?

SPIDER-MAN IS HERE! SPIDER-MAN!

SPIDER-MAN!

YOU'RE BEING CRAZY!

SCORPION! STOP!

WE HAVE TO GET OUT OF HERE!

WE CAN'T HURT SPIDER-MAN!

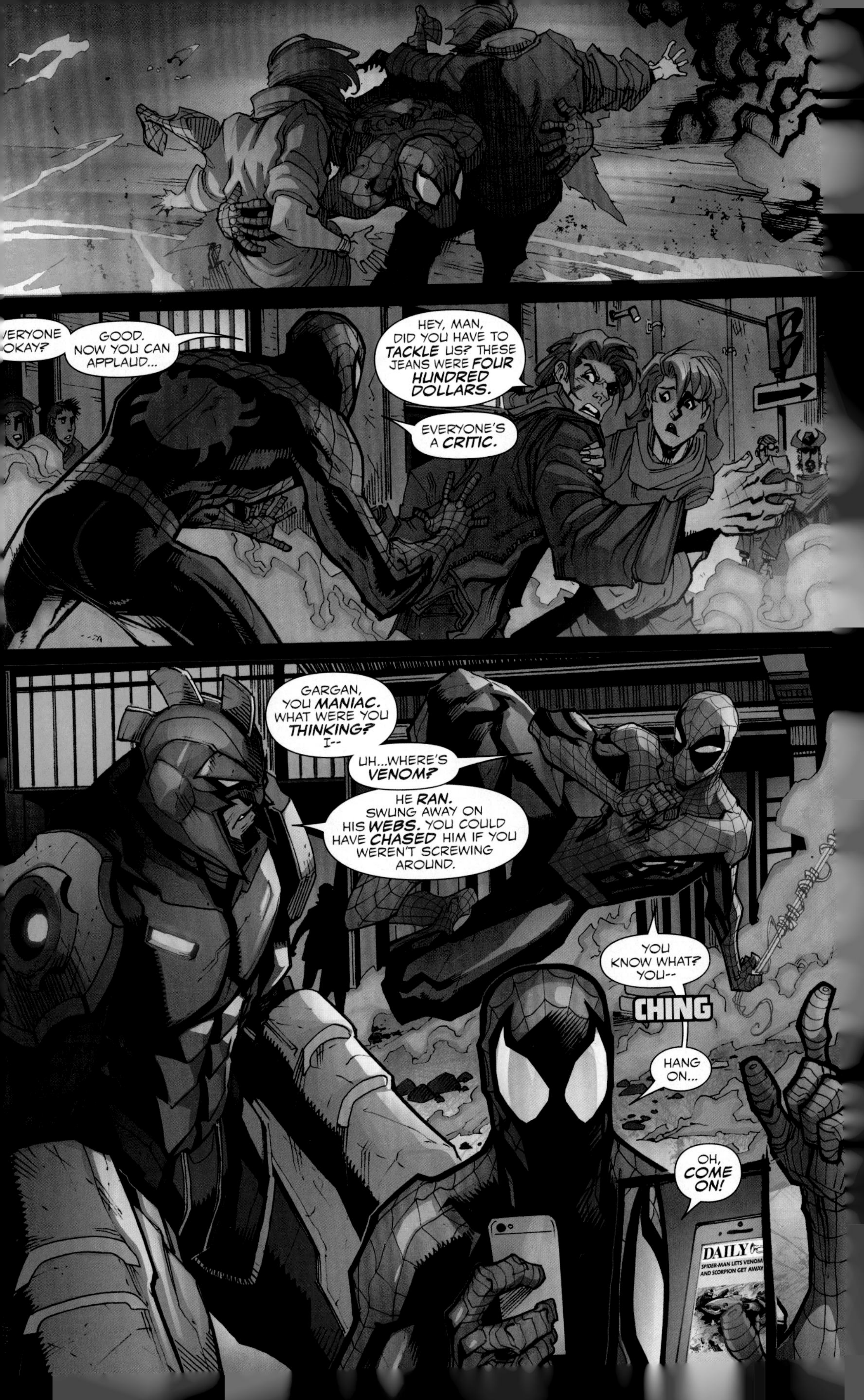

VERYONE OKAY?
GOOD. NOW YOU CAN APPLAUD...
HEY, MAN, DID YOU HAVE TO TACKLE US? THESE JEANS WERE FOUR HUNDRED DOLLARS.
EVERYONE'S A CRITIC.
GARGAN, YOU MANIAC. WHAT WERE YOU THINKING? I--
UH...WHERE'S VENOM?
HE RAN. SWUNG AWAY ON HIS WEBS. YOU COULD HAVE CHASED HIM IF YOU WEREN'T SCREWING AROUND.
YOU KNOW WHAT? YOU--
CHING
HANG ON...
OH, COME ON!
DAILY
SPIDER-MAN LETS VENOM AND SCORPION GET AWAY

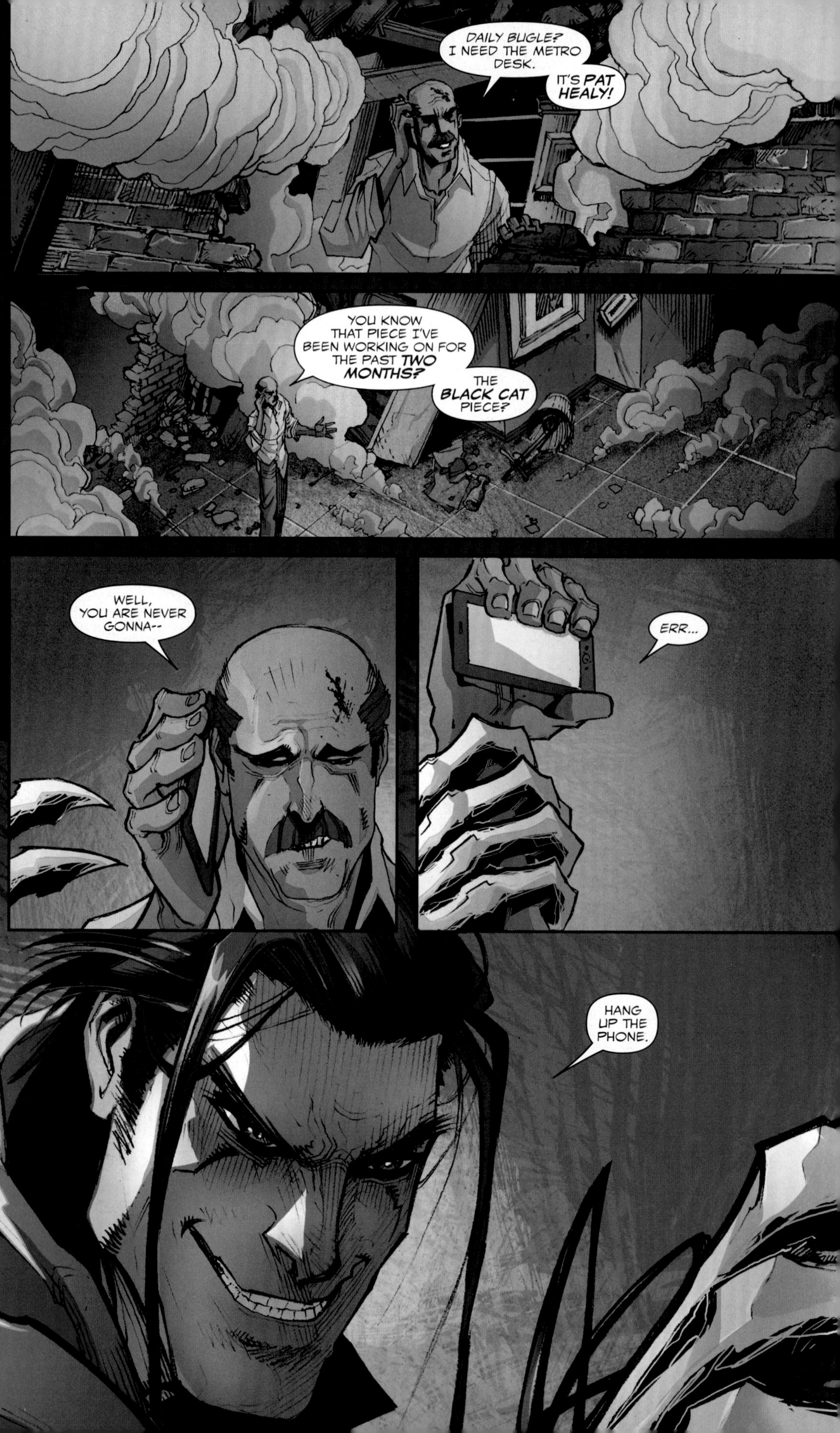
DAILY BUGLE? I NEED THE METRO DESK.
IT'S PAT HEALY!
YOU KNOW THAT PIECE I'VE BEEN WORKING ON FOR THE PAST TWO MONTHS?
THE BLACK CAT PIECE?
WELL, YOU ARE NEVER GONNA--
ERR...
HANG UP THE PHONE.

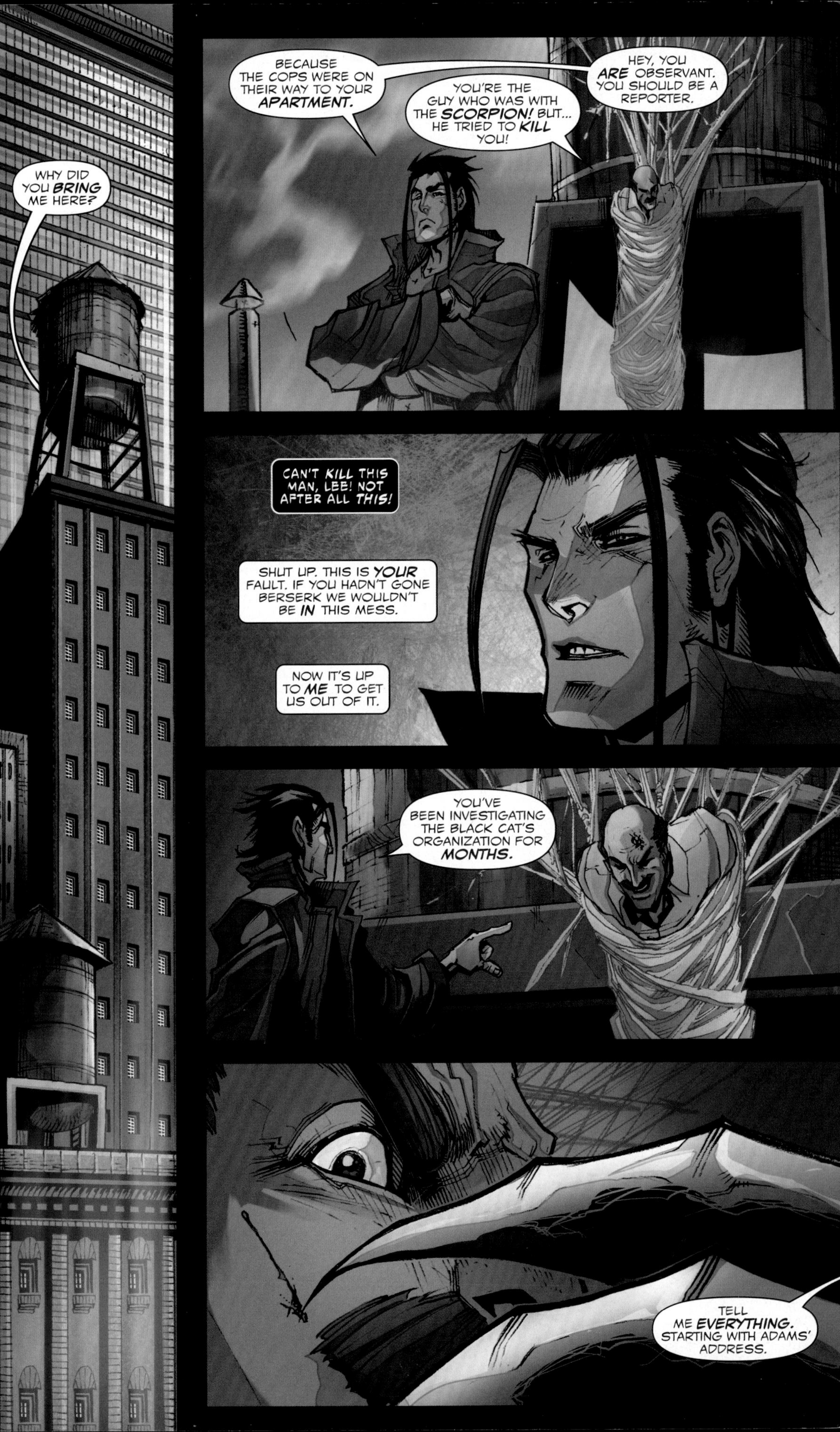
WHY DID YOU BRING ME HERE?
BECAUSE THE COPS WERE ON THEIR WAY TO YOUR APARTMENT.
YOU'RE THE GUY WHO WAS WITH THE SCORPION! BUT... HE TRIED TO KILL YOU!
HEY, YOU ARE OBSERVANT. YOU SHOULD BE A REPORTER.
CAN'T KILL THIS MAN, LEE! NOT AFTER ALL THIS!
SHUT UP. THIS IS YOUR FAULT. IF YOU HADN'T GONE BERSERK WE WOULDN'T BE IN THIS MESS.
NOW IT'S UP TO ME TO GET US OUT OF IT.
YOU'VE BEEN INVESTIGATING THE BLACK CAT'S ORGANIZATION FOR MONTHS.
TELL ME EVERYTHING. STARTING WITH ADAMS' ADDRESS.

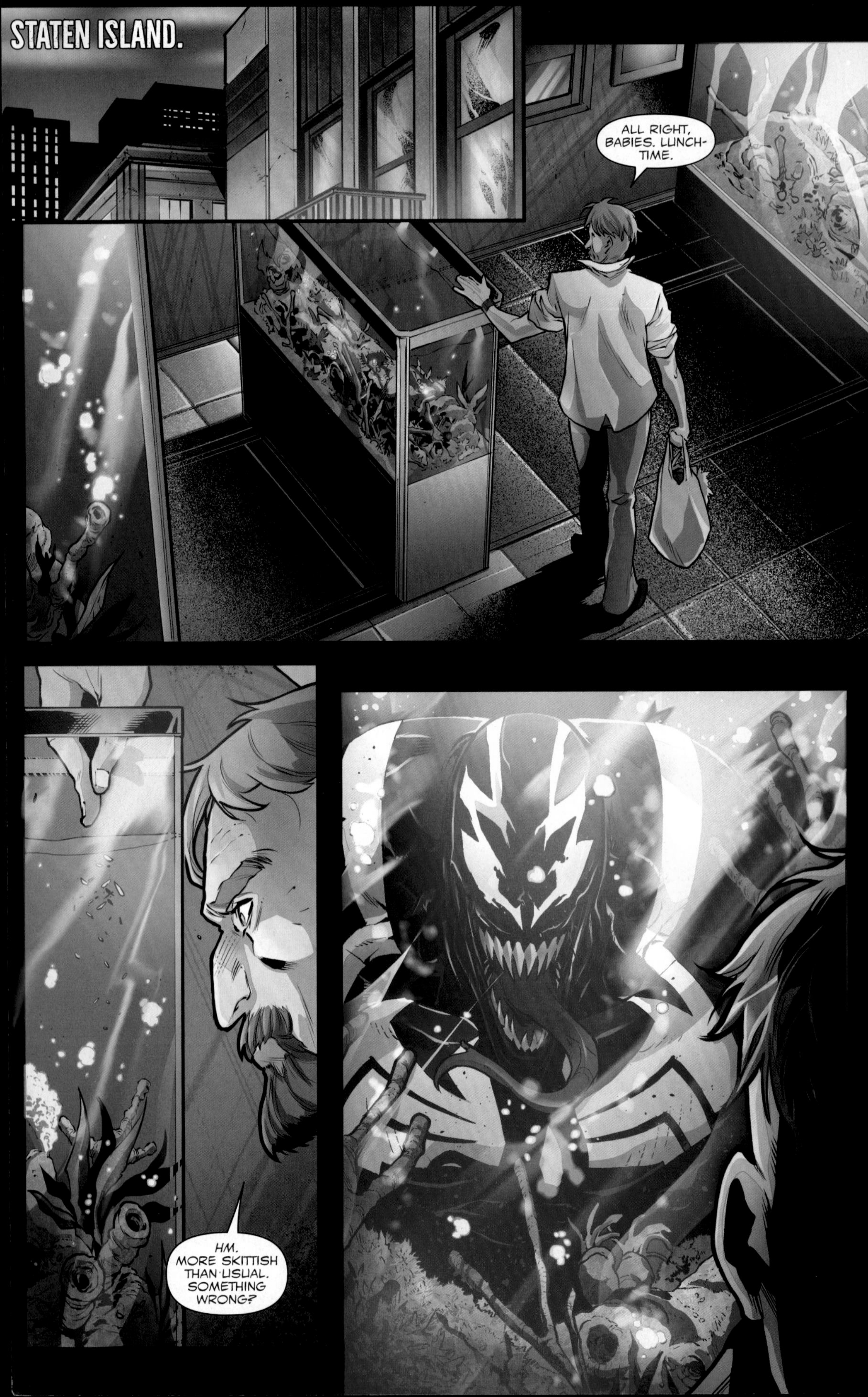
STATEN ISLAND.
ALL RIGHT, BABIES. LUNCH-TIME.
HM. MORE SKITTISH THAN USUAL. SOMETHING WRONG?

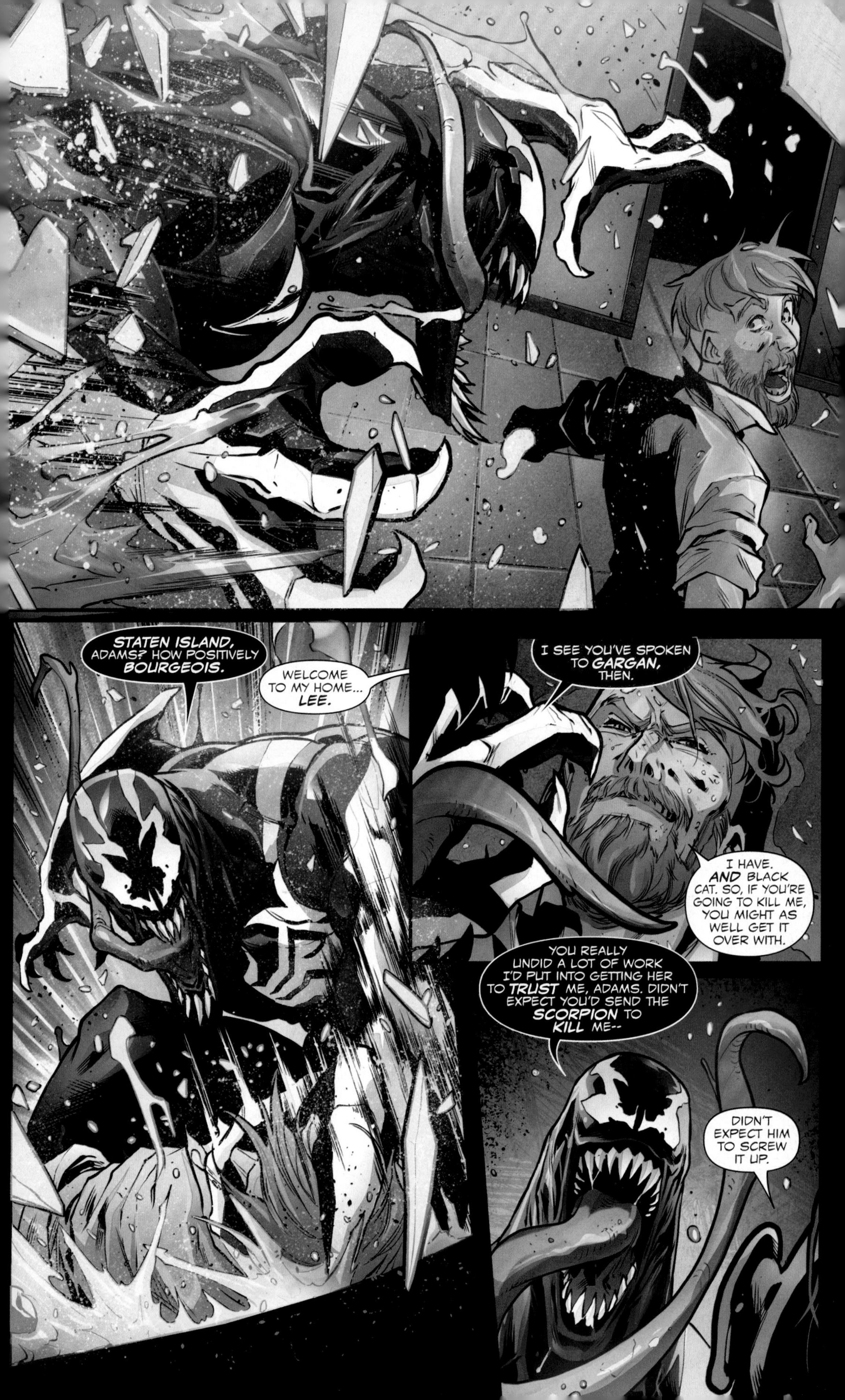

STATEN ISLAND, ADAMS? HOW POSITIVELY BOURGEOIS.
WELCOME TO MY HOME... LEE.
I SEE YOU'VE SPOKEN TO GARGAN, THEN.
I HAVE. AND BLACK CAT. SO, IF YOU'RE GOING TO KILL ME, YOU MIGHT AS WELL GET IT OVER WITH.
YOU REALLY UNDID A LOT OF WORK I'D PUT INTO GETTING HER TO TRUST ME, ADAMS. DIDN'T EXPECT YOU'D SEND THE SCORPION TO KILL ME--
DIDN'T EXPECT HIM TO SCREW IT UP.

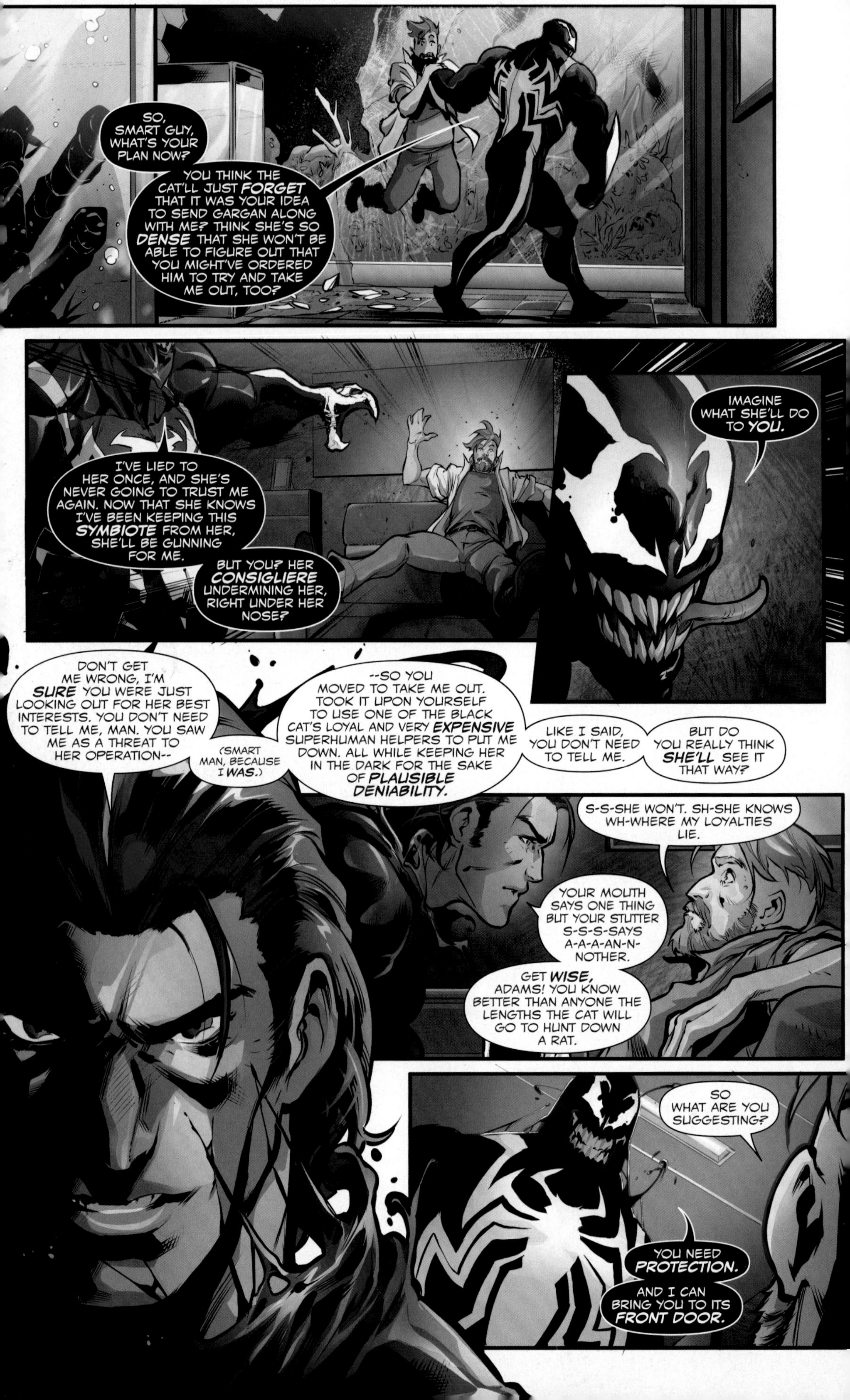
SO, SMART GUY, WHAT'S YOUR PLAN NOW?
YOU THINK THE CAT'LL JUST FORGET THAT IT WAS YOUR IDEA TO SEND GARGAN ALONG WITH ME? THINK SHE'S SO DENSE THAT SHE WON'T BE ABLE TO FIGURE OUT THAT YOU MIGHT'VE ORDERED HIM TO TRY AND TAKE ME OUT, TOO?
I'VE LIED TO HER ONCE, AND SHE'S NEVER GOING TO TRUST ME AGAIN. NOW THAT SHE KNOWS I'VE BEEN KEEPING THIS SYMBIOTE FROM HER, SHE'LL BE GUNNING FOR ME.
BUT YOU? HER CONSIGLIERE UNDERMINING HER, RIGHT UNDER HER NOSE?
IMAGINE WHAT SHE'LL DO TO YOU.
DON'T GET ME WRONG, I'M SURE YOU WERE JUST LOOKING OUT FOR HER BEST INTERESTS. YOU DON'T NEED TO TELL ME, MAN. YOU SAW ME AS A THREAT TO HER OPERATION--
(SMART MAN, BECAUSE I WAS.)
--SO YOU MOVED TO TAKE ME OUT. TOOK IT UPON YOURSELF TO USE ONE OF THE BLACK CAT'S LOYAL AND VERY EXPENSIVE SUPERHUMAN HELPERS TO PUT ME DOWN. ALL WHILE KEEPING HER IN THE DARK FOR THE SAKE OF PLAUSIBLE DENIABILITY.
LIKE I SAID, YOU DON'T NEED TO TELL ME.
BUT DO YOU REALLY THINK SHE'LL SEE IT THAT WAY?
S-S-SHE WON'T. SH-SHE KNOWS WH-WHERE MY LOYALTIES LIE.
YOUR MOUTH SAYS ONE THING BUT YOUR STUTTER S-S-S-SAYS A-A-A-AN-N-NOTHER.
GET WISE, ADAMS! YOU KNOW BETTER THAN ANYONE THE LENGTHS THE CAT WILL GO TO HUNT DOWN A RAT.
SO WHAT ARE YOU SUGGESTING?
YOU NEED PROTECTION.
AND I CAN BRING YOU TO ITS FRONT DOOR.

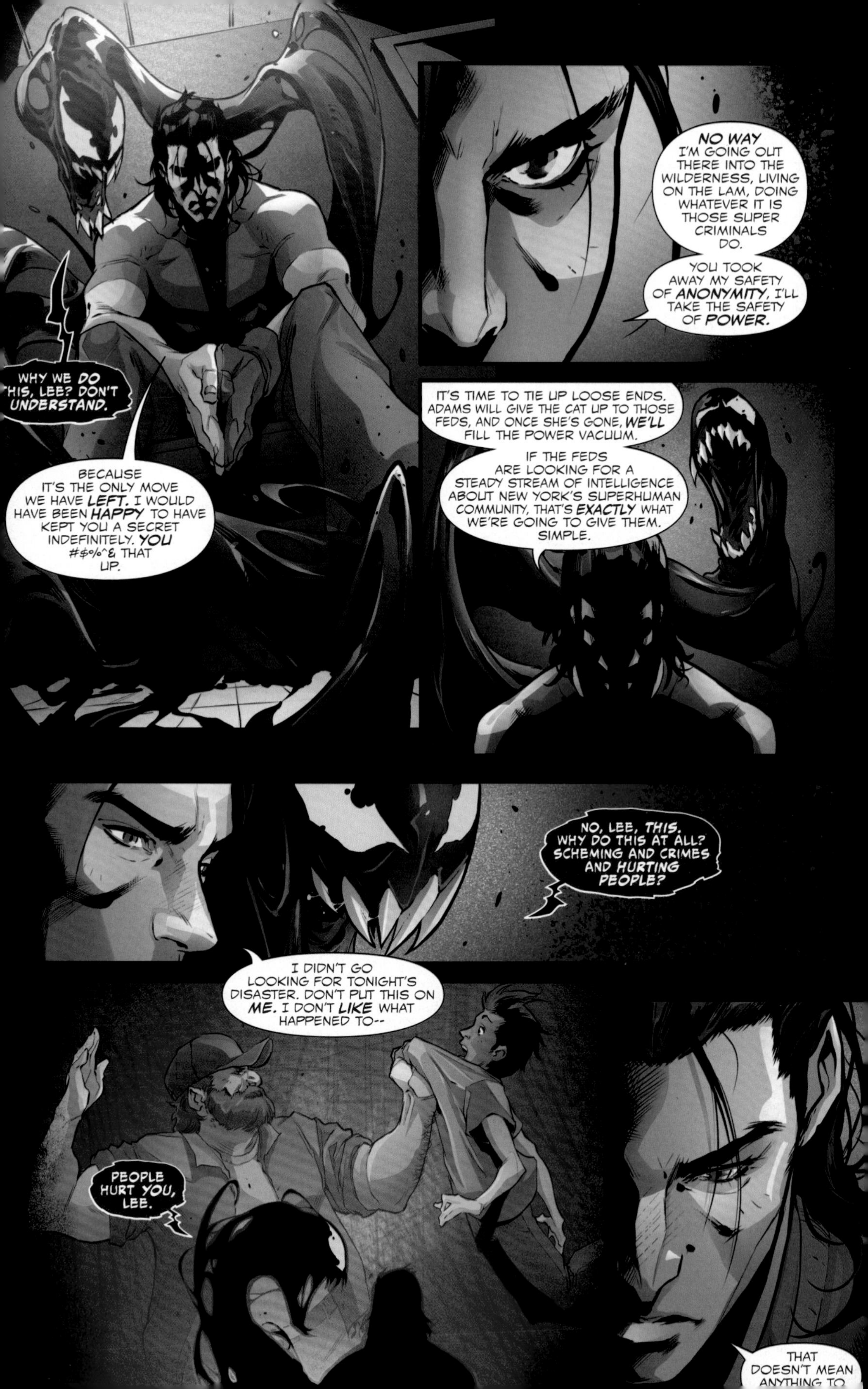
NO WAY I'M GOING OUT THERE INTO THE WILDERNESS, LIVING ON THE LAM, DOING WHATEVER IT IS THOSE SUPER CRIMINALS DO.
YOU TOOK AWAY MY SAFETY OF ANONYMITY, I'LL TAKE THE SAFETY OF POWER.
WHY WE DO THIS, LEE? DON'T UNDERSTAND.
BECAUSE IT'S THE ONLY MOVE WE HAVE LEFT. I WOULD HAVE BEEN HAPPY TO HAVE KEPT YOU A SECRET INDEFINITELY. YOU #$%^& THAT UP.
IT'S TIME TO TIE UP LOOSE ENDS. ADAMS WILL GIVE THE CAT UP TO THOSE FEDS, AND ONCE SHE'S GONE, WE'LL FILL THE POWER VACUUM.
IF THE FEDS ARE LOOKING FOR A STEADY STREAM OF INTELLIGENCE ABOUT NEW YORK'S SUPERHUMAN COMMUNITY, THAT'S EXACTLY WHAT WE'RE GOING TO GIVE THEM. SIMPLE.
NO, LEE, THIS. WHY DO THIS AT ALL? SCHEMING AND CRIMES AND HURTING PEOPLE?
I DIDN'T GO LOOKING FOR TONIGHT'S DISASTER. DON'T PUT THIS ON ME. I DON'T LIKE WHAT HAPPENED TO--
PEOPLE HURT YOU, LEE.
THAT DOESN'T MEAN ANYTHING TO

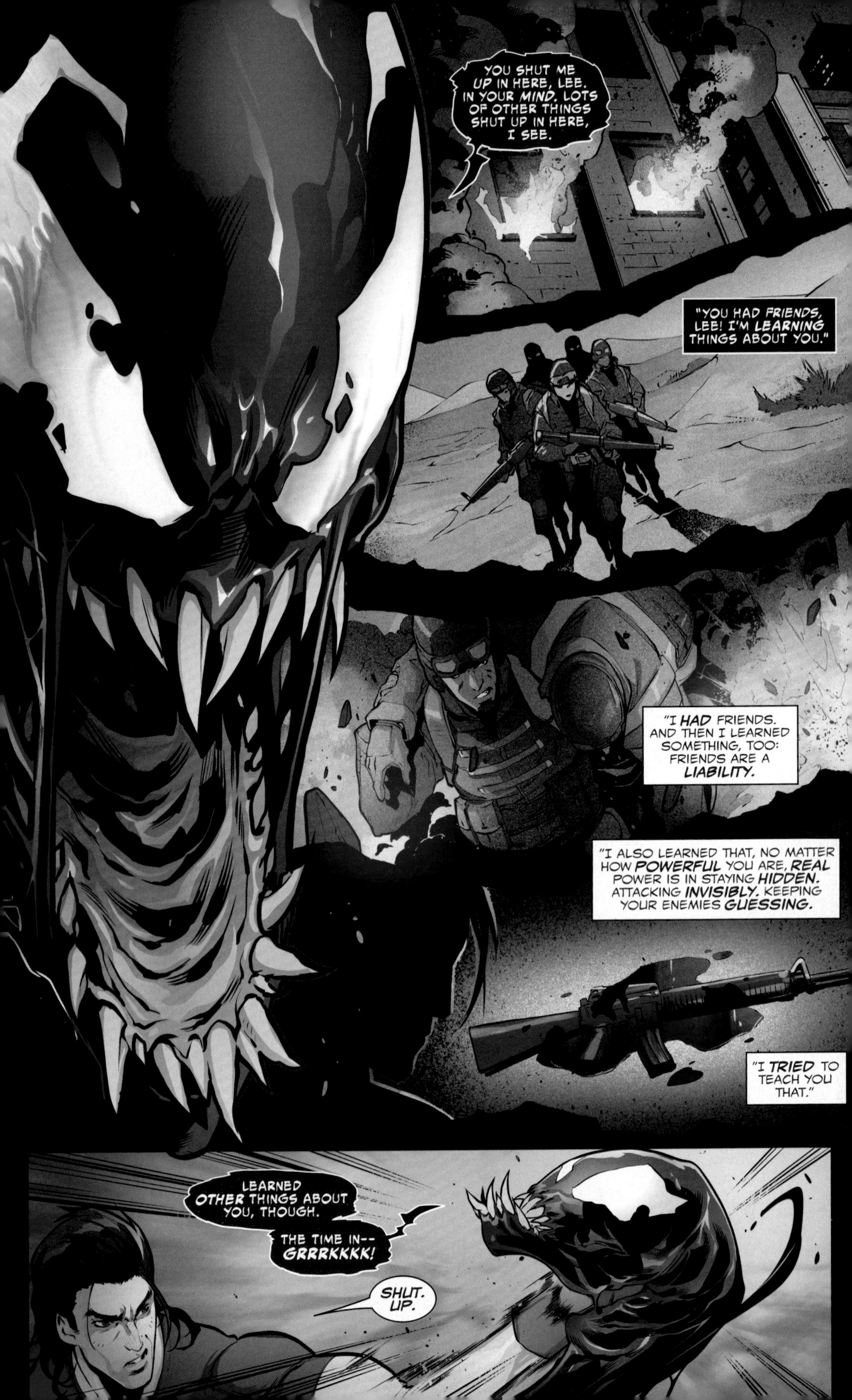

YOU SHUT ME UP IN HERE, LEE. IN YOUR MIND. LOTS OF OTHER THINGS SHUT UP IN HERE, I SEE.
"YOU HAD FRIENDS, LEE! I'M LEARNING THINGS ABOUT YOU."
"I HAD FRIENDS. AND THEN I LEARNED SOMETHING, TOO: FRIENDS ARE A LIABILITY.
"I ALSO LEARNED THAT, NO MATTER HOW POWERFUL YOU ARE, REAL POWER IS IN STAYING HIDDEN. ATTACKING INVISIBLY. KEEPING YOUR ENEMIES GUESSING.
"I TRIED TO TEACH YOU THAT."
LEARNED OTHER THINGS ABOUT YOU, THOUGH.
THE TIME IN-- GRRRKKKK!
SHUT. UP.

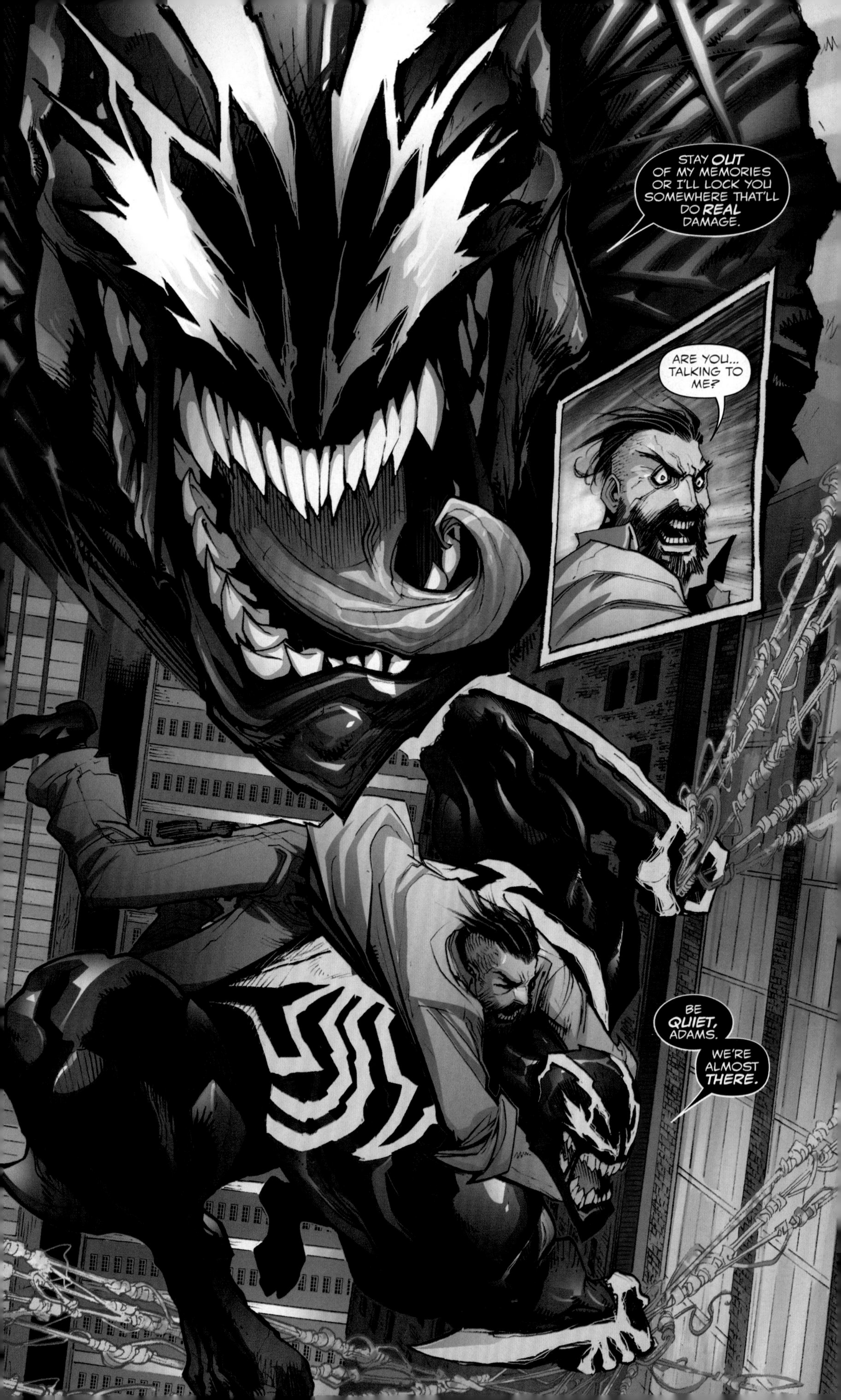
STAY OUT OF MY MEMORIES OR I'LL LOCK YOU SOMEWHERE THAT'LL DO REAL DAMAGE.
ARE YOU... TALKING TO ME?
BE QUIET, ADAMS.
WE'RE ALMOST THERE.

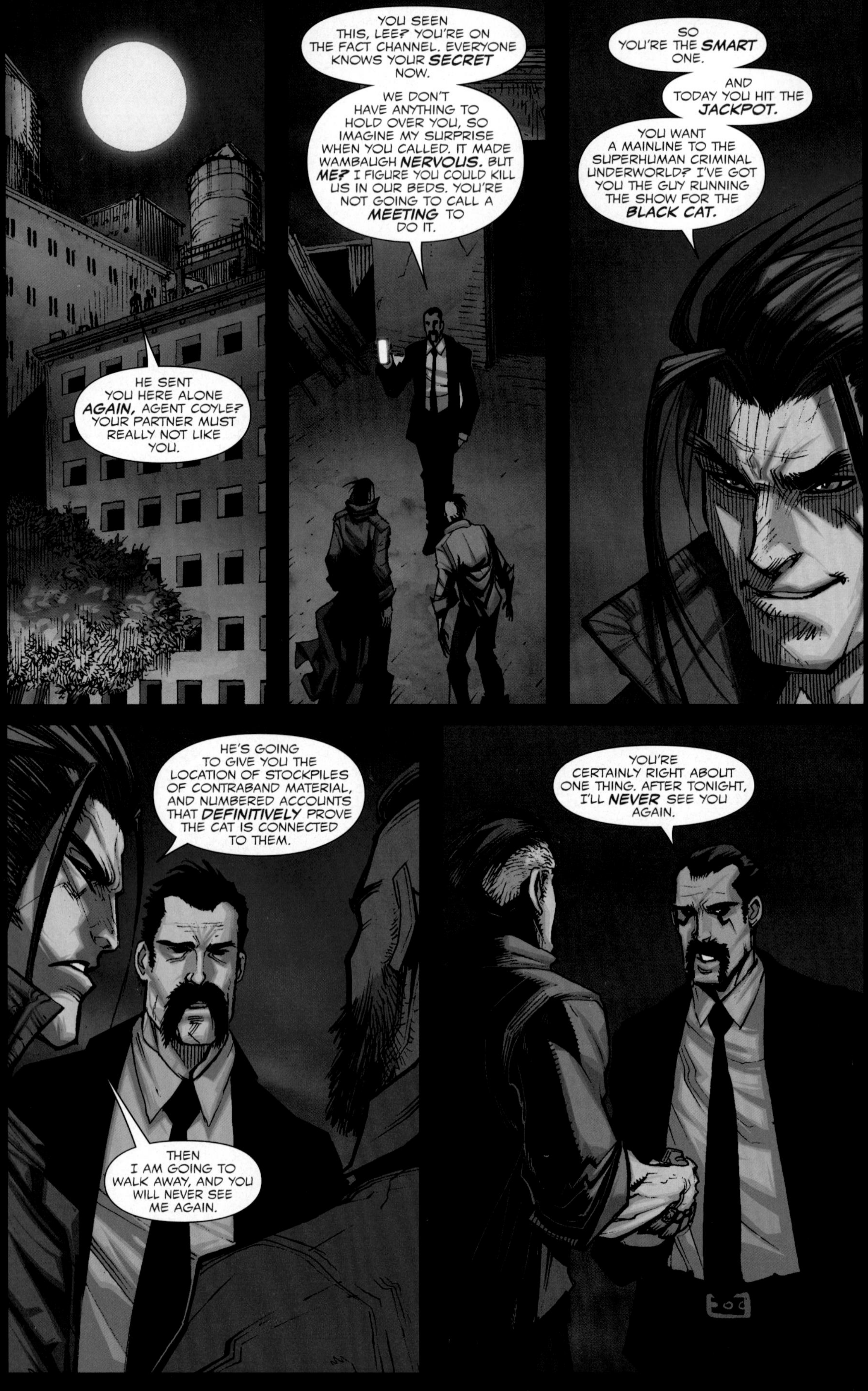
HE SENT YOU HERE ALONE AGAIN, AGENT COYLE? YOUR PARTNER MUST REALLY NOT LIKE YOU.
YOU SEEN THIS, LEE? YOU'RE ON THE FACT CHANNEL. EVERYONE KNOWS YOUR SECRET NOW.
WE DON'T HAVE ANYTHING TO HOLD OVER YOU, SO IMAGINE MY SURPRISE WHEN YOU CALLED. IT MADE WAMBAUGH NERVOUS. BUT ME? I FIGURE YOU COULD KILL US IN OUR BEDS. YOU'RE NOT GOING TO CALL A MEETING TO DO IT.
SO YOU'RE THE SMART ONE.
AND TODAY YOU HIT THE JACKPOT.
YOU WANT A MAINLINE TO THE SUPERHUMAN CRIMINAL UNDERWORLD? I'VE GOT YOU THE GUY RUNNING THE SHOW FOR THE BLACK CAT.
HE'S GOING TO GIVE YOU THE LOCATION OF STOCKPILES OF CONTRABAND MATERIAL, AND NUMBERED ACCOUNTS THAT DEFINITIVELY PROVE THE CAT IS CONNECTED TO THEM.
THEN I AM GOING TO WALK AWAY, AND YOU WILL NEVER SEE ME AGAIN.
YOU'RE CERTAINLY RIGHT ABOUT ONE THING. AFTER TONIGHT, I'LL NEVER SEE YOU AGAIN.

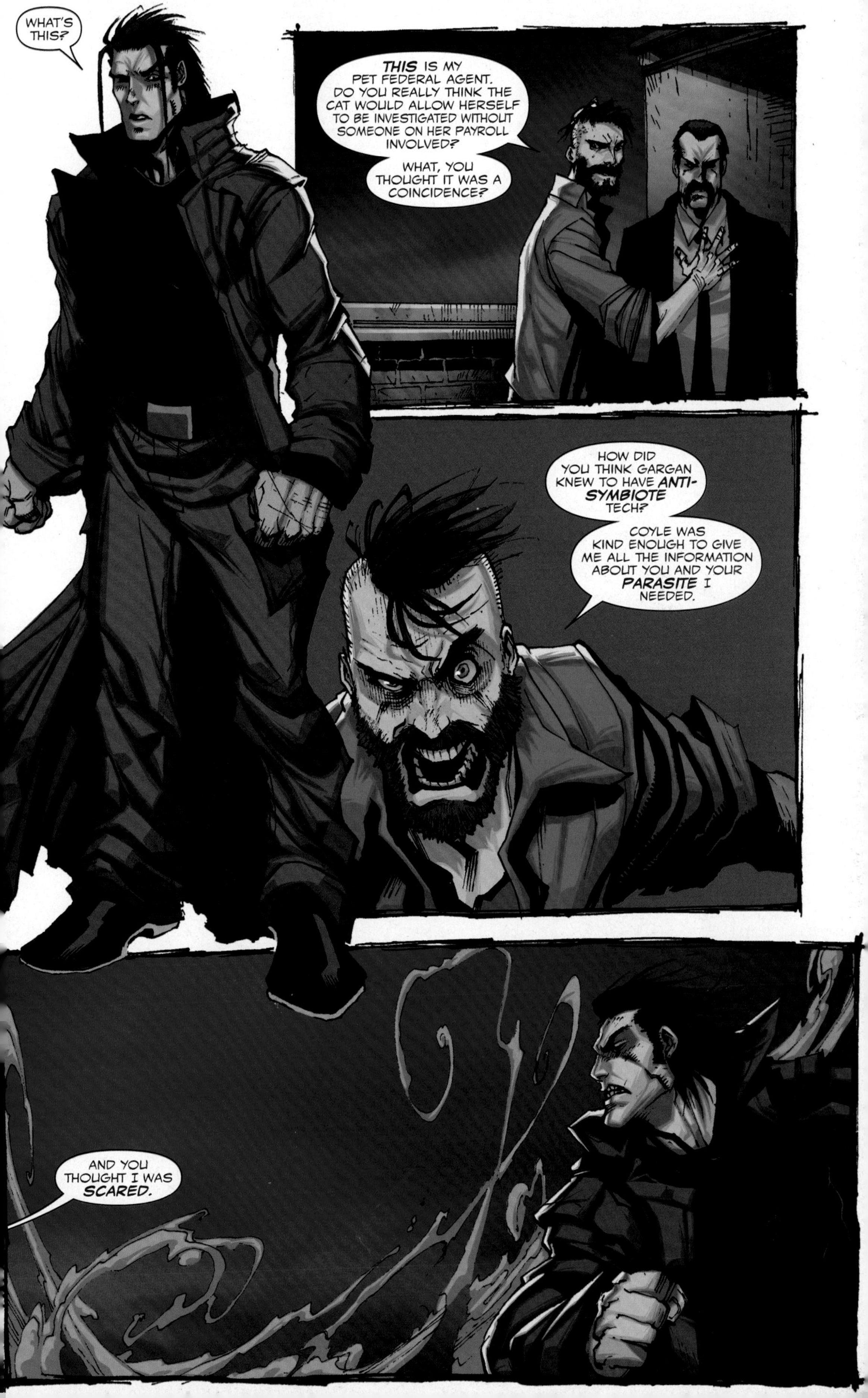
WHAT'S THIS?
THIS IS MY PET FEDERAL AGENT. DO YOU REALLY THINK THE CAT WOULD ALLOW HERSELF TO BE INVESTIGATED WITHOUT SOMEONE ON HER PAYROLL INVOLVED?
WHAT, YOU THOUGHT IT WAS A COINCIDENCE?
HOW DID YOU THINK GARGAN KNEW TO HAVE ANTI-SYMBIOTE TECH?
COYLE WAS KIND ENOUGH TO GIVE ME ALL THE INFORMATION ABOUT YOU AND YOUR PARASITE I NEEDED.
AND YOU THOUGHT I WAS SCARED.

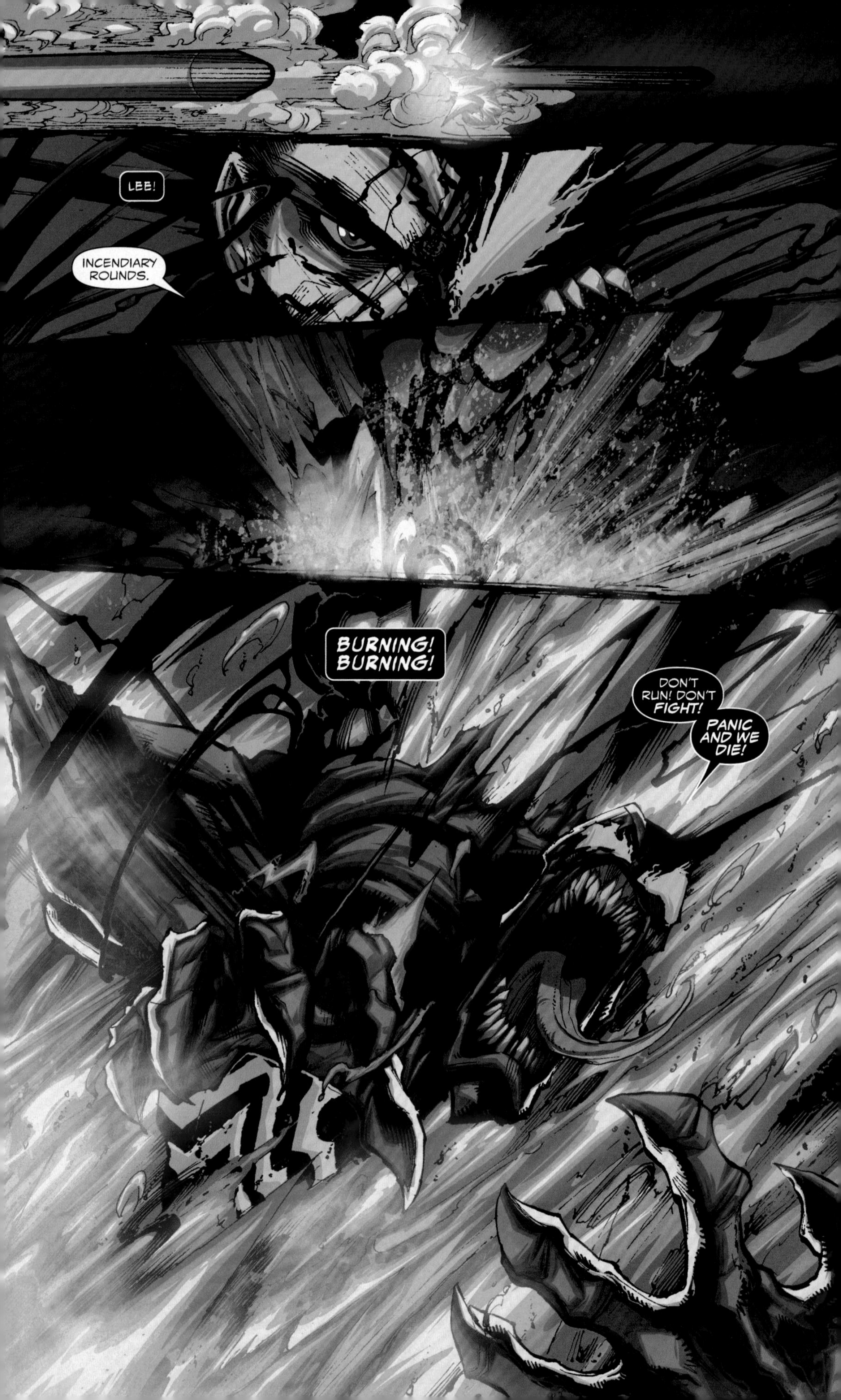
LEE!
INCENDIARY ROUNDS.
BURNING! BURNING!
DON'T RUN! DON'T FIGHT!
PANIC AND WE DIE!

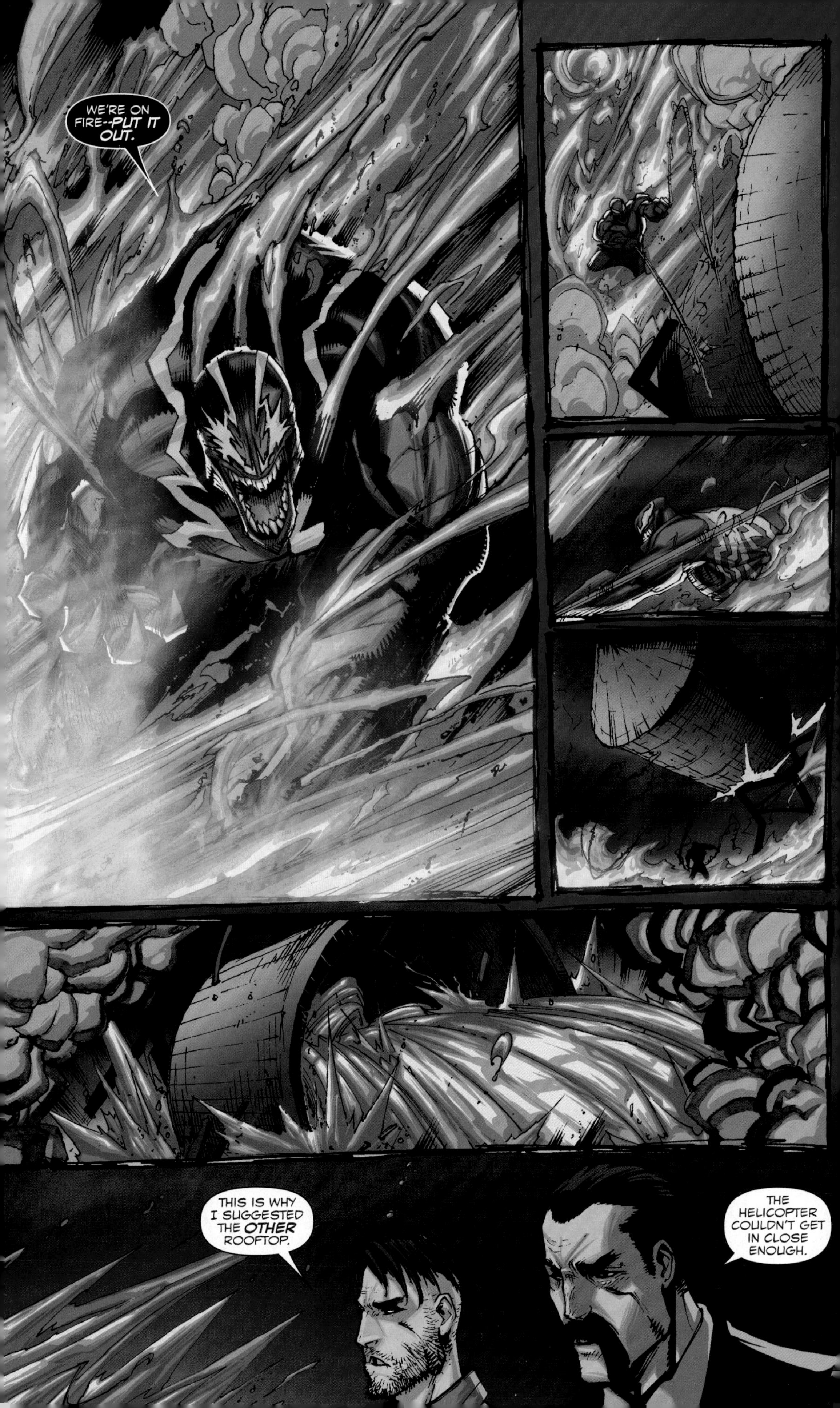
WE'RE ON FIRE--PUT IT OUT.
THIS IS WHY I SUGGESTED THE OTHER ROOFTOP.
THE HELICOPTER COULDN'T GET IN CLOSE ENOUGH.

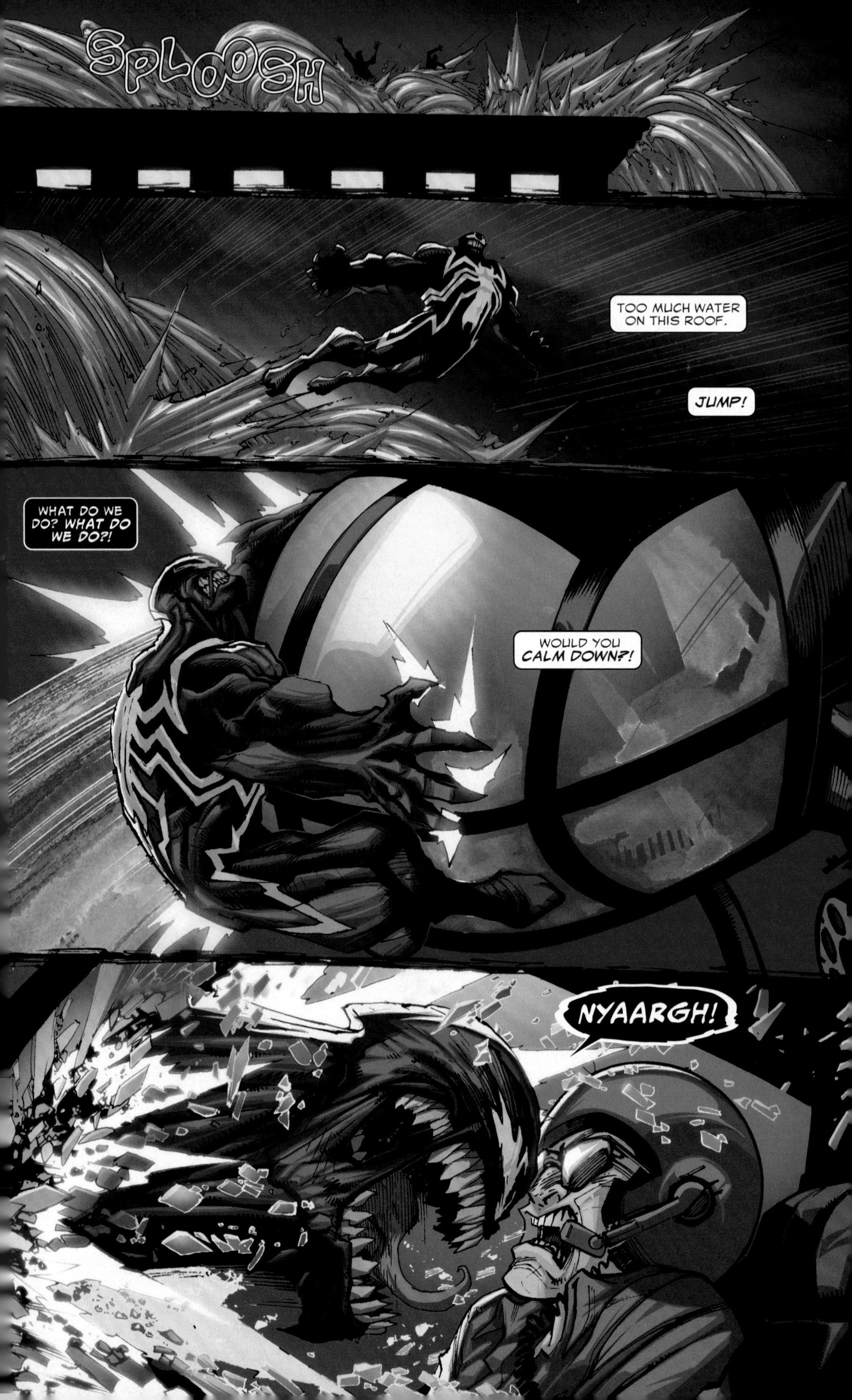
SPLOOSH
TOO MUCH WATER ON THIS ROOF.
JUMP!
WHAT DO WE DO? WHAT DO WE DO?!
WOULD YOU CALM DOWN?!
NYAARGH!

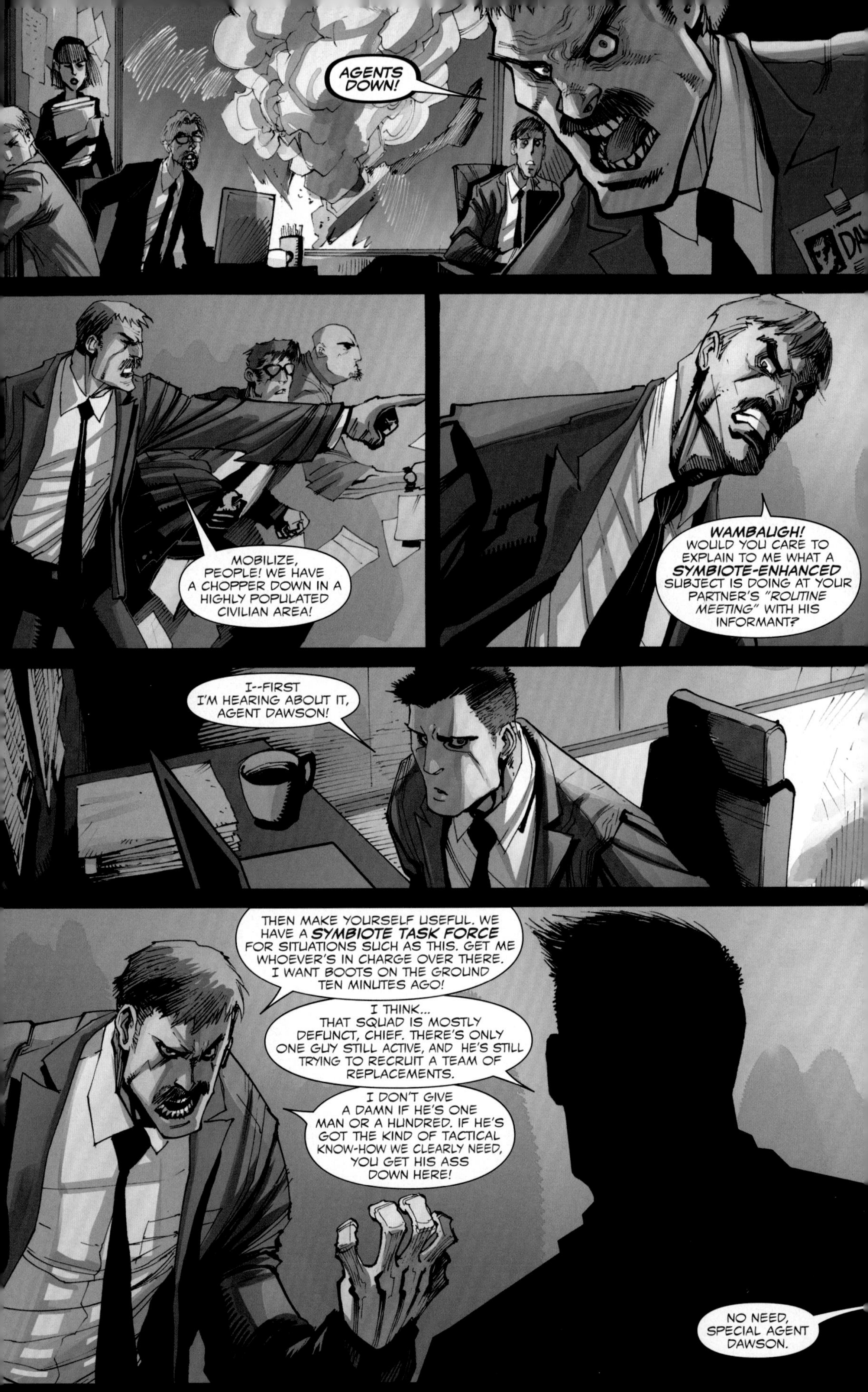
AGENTS DOWN!
MOBILIZE, PEOPLE! WE HAVE A CHOPPER DOWN IN A HIGHLY POPULATED CIVILIAN AREA!
WAMBAUGH! WOULD YOU CARE TO EXPLAIN TO ME WHAT A SYMBIOTE-ENHANCED SUBJECT IS DOING AT YOUR PARTNER'S "ROUTINE MEETING" WITH HIS INFORMANT?
I--FIRST I'M HEARING ABOUT IT, AGENT DAWSON!
THEN MAKE YOURSELF USEFUL. WE HAVE A SYMBIOTE TASK FORCE FOR SITUATIONS SUCH AS THIS. GET ME WHOEVER'S IN CHARGE OVER THERE. I WANT BOOTS ON THE GROUND TEN MINUTES AGO!
I THINK... THAT SQUAD IS MOSTLY DEFUNCT, CHIEF. THERE'S ONLY ONE GUY STILL ACTIVE, AND HE'S STILL TRYING TO RECRUIT A TEAM OF REPLACEMENTS.
I DON'T GIVE A DAMN IF HE'S ONE MAN OR A HUNDRED. IF HE'S GOT THE KIND OF TACTICAL KNOW-HOW WE CLEARLY NEED, YOU GET HIS ASS DOWN HERE!
NO NEED, SPECIAL AGENT DAWSON.

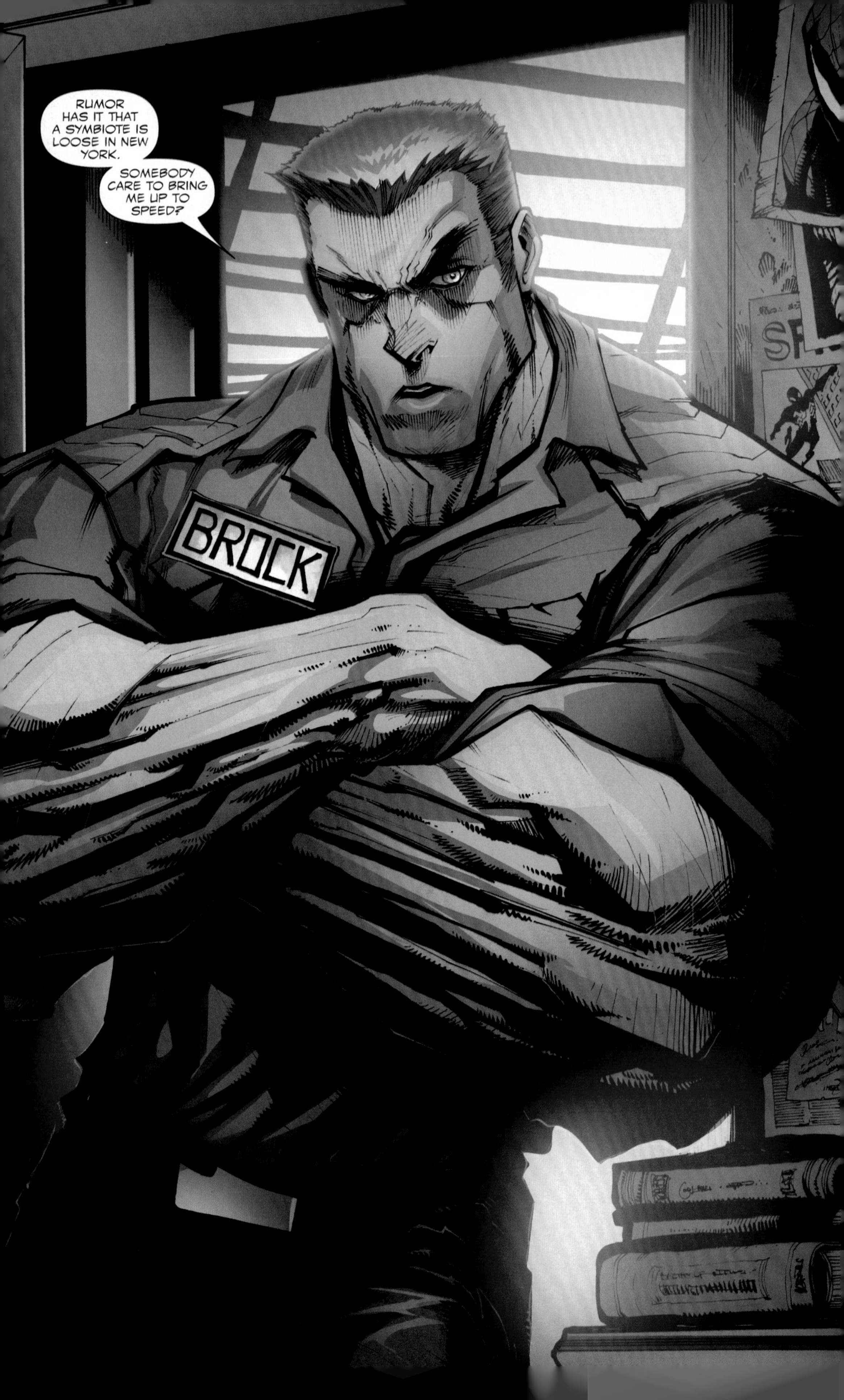
RUMOR HAS IT THAT A SYMBIOTE IS LOOSE IN NEW YORK.
SOMEBODY CARE TO BRING ME UP TO SPEED?
BROCK

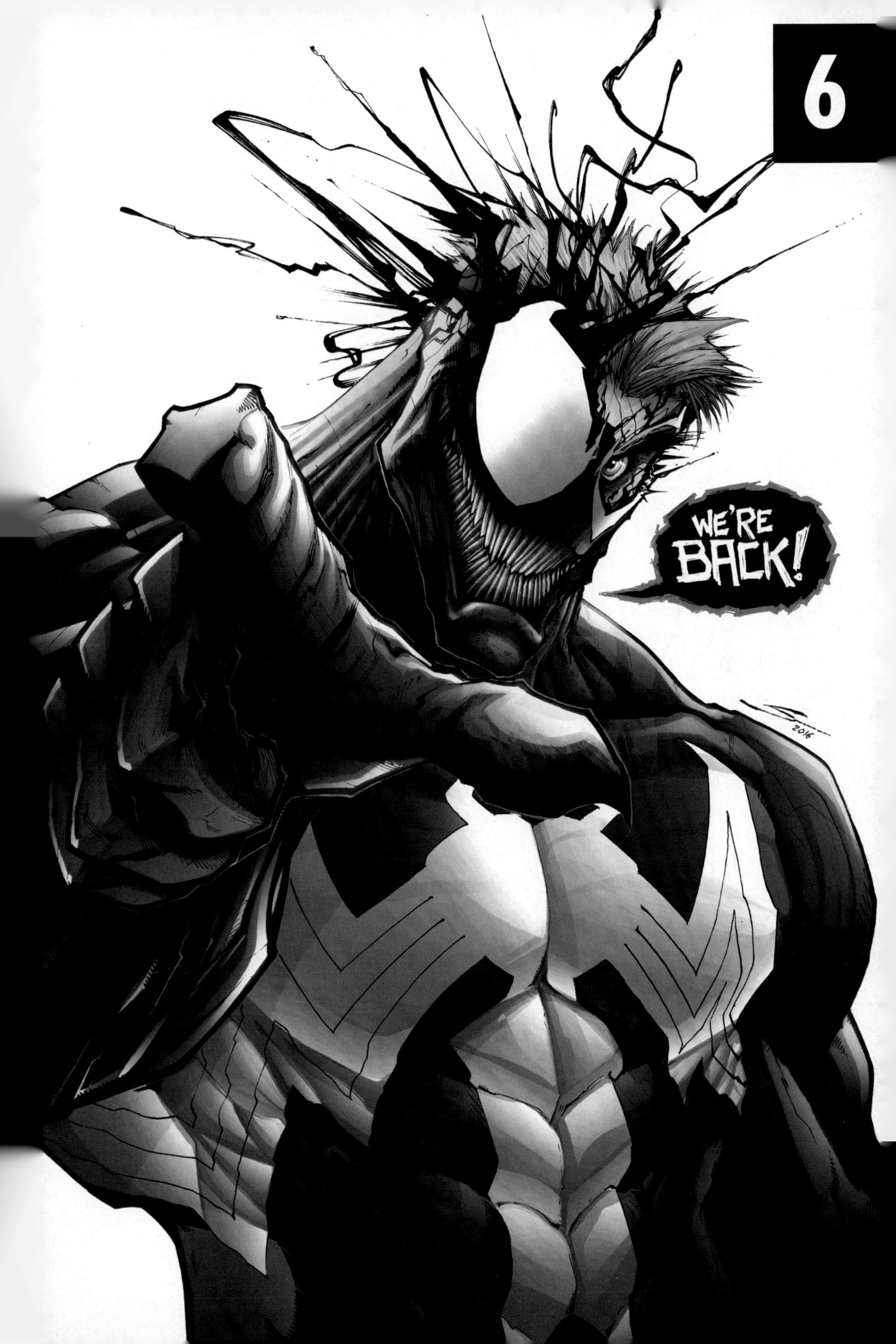
6
WE'RE BACK!

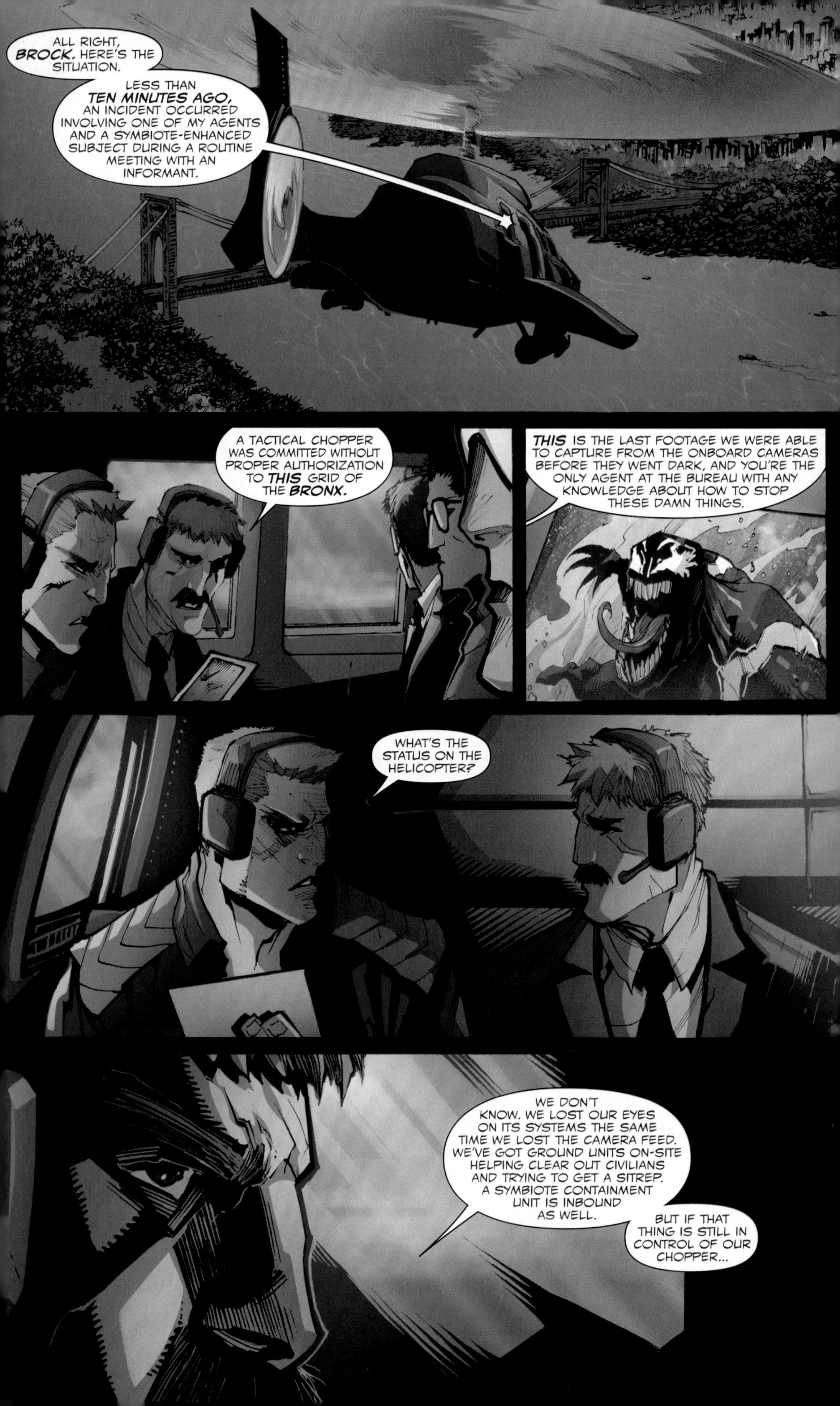

ALL RIGHT, BROCK. HERE'S THE SITUATION.
LESS THAN TEN MINUTES AGO, AN INCIDENT OCCURRED INVOLVING ONE OF MY AGENTS AND A SYMBIOTE-ENHANCED SUBJECT DURING A ROUTINE MEETING WITH AN INFORMANT.
A TACTICAL CHOPPER WAS COMMITTED WITHOUT PROPER AUTHORIZATION TO THIS GRID OF THE BRONX.
THIS IS THE LAST FOOTAGE WE WERE ABLE TO CAPTURE FROM THE ONBOARD CAMERAS BEFORE THEY WENT DARK, AND YOU'RE THE ONLY AGENT AT THE BUREAU WITH ANY KNOWLEDGE ABOUT HOW TO STOP THESE DAMN THINGS.
WHAT'S THE STATUS ON THE HELICOPTER?
WE DON'T KNOW. WE LOST OUR EYES ON ITS SYSTEMS THE SAME TIME WE LOST THE CAMERA FEED. WE'VE GOT GROUND UNITS ON-SITE HELPING CLEAR OUT CIVILIANS AND TRYING TO GET A SITREP. A SYMBIOTE CONTAINMENT UNIT IS INBOUND AS WELL.
BUT IF THAT THING IS STILL IN CONTROL OF OUR CHOPPER...

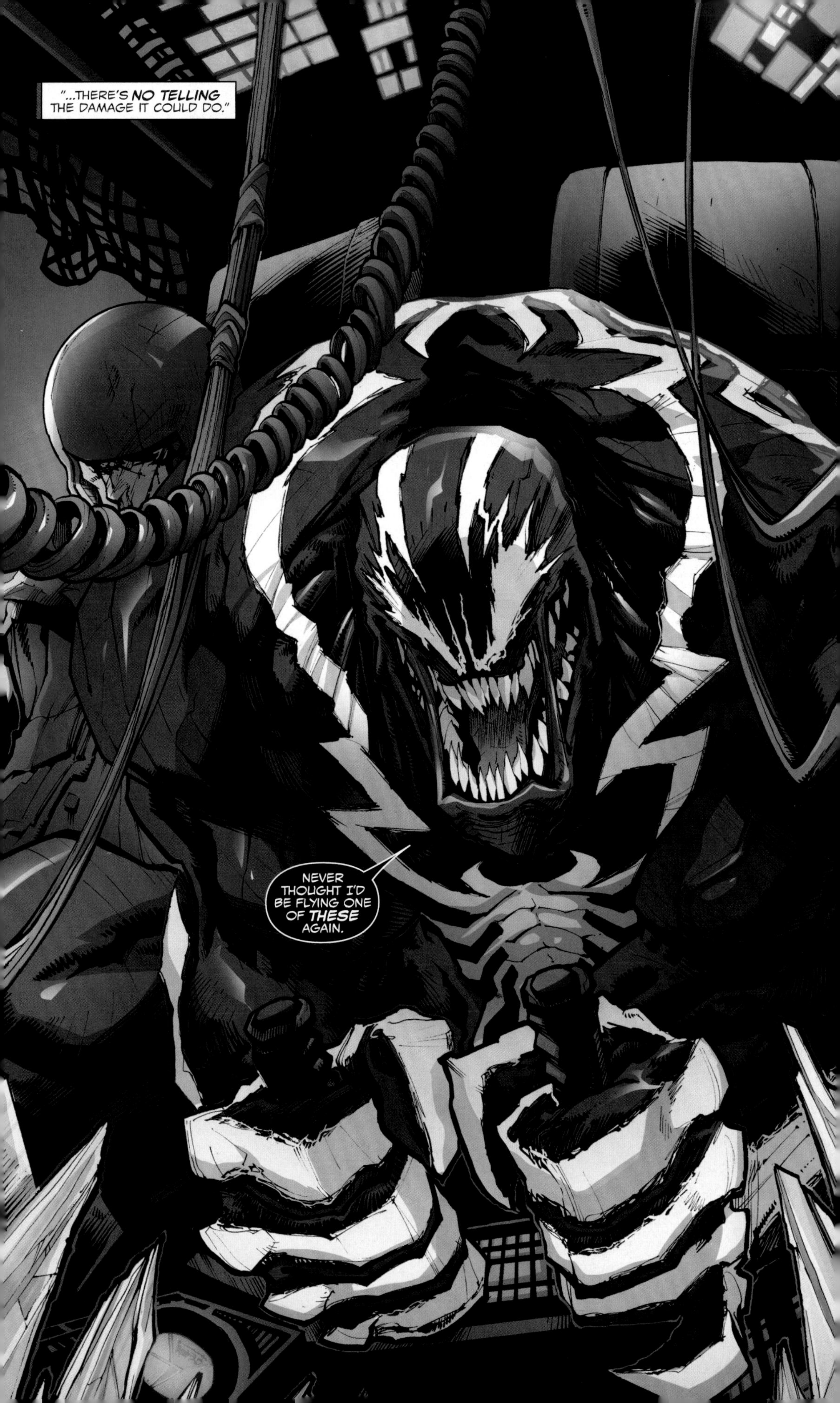
"...THERE'S **NO TELLING** THE DAMAGE IT COULD DO."
NEVER THOUGHT I'D BE FLYING ONE OF ***THESE*** AGAIN.

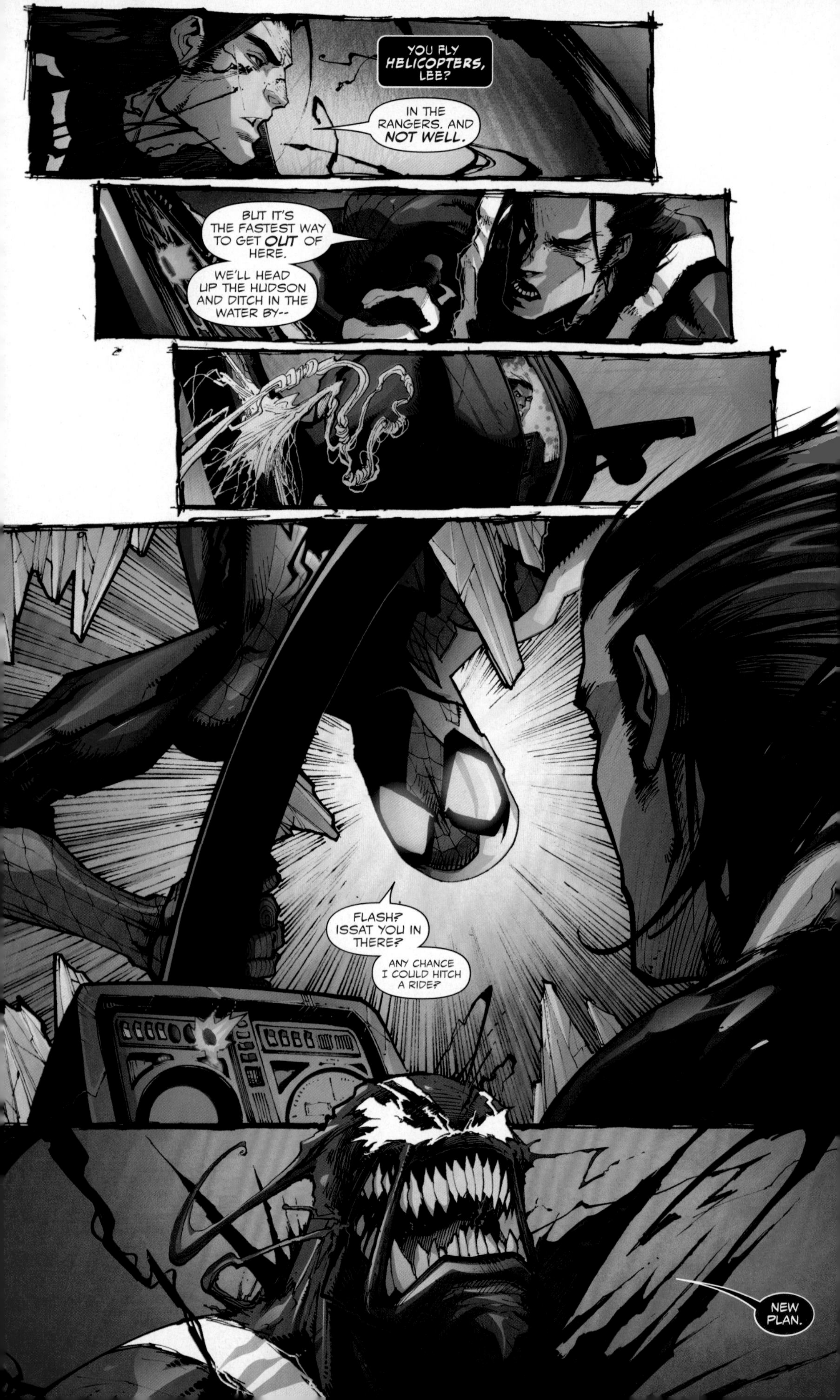
YOU FLY HELICOPTERS, LEE?
IN THE RANGERS. AND NOT WELL.
BUT IT'S THE FASTEST WAY TO GET OUT OF HERE.
WE'LL HEAD UP THE HUDSON AND DITCH IN THE WATER BY--
FLASH? ISSAT YOU IN THERE?
ANY CHANCE I COULD HITCH A RIDE?
NEW PLAN.

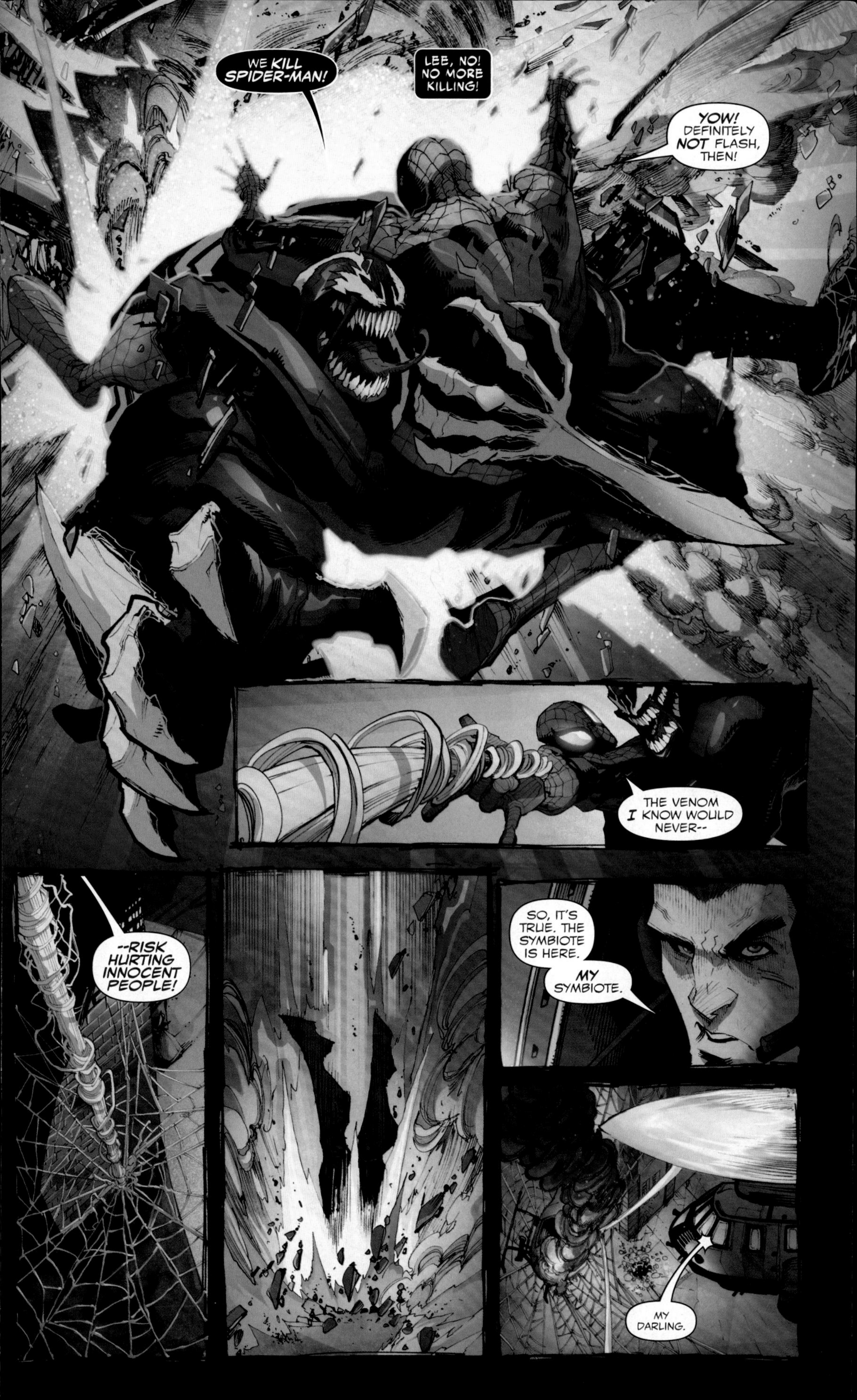
WE KILL SPIDER-MAN!
LEE, NO! NO MORE KILLING!
YOW! DEFINITELY NOT FLASH, THEN!
THE VENOM I KNOW WOULD NEVER--
--RISK HURTING INNOCENT PEOPLE!
SO, IT'S TRUE. THE SYMBIOTE IS HERE.
MY SYMBIOTE.
MY DARLING.

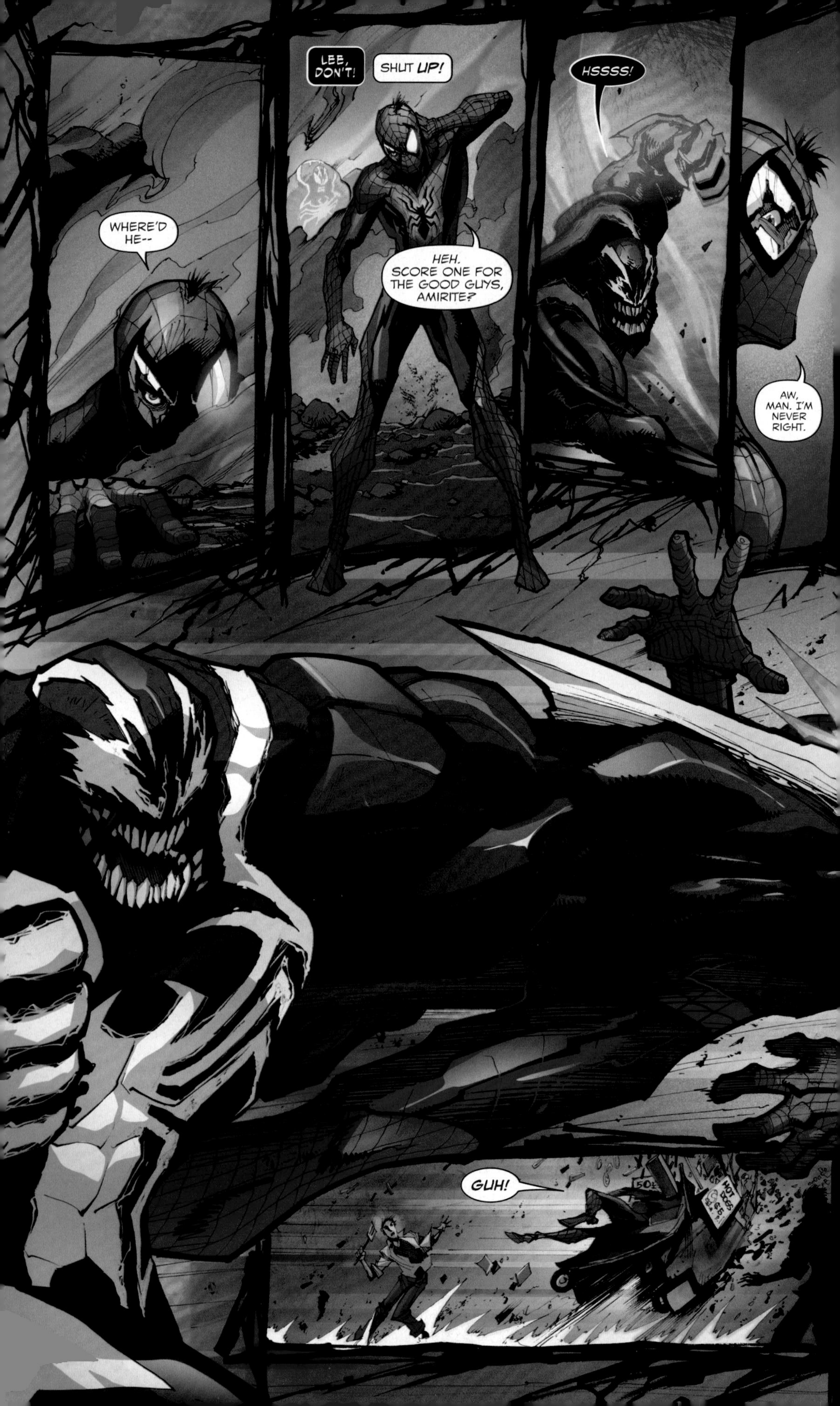
WHERE'D HE--
LEE, DON'T!
SHUT UP!
HEH. SCORE ONE FOR THE GOOD GUYS, AMIRITE?
HSSSS!
AW, MAN. I'M NEVER RIGHT.
GUH!

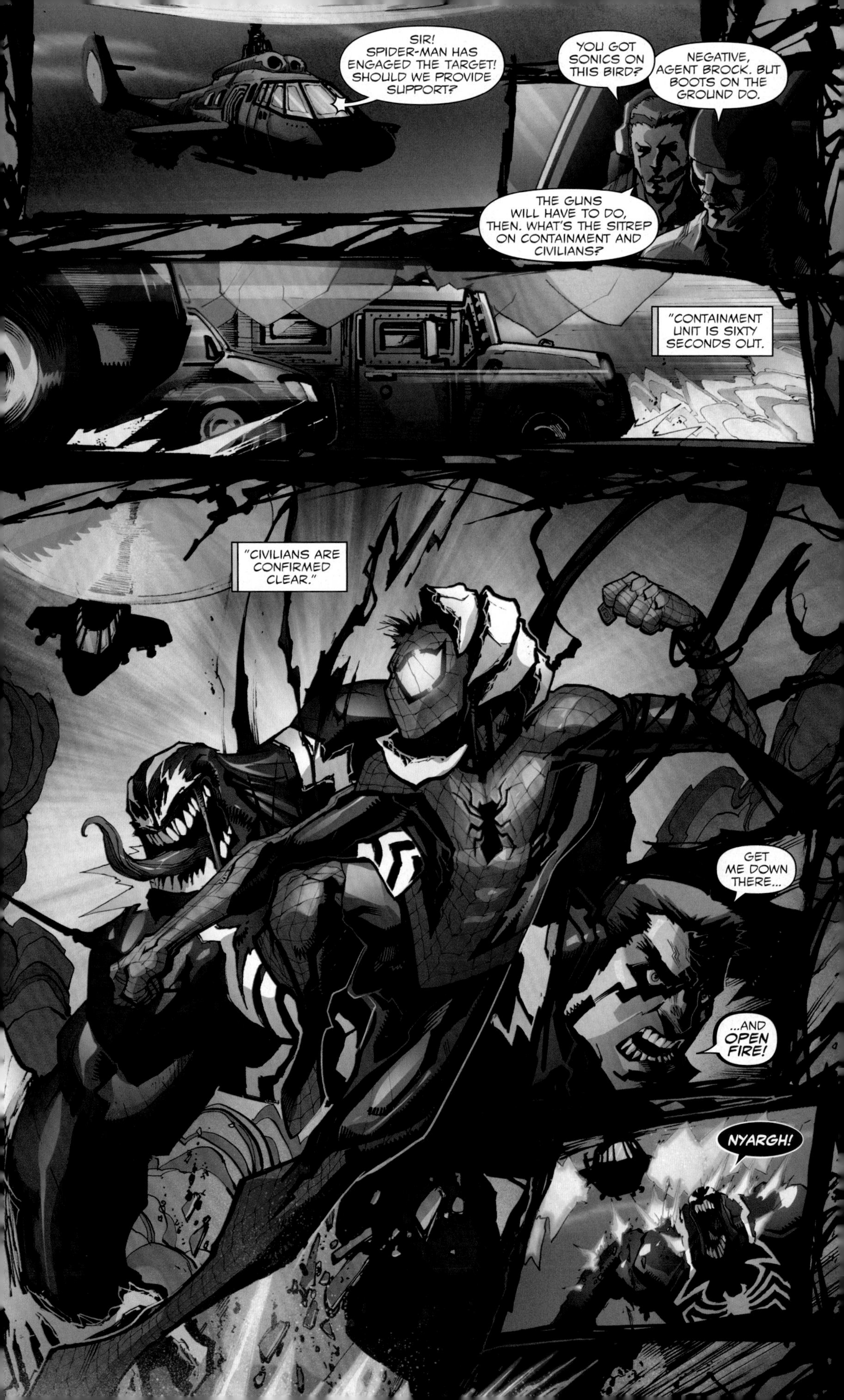
SIR! SPIDER-MAN HAS ENGAGED THE TARGET! SHOULD WE PROVIDE SUPPORT?
YOU GOT SONICS ON THIS BIRD?
NEGATIVE, AGENT BROCK. BUT BOOTS ON THE GROUND DO.
THE GUNS WILL HAVE TO DO, THEN. WHAT'S THE SITREP ON CONTAINMENT AND CIVILIANS?
"CONTAINMENT UNIT IS SIXTY SECONDS OUT.
"CIVILIANS ARE CONFIRMED CLEAR."
GET ME DOWN THERE...
...AND OPEN FIRE!
NYARGH!

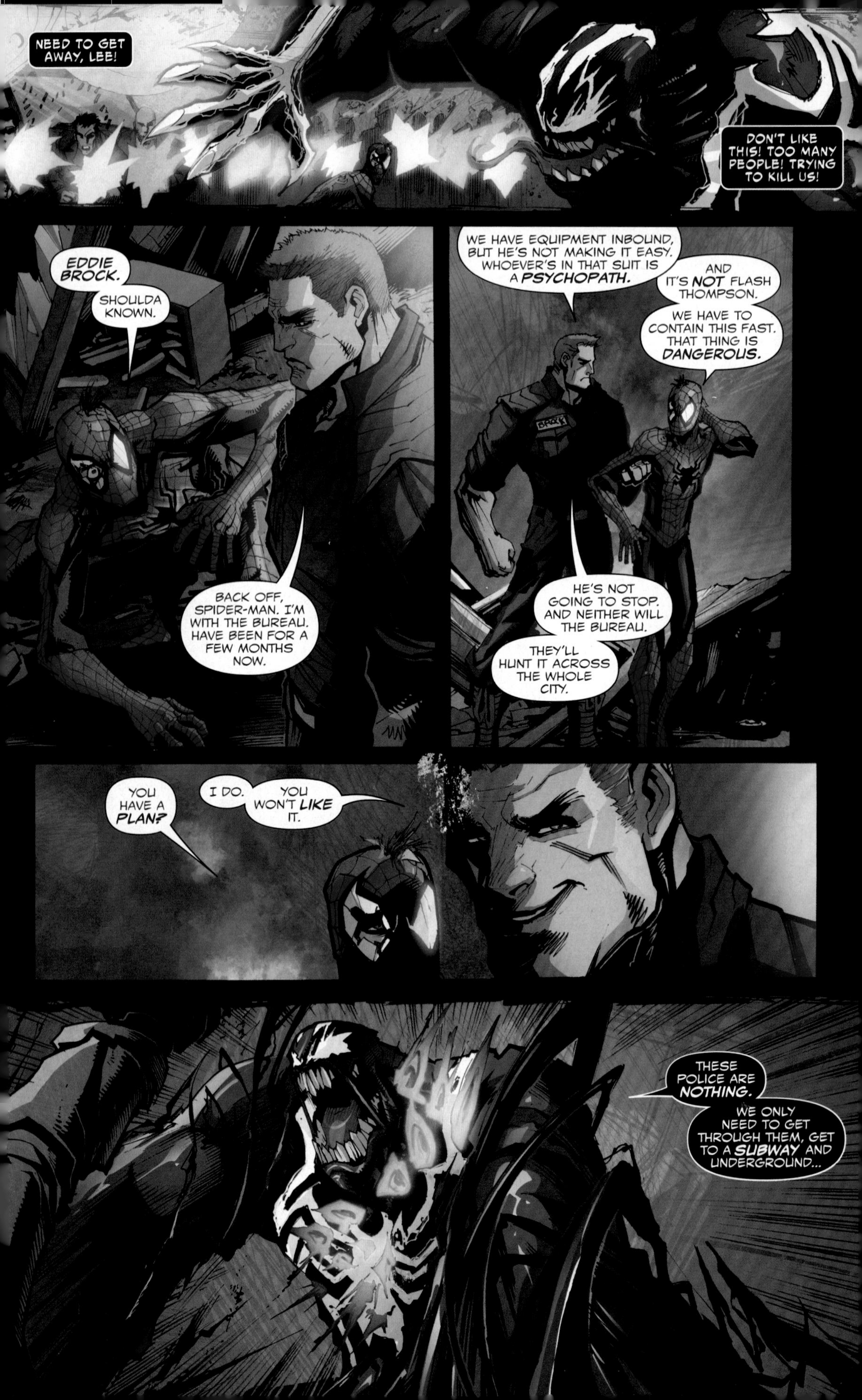
NEED TO GET AWAY, LEE!
DON'T LIKE THIS! TOO MANY PEOPLE! TRYING TO KILL US!
EDDIE BROCK.
SHOULDA KNOWN.
BACK OFF, SPIDER-MAN. I'M WITH THE BUREAU. HAVE BEEN FOR A FEW MONTHS NOW.
WE HAVE EQUIPMENT INBOUND, BUT HE'S NOT MAKING IT EASY. WHOEVER'S IN THAT SUIT IS A PSYCHOPATH.
AND IT'S NOT FLASH THOMPSON.
WE HAVE TO CONTAIN THIS FAST. THAT THING IS DANGEROUS.
HE'S NOT GOING TO STOP. AND NEITHER WILL THE BUREAU.
THEY'LL HUNT IT ACROSS THE WHOLE CITY.
YOU HAVE A PLAN?
I DO.
YOU WON'T LIKE IT.
THESE POLICE ARE NOTHING.
WE ONLY NEED TO GET THROUGH THEM, GET TO A SUBWAY AND UNDERGROUND...

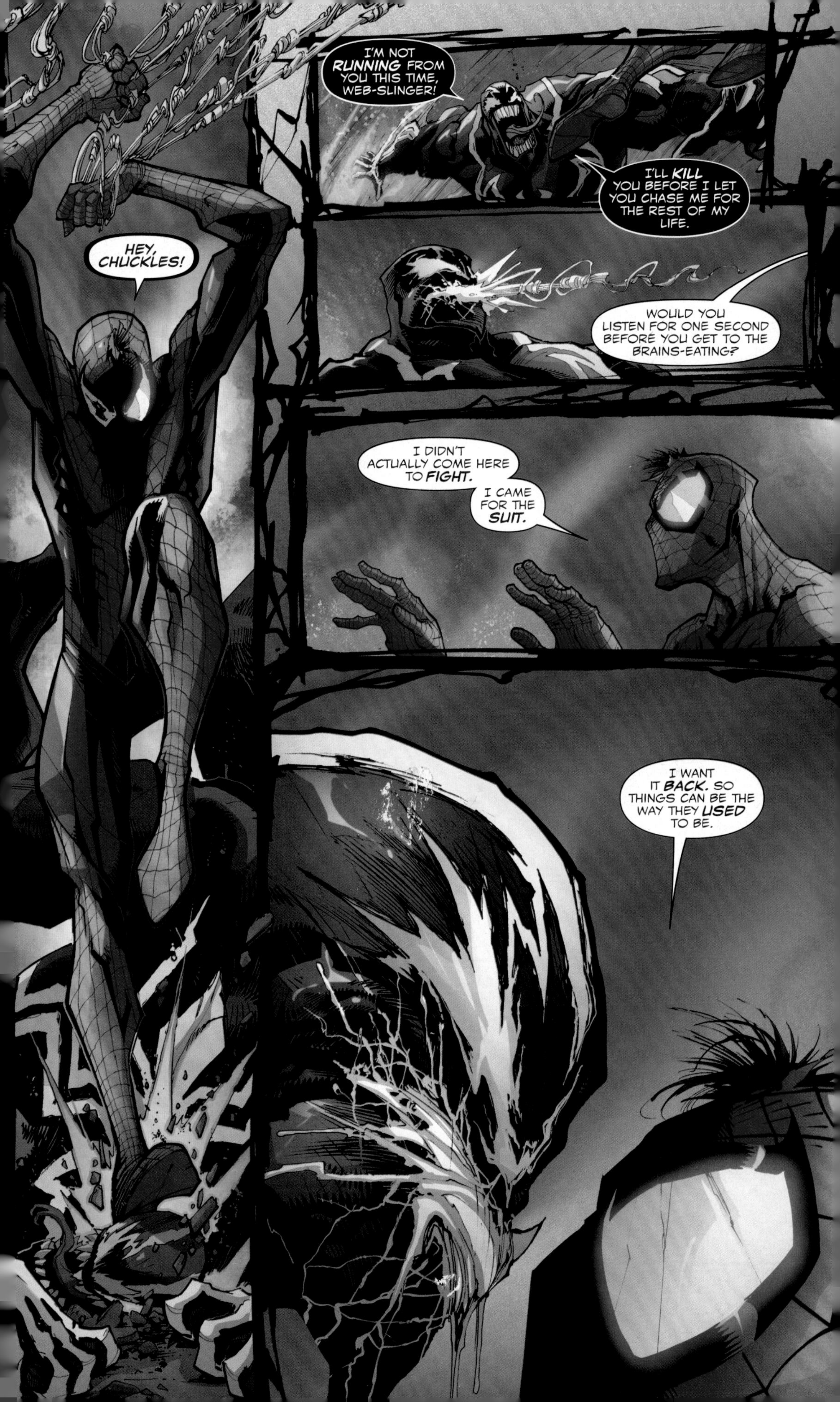
HEY, CHUCKLES!
I'M NOT RUNNING FROM YOU THIS TIME, WEB-SLINGER!
I'LL KILL YOU BEFORE I LET YOU CHASE ME FOR THE REST OF MY LIFE.
WOULD YOU LISTEN FOR ONE SECOND BEFORE YOU GET TO THE BRAINS-EATING?
I DIDN'T ACTUALLY COME HERE TO FIGHT.
I CAME FOR THE SUIT.
I WANT IT BACK. SO THINGS CAN BE THE WAY THEY USED TO BE.

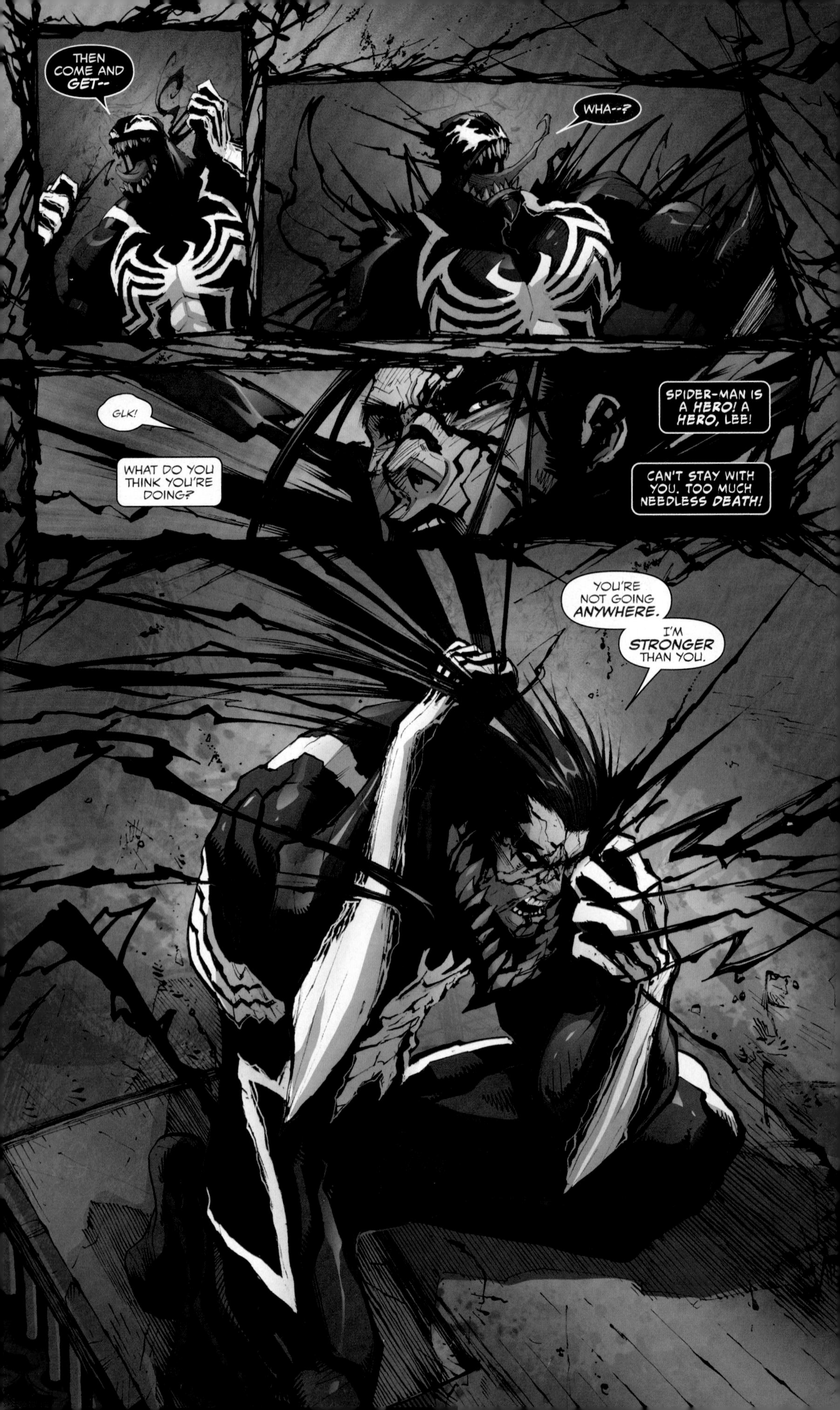

THEN COME AND GET--
WHA--?
GLK!
WHAT DO YOU THINK YOU'RE DOING?
SPIDER-MAN IS A HERO! A HERO, LEE!
CAN'T STAY WITH YOU. TOO MUCH NEEDLESS DEATH!
YOU'RE NOT GOING ANYWHERE.
I'M STRONGER THAN YOU.

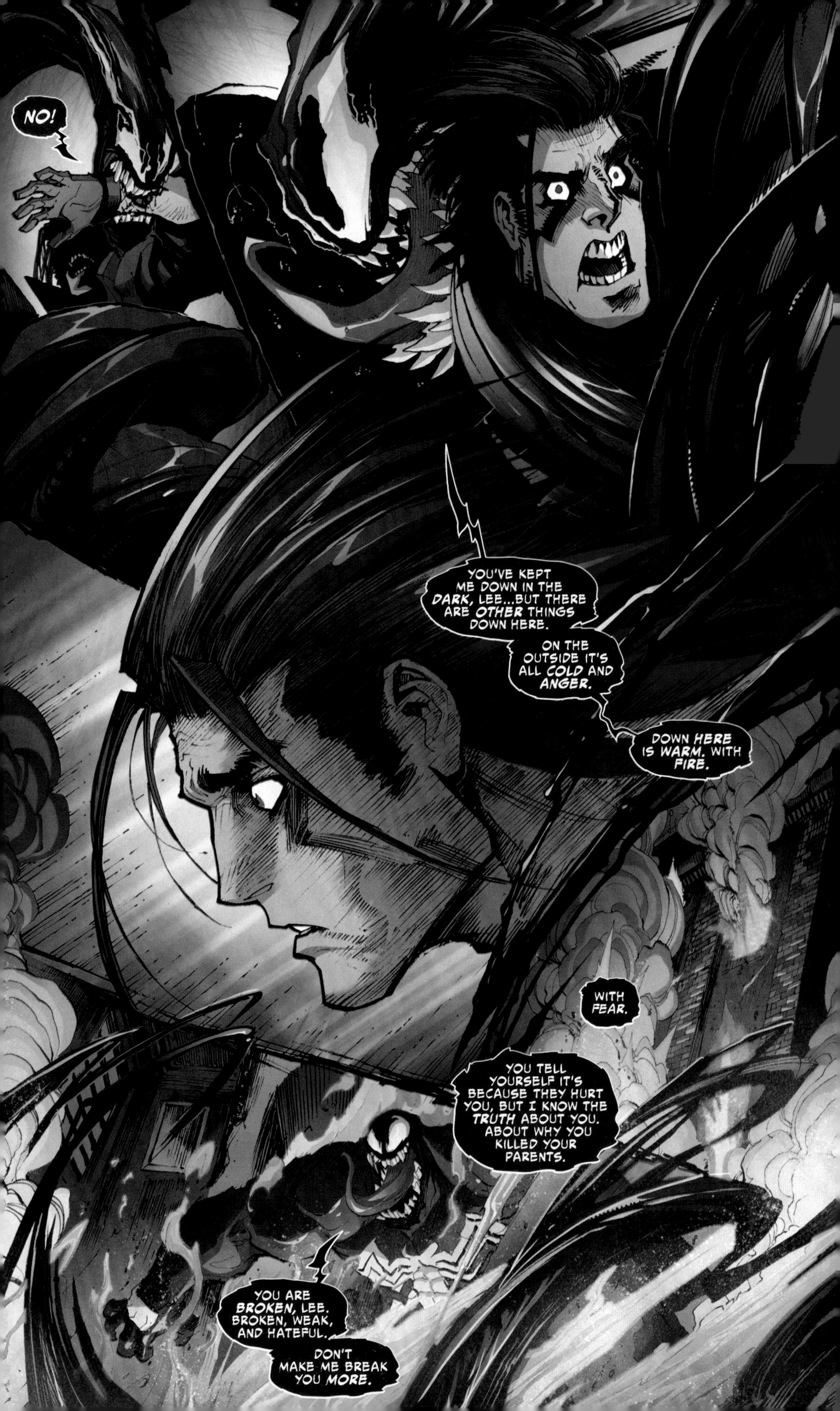
NO!
YOU'VE KEPT ME DOWN IN THE DARK, LEE...BUT THERE ARE OTHER THINGS DOWN HERE.
ON THE OUTSIDE IT'S ALL COLD AND ANGER.
DOWN HERE IS WARM. WITH FIRE.
WITH FEAR.
YOU TELL YOURSELF IT'S BECAUSE THEY HURT YOU, BUT I KNOW THE TRUTH ABOUT YOU. ABOUT WHY YOU KILLED YOUR PARENTS.
YOU ARE BROKEN, LEE. BROKEN, WEAK, AND HATEFUL.
DON'T MAKE ME BREAK YOU MORE.

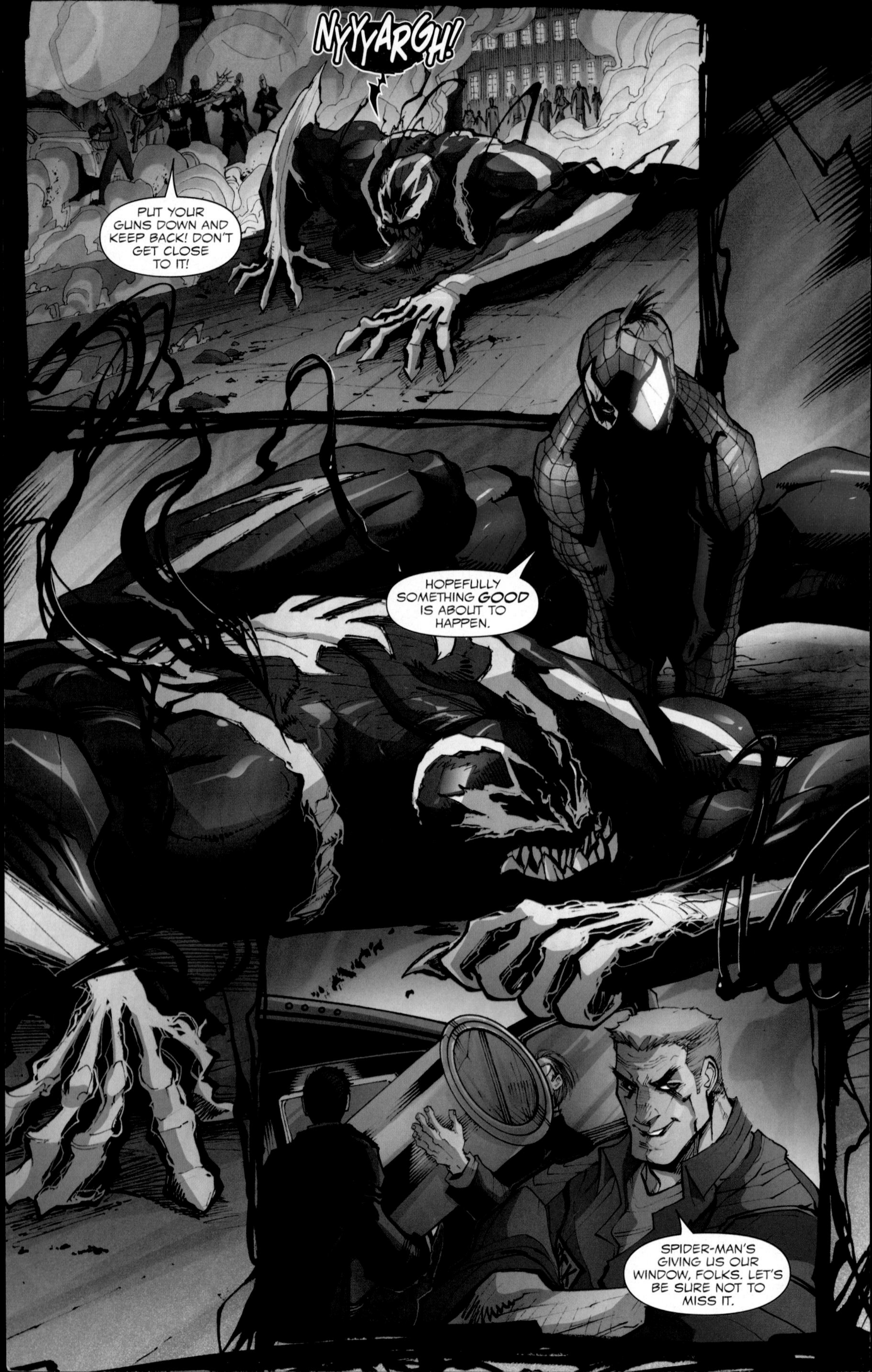
NYYYARGH!
PUT YOUR GUNS DOWN AND KEEP BACK! DON'T GET CLOSE TO IT!
HOPEFULLY SOMETHING **GOOD** IS ABOUT TO HAPPEN.
SPIDER-MAN'S GIVING US OUR WINDOW, FOLKS. LET'S BE SURE NOT TO MISS IT.

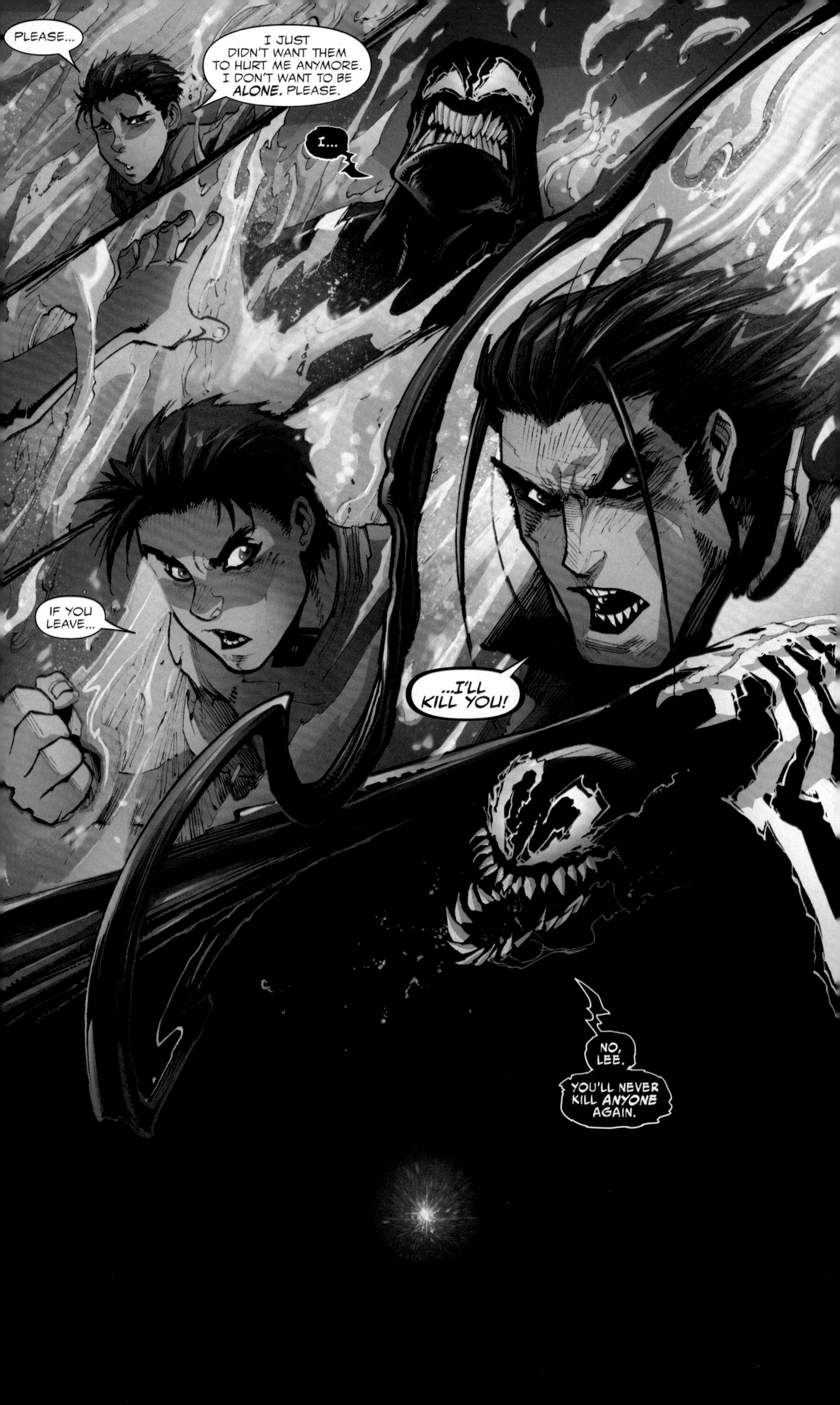
PLEASE...
I JUST DIDN'T WANT THEM TO HURT ME ANYMORE. I DON'T WANT TO BE ALONE. PLEASE.
I...
IF YOU LEAVE...
...I'LL KILL YOU!
NO, LEE.
YOU'LL NEVER KILL ANYONE AGAIN.

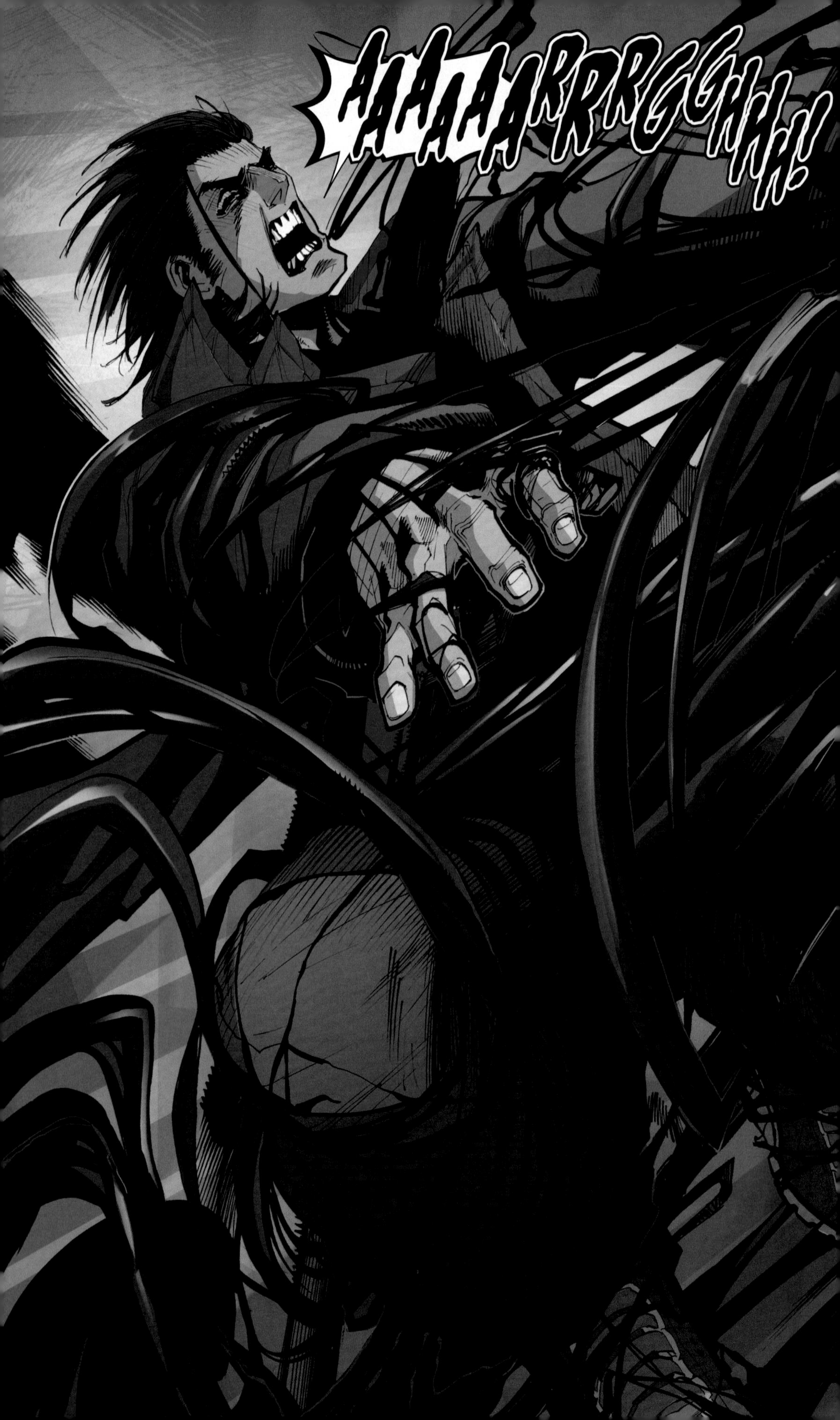
AAAAARRRGGHHH!

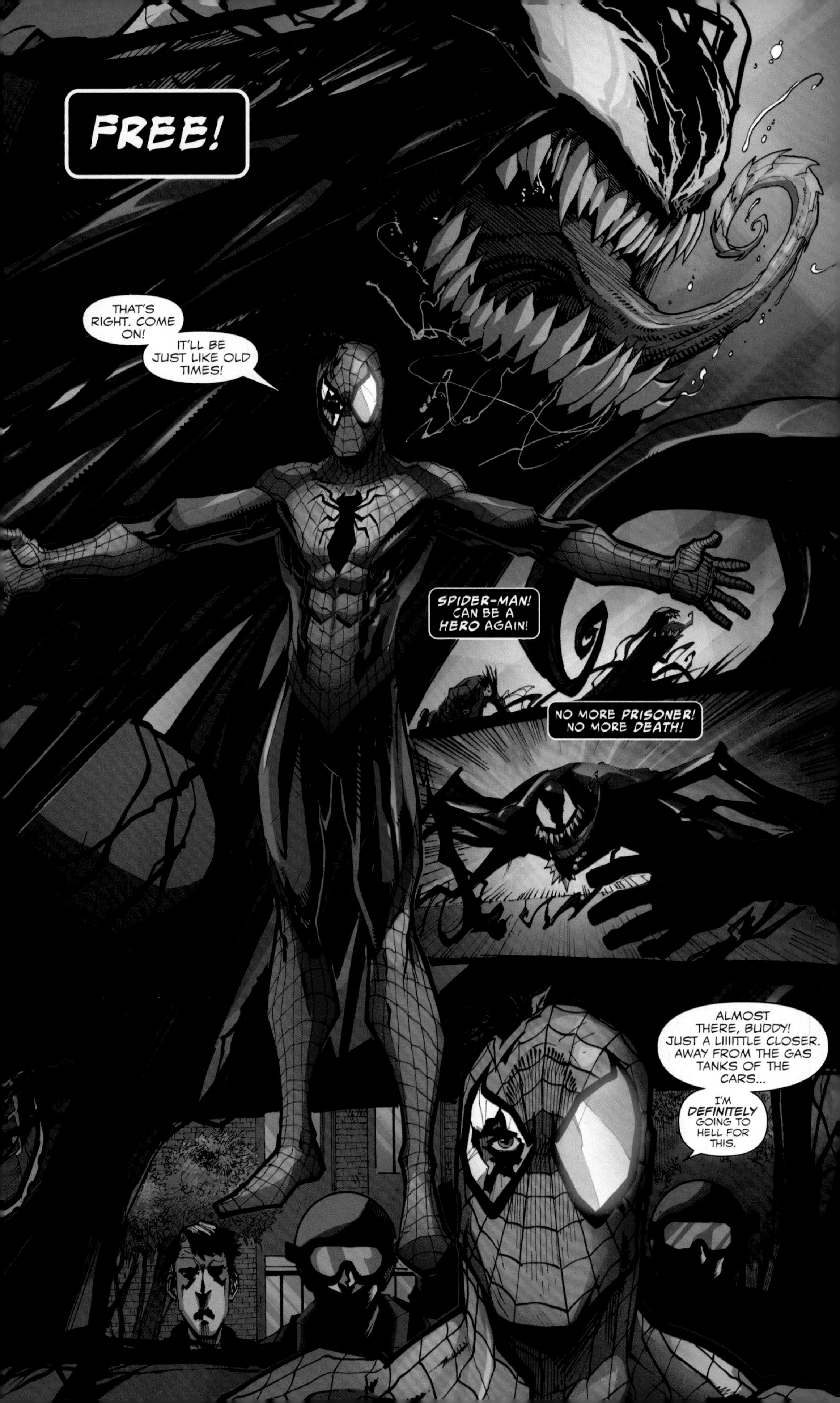
FREE!
THAT'S RIGHT. COME ON!
IT'LL BE JUST LIKE OLD TIMES!
SPIDER-MAN! CAN BE A HERO AGAIN!
NO MORE PRISONER! NO MORE DEATH!
ALMOST THERE, BUDDY! JUST A LIIIITTLE CLOSER. AWAY FROM THE GAS TANKS OF THE CARS...
I'M DEFINITELY GOING TO HELL FOR THIS.

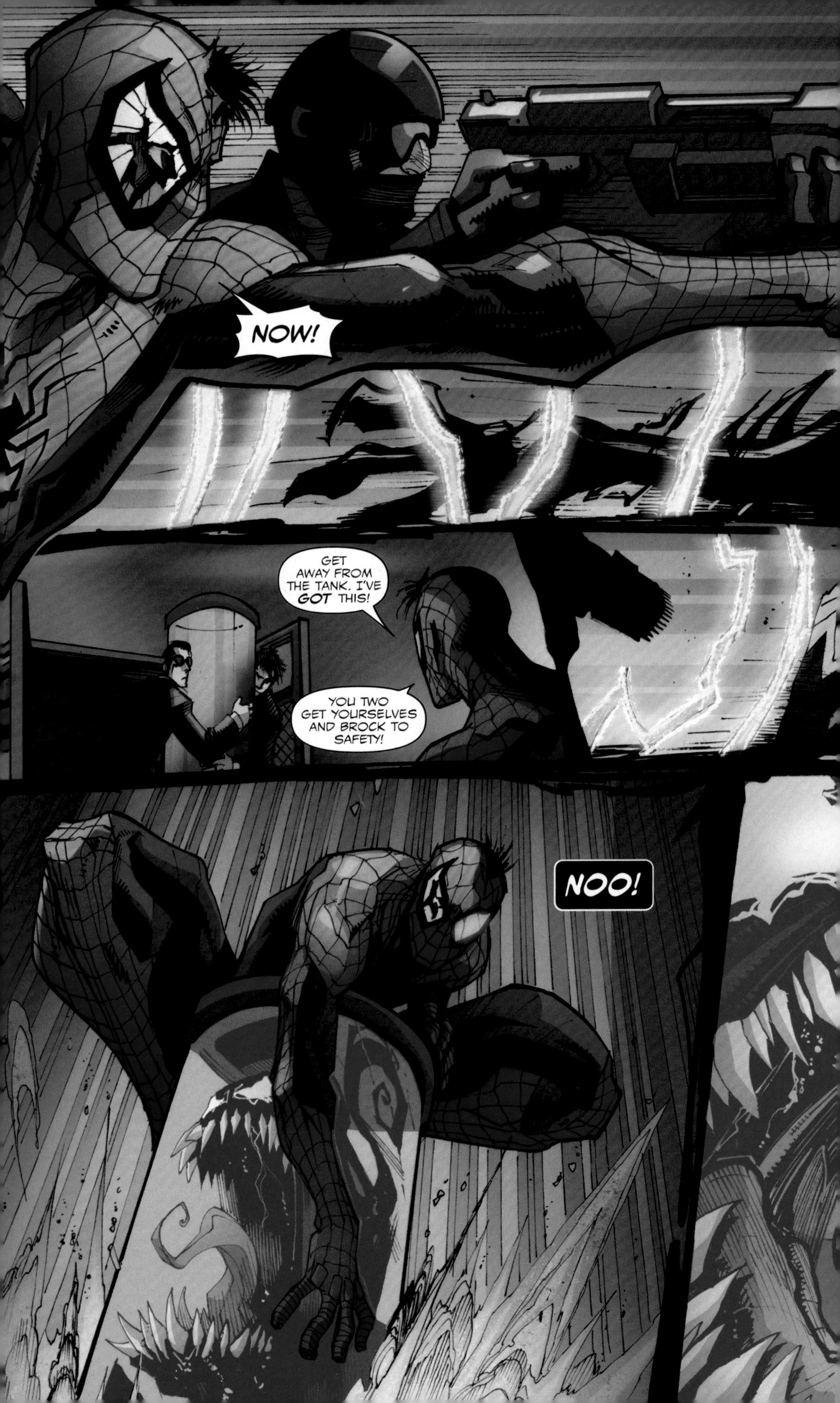
NOW!
GET AWAY FROM THE TANK. I'VE GOT THIS!
YOU TWO GET YOURSELVES AND BROCK TO SAFETY!
NOO!

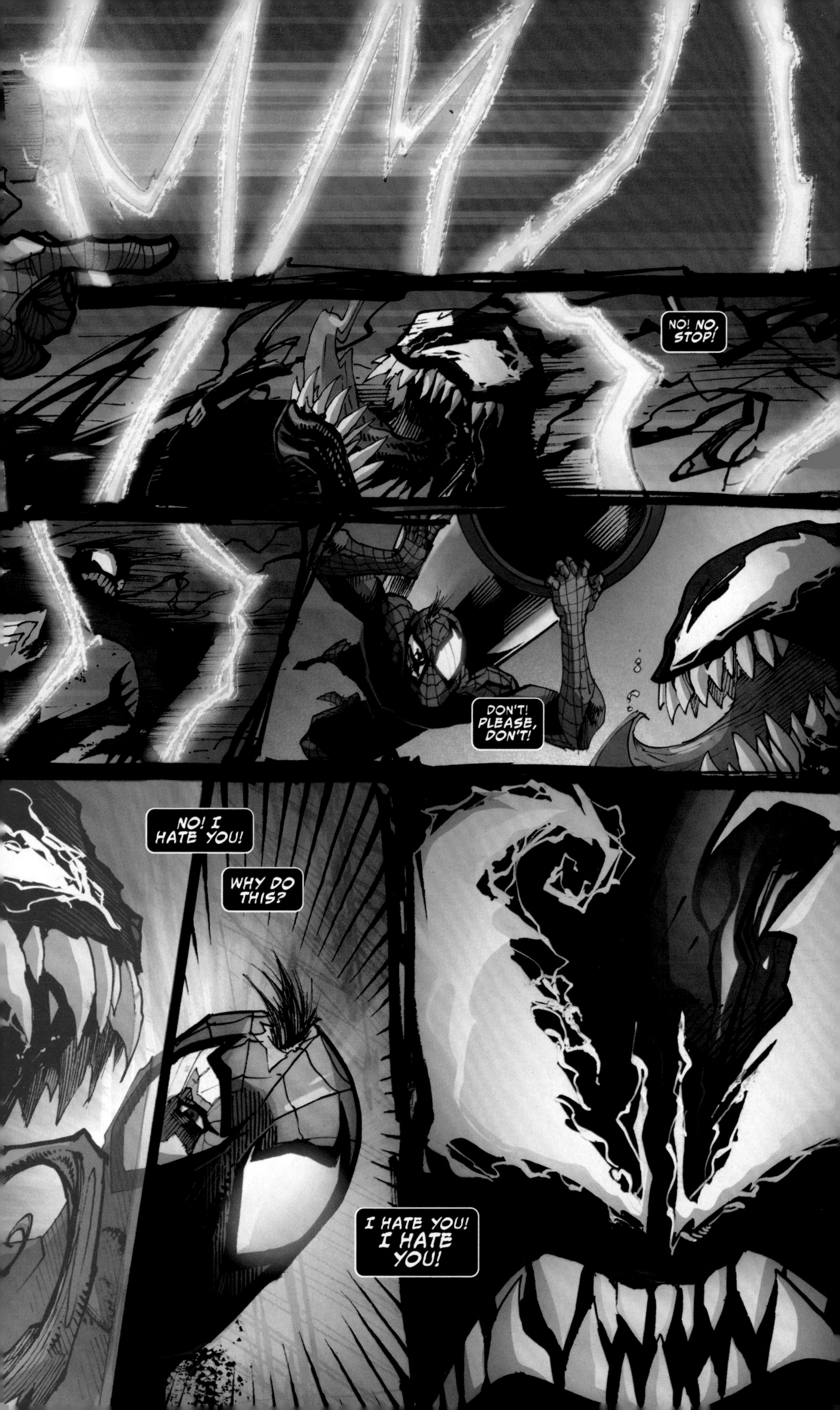
NO! NO, STOP!
DON'T! PLEASE, DON'T!
NO! I HATE YOU!
WHY DO THIS?
I HATE YOU! I HATE YOU!

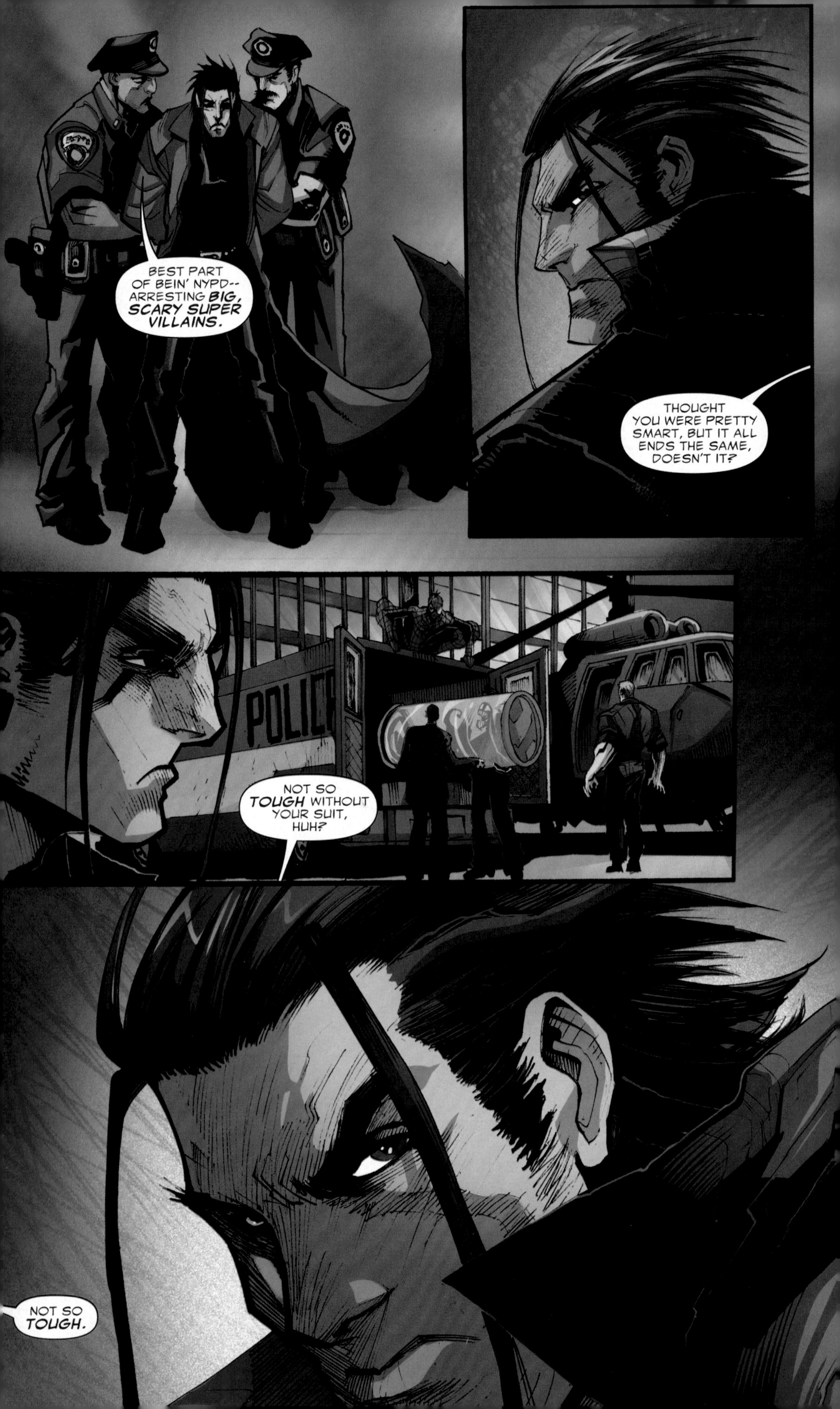
BEST PART OF BEIN' NYPD-- ARRESTING BIG, SCARY SUPER VILLAINS.
THOUGHT YOU WERE PRETTY SMART, BUT IT ALL ENDS THE SAME, DOESN'T IT?
POLIC
NOT SO TOUGH WITHOUT YOUR SUIT, HUH?
NOT SO TOUGH.

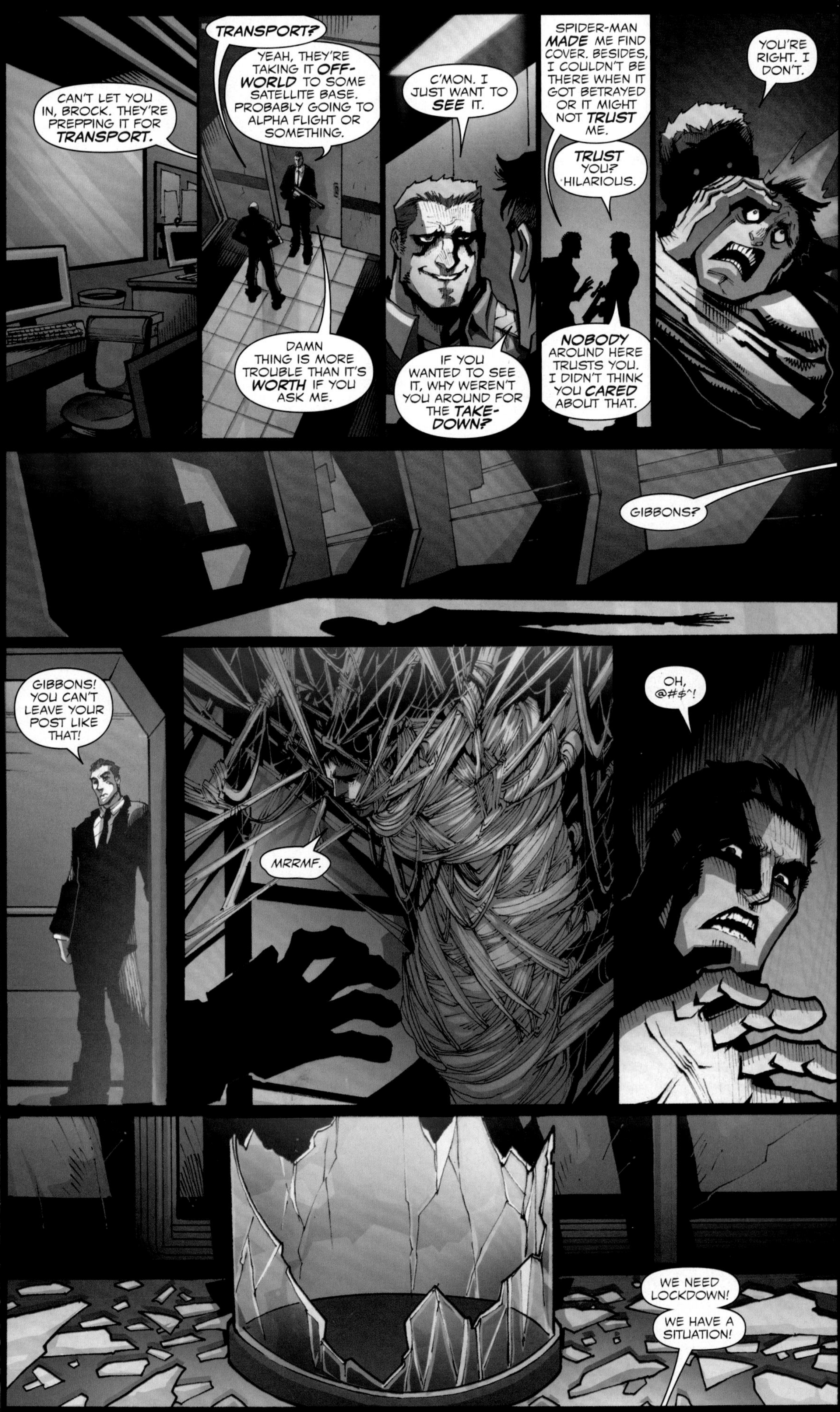
CAN'T LET YOU IN, BROCK. THEY'RE PREPPING IT FOR TRANSPORT.
TRANSPORT?
YEAH, THEY'RE TAKING IT OFF-WORLD TO SOME SATELLITE BASE. PROBABLY GOING TO ALPHA FLIGHT OR SOMETHING.
DAMN THING IS MORE TROUBLE THAN IT'S WORTH IF YOU ASK ME.
C'MON. I JUST WANT TO SEE IT.
IF YOU WANTED TO SEE IT, WHY WEREN'T YOU AROUND FOR THE TAKE-DOWN?
SPIDER-MAN MADE ME FIND COVER. BESIDES, I COULDN'T BE THERE WHEN IT GOT BETRAYED OR IT MIGHT NOT TRUST ME.
TRUST YOU? HILARIOUS.
NOBODY AROUND HERE TRUSTS YOU. I DIDN'T THINK YOU CARED ABOUT THAT.
YOU'RE RIGHT. I DON'T.
GIBBONS?
GIBBONS! YOU CAN'T LEAVE YOUR POST LIKE THAT!
MRRMF.
OH, @#$^!
WE NEED LOCKDOWN!
WE HAVE A SITUATION!

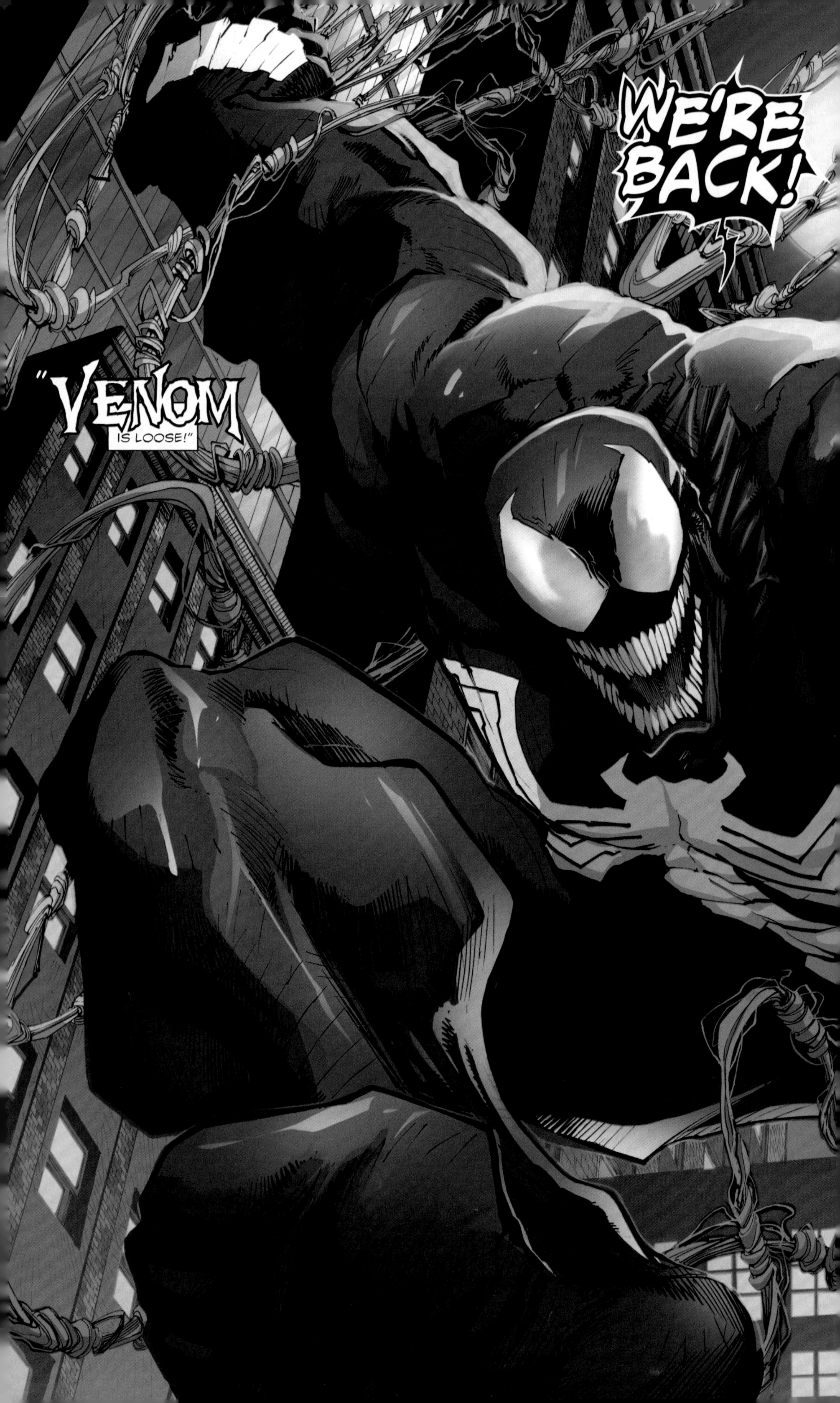

WE'RE BACK!
"VENOM IS LOOSE!"

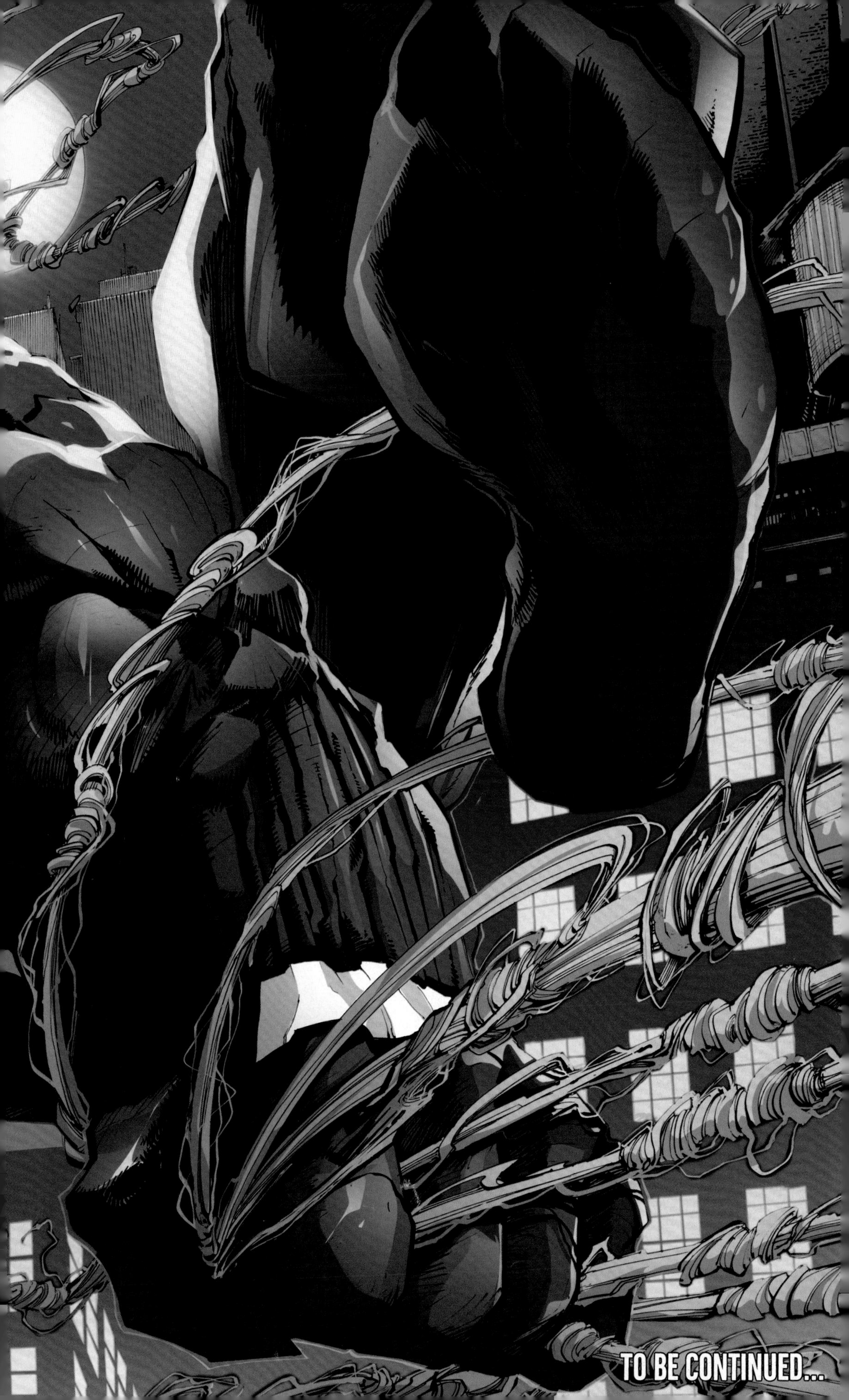
TO BE CONTINUED...

#1 VARIANT BY **RON LIM**
& **ANDREW CROSSLEY**

#1 REMASTERED VARIANT
BY **TODD McFARLANE**
& **RICHARD ISANOVE**

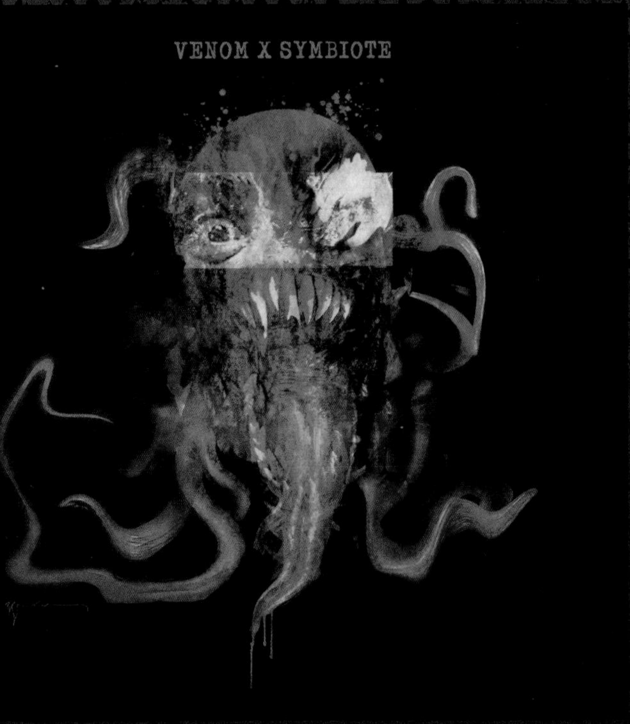
VENOM X SYMBIOTE

#1 HIP-HOP VARIANT BY **BILL SIENKIEWICZ**

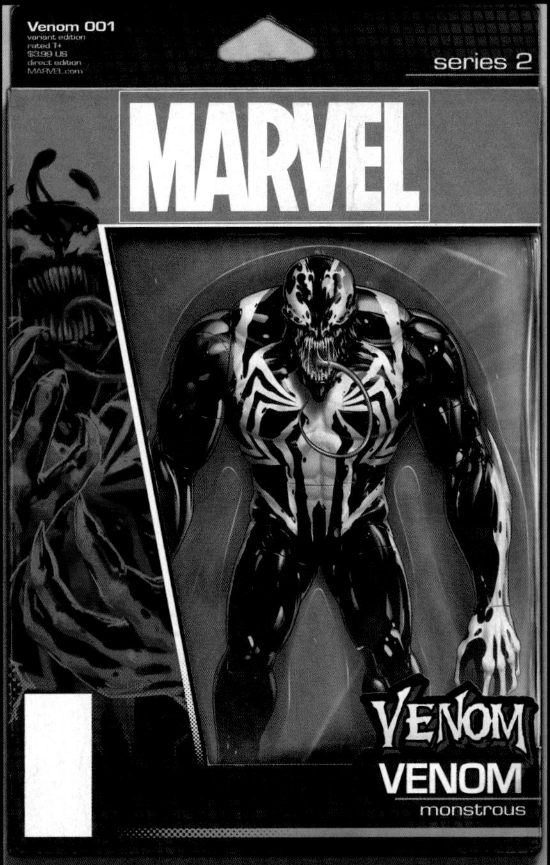
Venom 001
variant edition
rated T+
$3.99 US
direct edition
MARVEL.com
series 2
MARVEL
VENOM
VENOM
monstrous

#1 ACTION FIGURE VARIANT
BY **JOHN TYLER CHRISTOPHER**

#2 VARIANT BY **TRADD MOORE**

#3 VARIANT BY **J. SCOTT CAMPBELL**
& PETER STEIGERWALD